Housing and the Welfare State

Also by Peter Malpass

Housing Policy and Practice (5th edn) (with Alan Murie)
The Housing Crisis (editor)
Reshaping Housing Policy
Implementing Housing Policy (editor with Robin Means)
Ownership, Control and Accountability (editor)
Housing Finance: A Basic Guide (5th edn) (with Henry Aughton)
Housing Associations and Housing Policy

Housing and the Welfare State

The Development of Housing Policy in Britain

Peter Malpass

First published in 2005 by
PALGRAVE MACMILLAN
Houndmills, Basingstoke, Hampshire RG21 6XS and
175 Fifth Avenue, New York, N.Y. 10010
Companies and representatives throughout the world.

PALGRAVE MACMILLAN is the global academic imprint of the Palgrave
Macmillan division of St. Martin's Press, LLC and of Palgrave Macmillan Ltd.
Macmillan® is a registered trademark in the United States, United Kingdom
and other countries. Palgrave is a registered trademark in the European
Union and other countries.

ISBN-13: 9780–333–96208–4 hardback
ISBN-10: 0–333–96208–7 hardback
ISBN-13: 9780–333–96209–1 paperback
ISBN-10: 0–333–96209–5 paperback

This book is printed on paper suitable for recycling and made from fully
managed and sustained forest sources.

A catalogue record for this book is available from the British Library.

A catalog record for this book is available from the Library of Congress.

10 9 8 7 6 5 4 3 2 1
14 13 12 11 10 09 08 07 06 05

Printed in China

Contents

List of Tables

Preface and Acknowledgements

As an undergraduate in Newcastle upon Tyne in the late 1960s I learned from Norman Dennis the importance of that basic social science question: who gets what, when and how? It was Norman, along with Jon Davies and Betty Gittus, who fired and encouraged my interest in housing. At that time housing was still a high profile policy area, with governments committed to high levels of new building, and local authorities actively engaged in large scale urban redevelopment. It was an exciting time to be living in a big city undergoing extensive physical reconstruction, with entire neighbourhoods being demolished and rebuilt. Housing was therefore a good context within which to explore issues of the distribution of power and material resources, and the social, economic and political processes underpinning or modifying existing patterns of inequality. In those days I think I took it for granted that housing was part of the welfare state, and I certainly believed then (and I still do) that building council houses was a good thing to do; it was one very effective way of breaking the link between poverty and poor housing. The welfare state itself also seemed to be a permanent fixture, something else that could be taken for granted. It was, and to some extent remains, a mechanism for moderating the distribution of resources in capitalist, market based societies. Without some kind of redistributive apparatus the inequalities generated in the labour market and elsewhere would be even starker.

I have spent most of my working life thinking about, researching and teaching aspects of housing and housing policy. For eighteen years, of course, this was an activity carried out against the backdrop of Conservative governments that seemed determined to undermine the welfare state, attack local government and sell off as many council houses as possible. But Thatcherism and its successors in Britain are part of a global transformation which has produced conditions in which welfare states are everywhere on the defensive if not in actual retreat. And housing appears to have retreated further than other services.

This book is, therefore, an attempt to come to terms with, to make some sense of, the changes affecting housing and the welfare state. It is an attempt to write a history of housing policy in Britain, concentrating on the sixty years since the Second World War. That war not only helped to create the conditions that made possible the series of reforms that came to be known as the welfare state, it also had a huge impact on housing policy for several decades as successive governments sought to restore the construction industry to health and to overcome serious problems of shortages and poor quality housing. The book is also an attempt to reassess and reinterpret the housing–welfare state relationship, questioning some popular assumptions and developing a new perspective.

Over the years I have discussed the ideas explored in the book with many friends and colleagues in both academic and practice settings. In addition to those mentioned above I would like to identify and thank the following: Alan Murie, Peter Williams, Alex Marsh, David Mullins, David Garnett, Geoff Winn, Judith Ritchie, Nancy Holman, Rob Atkinson, Christine Lambert, Dave Cowan, Morag McDermont, Nancy Carlton, Rob Furbey, Ian Cole, Hal Pawson and Mark Kleinman. Several of those listed have been kind enough to read and comment on draft chapters, although of course none of them can be held responsible for what follows. Finally, thanks to Steven Kennedy at Palgrave Macmillan for encouraging me to write the book, and for his patience in waiting for it to arrive.

PETER MALPASS

List of Acronyms and Abbreviations

ADP	Approved Development Programme
ALMO	Arm's Length Management Organization
BV	Best Value
CCT	Compulsory Competitive Tendering
CHAC	Central Housing Advisory Committee
DETR	Department of the Environment, Transport and the Regions
DoE	Department of the Environment
ERCF	Estates Renewal Challenge Fund
HAG	Housing Association Grant
HAT	Housing Action Trust
ISMI	Income Support for Mortgage Interest
LSVT	Large Scale Voluntary Transfer
MITR	Mortgage Interest Tax Relief
MoHLG	Ministry of Housing and Local Government
NFHS	National Federation of Housing Societies
NHF	National Housing Federation
NHFA	National Federation of Housing Associations
NHS	National Health Service
NPM	New Public Management
ODPM	Office of the Deputy Prime Minister
PFI	Private Finance Initiative
PRO	Public Record Office
PUS	Public Utility Society
PWLB	Public Works Loans Board
RTB	Right to Buy
RSL	Registered Social Landlord
SERPS	State Earnings Related Pension Scheme
WNHC	Workmen's National Housing Council

Chapter 1

Introduction

The intention of this book is to examine the housing–welfare state relationship in Britain since the end of the Second World War. In July 1945 Britain emerged from six years of war with the worst housing shortage of the whole of the twentieth century (Holmans, 1987: 93) and not surprisingly the number of new houses built each year became a key indicator of government performance during the next twenty years or so. Much has changed since those days, not least the housing situation. The people of Britain are, on the whole, much better housed, and more than two-thirds enjoy the benefits (and risks) of buying their own homes. Housing is now seen in a very different light; in the early postwar years its high political profile meant that it was considered to be a mainstream part of the nascent welfare state, but more recently housing has been identified as the 'wobbly pillar' under the welfare state (Torgersen, 1987), which is itself undergoing prolonged and profound change. The housing–welfare state relationship must therefore be understood as dynamic, and a central task of the book is to show how that relationship has changed over time. In the course of the analysis it will be argued that we need to revise commonly held notions of the welfare state and the place of housing within it.

The reforms that established Britain as a welfare state were part of postwar reconstruction and a potent symbol of government commitment to the idea of building a better society after the bitterness and hardship of the 1920s and 1930s, and the sacrifices of the war years. But as society and the economy have changed so have attitudes to the welfare state. For a long time now academic commentators have been depicting the welfare state in terms of crisis or transition (Ellison and Pierson, 2003; Esping-Andersen, 1996; Huber and Stephens, 2001; Mishra, 1984). 'The half-century experiment of the British welfare state is everywhere in retreat' (Taylor-Gooby, 2000: 2). Bauman (1998: 51) refers to 'the present day implosion of the welfare state, the fast evaporation of support in quarters once eager to make it work'. The continued development and expansion of the European Union, and economic changes variously understood in terms of globalization or the transition from Fordism to post-Fordism, have implications that need to be factored into theories of the welfare state (Burrows and Loader, 1994; Kleinman, 2002; Sykes, Palier and Prior, 2001). Others have referred to the emergence of 'risk society' as a perspective on change resulting from

1

rapid scientific and technological advances with uncertain implications (Beck, Giddens and Lash, 1994; Franklin, 1998). According to Giddens (1998: 33) 'The crisis of the welfare state is not purely fiscal, it is a crisis of risk management in a society dominated by a new type of risk.' Consumer society forces people constantly to make choices and take risks, and as Bauman (1998: 58) notes, consumerism and the welfare state are at cross-purposes. Changes in the class structure, in the role of women in society and in the demographic and ethnic composition of the British population also need to be taken into account (Ginsburg, 1992; F. Williams, 1989). In international comparative terms Britain has been identified as a country that has undergone more radical welfare state retrenchment and modernization than most other advanced market economies since the 1980s (Ellison and Pierson, 2003: 6; Esping-Andersen, 1996: 10, 15). And in the early 2000s the British government proclaimed itself to have embarked on 'the most ambitious programme of public service investment and reform since the 1940s' (Office of Public Service Reform, 2002: 7). It seems safe to assume, therefore, that the pace of change is unlikely to slow down in the foreseeable future.

Change proceeds differently and at different speeds in the various parts of the welfare state. This was most vividly revealed in the early 1980s when Margaret Thatcher simultaneously claimed to have won the 1979 general election partly on the promise to council tenants of a right to buy their homes, while pledging that the health service was safe in her hands. In the event the health service was subject to far-reaching changes during Thatcher's long term of office, but the National Health Service retains its iconic status as the jewel in the crown of the welfare state and ministers still claim allegiance to the idea of health care that is free at the point of consumption. Housing, on the other hand, has been at the forefront of retrenchment, restructuring and modernization for more than twenty-five years, although it now warrants barely a passing mention in official pronouncements on the reform of public services (Blair, 1998, 2002). This stands in marked contrast to the way it was perceived in the years after the Second World War. In those days both the Labour and Conservative parties were committed to building very large numbers of new houses, to be let at subsidized rents to families in need. The relative importance of housing in the early 1950s can be judged by the fact that the Minister of Housing and Local Government, Harold Macmillan, was a senior cabinet figure who went on to be prime minister in little over two years, while for most of the decade the Minister of Health was not even in the cabinet, an inconceivable arrangement in the present period. In the early postwar years it was the local authorities who supplied the majority of these new houses, and it was not until 1959 that they were overtaken by the private sector (Merrett, 1979: 247). Local authorities went on building at a relatively high level until the late 1970s. In the three decades after the war public housing seemed to have become a permanent and substantial social institution, increasing from less than 12 per cent of all housing in 1945 to 32 per cent by 1979. One respected academic commentator even expressed the view that:

> Public housing is so important a part of national policy that one could almost determine the claim of a country to be recognised as a welfare state by the magnitude of its effort in this sphere in relation to the total demand for housing. (Robson, 1976: 31)

Few would agree with that judgement today. Now, after years of under-investment and privatization through the right to buy, local authority housing amounts to less than a fifth of the total stock, and what remains has been judged to require huge amounts of investment to bring all dwellings up to a decent standard for the twenty-first century (Department of the Environment, Transport and the Regions, or DETR, 2000: 8). Moreover, social rented housing as a whole has drifted, or been driven, towards a position where it is seen as a tenure of last resort, a residual sector for what Margaret Thatcher once disparagingly referred to as 'the elderly and social cases'. In this context, therefore, it is tempting to agree that housing is, or has become, the wobbly pillar under the welfare state. However, a settled view on the relationship between housing and the welfare state requires consideration of the notion of the welfare state itself and its manifestation in particular times and places. As a precursor to the more detailed housing-focused discussion, this opening chapter looks at ways of thinking about the welfare state and outlines a framework for analysing developments and changes since its creation after the war.

'An indefinable abstraction'

William Beveridge, the man widely seen as the architect of social reform in Britain after the Second World War, is said by his biographer to have hated the term 'welfare state' (J. Harris, 1977: 448). And Richard Titmuss, one of the leading academic analysts and defenders of public services in the postwar period, expressed a similar sentiment, describing it as an indefinable abstraction (Abel-Smith and Titmuss, 1987: 141). More recently the welfare state has been identified as a political representation, not an organizational reality (Clarke and Newman, 1997: 17n). R. Lowe (1993: 9; 1999: 5) has pointed out that there is no agreement among social scientists and historians as to when the first welfare states were established or what the term means, while Viet-Wilson (2000) has lamented the undifferentiated adoption of welfare state as a label for all advanced capitalist societies. As Viet-Wilson says, unless there is some agreement about how to distinguish welfare states from non-welfare states then the word 'welfare' has no meaning in this context. Some sort of essay in definition of terms is essential, for without it we cannot be clear about what it is that housing is standing under, nor what counts as housing in this context.

The welfare state is a difficult subject to write about, partly because of the lack of scholarly agreement about what it means, but also because it is, at the same time, such a familiar, taken-for-granted feature of society. The welfare state is, and always has been, contested, contradictory, complex and dynamic, and therefore is not easily encapsulated in a simple definition or list of principles. The very term welfare state is emotive and loaded, implying to some observers a warm and positive role for the state in promoting wellbeing, while for others it suggests dependency, support for idleness and a burden on the economy. Writers such as Charles Murray (1990), for example, have argued that the welfare state has been counter-productive, seeking to tackle poverty but creating more of it. However, an important role of the social security system, for example, is to discipline the labour force, with benefits being contingent on past employment record and future availability for work. The management of social housing can be seen in the same way, with its emphasis on regular payment of rent and threat of sanctions against 'anti-social behaviour'. Welfare services can be aimed at meeting basic human requirements and yet be alienating and stigmatizing in their impact on their nominal beneficiaries (F. Williams, 1989: 10).

The welfare state has been contested both politically, because of the way that it involves attempts to modify command over scarce resources, and theoretically, for reasons including the problem of explaining its contradictoriness: is the welfare state a burden that capitalist societies cannot afford, or is it a necessary underpinning of such societies, or is it, in fact, both of these (Offe, 1984)? The welfare state is complex at a number of different levels: the administration of the benefits system is famously complicated, even for the people delivering the service; at another level it is complex in the sense that different parts of the welfare state are structured, funded and run in quite different ways; and at a third level the complexity of the welfare state is reflected in the difficulty of measuring the relationship between inputs and outcomes in terms of who actually benefits. The contested, contradictory and complex nature of the welfare state has helped to ensure that it is also dynamic, constantly under pressure to change, and in the early years of the twenty-first century it is very different from the form it took more than fifty years ago in the aftermath of the war.

In this situation it can be helpful to distinguish between broad and narrow definitions of the welfare state. The narrow approach tends to focus on what Esping-Andersen (1990: 1) calls the traditional terrain of social amelioration, and concentrates on a defined set of public services. An example of such a definition would be that offered by Glennerster and Hills (1998: 3), who say that for their purposes the welfare state consists of public policy in the areas of education, the National Health Service (NHS), housing, the personal social services and social security. Many more or less similar definitions could be listed, in contrast to broader approaches such as the one put forward by Pierson (1991: 7), who defines the welfare state as a specific type of society in which the state intervenes within the processes of economic reproduction and distribution to reallocate life chances between individuals and/or classes. Another example of this kind would be that the term refers to a concept of government in which the state plays a key role in the protection and promotion of the economic and social wellbeing of its citizens (quoted in Kleinman, 2002: 2). Or again, 'The concept of the "welfare state" conveys the idea that it is the duty and the obligation of the state to guarantee the "welfare" (that is, something more than sheer survival: survival with *dignity*, as understood in a given society at a given time) of all its subjects' (Bauman, 1998: 45).

Welfare needs (broadly defined) can be met in a number of different ways: informally within the family and local community, more or less formally by charitable or other voluntary activity (in contemporary society this includes a range of formally constituted not-for-profit organizations, such as housing associations), the private market and public services. A welfare state is one where the government accepts responsibility for ensuring that everyone has the opportunity to achieve at least a socially acceptable basic minimum level of material welfare. The definition of what constitutes the basic minimum is context specific, but typically the means of providing it will involve some combination of direct public service provision and state support for provision and/or consumption in a range of other areas. The balance between public and other forms of provision, and the degree of support provided for non-state services, will vary from service to service, from time to time, and from one jurisdiction to another.

This suggests that welfare states can be thought of in terms of two dimensions, one measuring commitment, or the extent to which governments accept responsibility for wellbeing, and the other referring to form, or the way in which commitment is operationalized. A given position on one axis does not necessarily imply a particular position on the other, but it is reasonable to expect that governments accepting a high level of responsibility for the wellbeing of citizens would opt for extensive public services and closely regulated markets. On the other hand, governments seeking to limit their commitment and to transfer risk and responsibility on to individuals would reduce the scale and scope of public services and encourage private initiative by moving to more open, lightly regulated markets. Thinking of welfare states in terms of continua has the advantage over typologies (such as that developed by Esping-Andersen, 1990) in that it is more dynamic, acknowledging that things change over time.

Narrow approaches to the welfare state lead to the conclusion that housing is the wobbly pillar, because the public sector is so small compared to the market, because within the public sector direct charges to service users remain significant and because of the residualized character of the service in the present period. Broader definitions, however, make no such clear distinction between public and private sectors. The question becomes, what is the range of factors affecting housing welfare, and what role does the state play in relation to these? On this view the important task is to identify all the various ways in which the state is involved in enhancing the wellbeing of its citizens, in this case through interventions that relate directly or indirectly to their consumption of housing. Harloe (1995: 3) has suggested that 'in capitalist societies there tends to be an inverse relationship between the degree to which there are major opportunities for private accumulation in various aspects of human needs provision, and the extent to which such provision may, in certain historical conjunctures, be wholly or partly decommodified'. He then suggests that in the case of housing the more interesting question concerns not the marginal position of housing in relation to the welfare state, but the problem of explaining why it has sometimes been provided through the agency of the state in a more or less decommodified form. However, another way of looking at housing and the welfare state is to say that precisely because housing is both a basic human need and a capitalist commodity that is relatively difficult to decommodify, the state is constrained to act through and with the market, in addition to direct public provision. Rather than approaching housing and the welfare state through a narrow focus on the public sector, it is necessary to look at a range of different forms of action taken by the state to influence the quality, quantity and price of dwellings across the system as a whole.

The narrow focus on the public services leaves unexamined and unexplained other crucial determinants of wellbeing. As Esping-Andersen (1990: 4) has argued:

> we cannot grasp the welfare state without locating its activities in relation to the private sector...it is a myth to think that either markets or the state are more naturally equipped to develop welfare. Instead, markets are often politically created and form an integral part of the overall welfare-state regime.

And in historical terms it is a mistake to concentrate exclusively on the public services because, as Richard Titmuss (1958) long ago pointed out, the state was heavily implicated in other forms of assistance, principally delivered through the tax system.

The broad view of the welfare state seems to have more to offer in general, not just in relation to an understanding of housing. In analytical terms the broader approach provides a way of looking at and explaining forms of state intervention that amount to working with and through markets (and other structures of provision such as voluntary and charitable organizations). The most important of these markets is the labour market, for in Britain and other capitalist economies with developed public services it has remained the case that income from employment is the main determinant of the material welfare of individuals and families (Glynn, 1999: 179). Much of what people spend their money on is complementary to, or a substitute for, public services provided free at the point of use. This includes not just expenditure on private health care, education, pensions and housing, but also the huge amounts spent on over-the-counter medicines and the consumption of education through books, magazines, the Internet and so forth. Traditional approaches to the welfare state tend to be input and output oriented (asking how much was spent and what was provided), but this wider approach shifts attention to outcomes, to achieved levels of wellbeing.

This is not to argue that private schools, book shops and supermarkets should be seen as parts of the welfare state, but that the levels of wellbeing achieved within the population reflect the choices that people make when spending their own money, as well as the expenditure on and quality of public services. Welfare states developed in the context of pre-existing market based economies, and were always predicated upon the assumption of continuing markets for all sorts of goods and services: even where the state undertook to provide a free service for all citizens (as in the case of the British NHS) private practice continued alongside. Welfare states, then, can be seen as representing a mixed economy of welfare, with some service areas dominated by the public sector, and others by the private market.

Therefore a key measure of government commitment to welfare is the stance taken on employment. Idleness was one of the 'five giants' identified by Beveridge, and full employment was a basic aim of postwar reconstruction. The importance of full employment to the postwar welfare state and to the general improvement in living standards observed in that period is widely accepted, although there is room to debate how far the levels of employment achieved between 1945 and the late 1960s would have happened in the absence of any such policy commitment. There is also scope to debate whether full employment should be analysed as an integral part of the welfare state or a separate but crucial underpinning for it. Service based approaches tend to see it as a necessary underpinning, whereas broader outcome related approaches imply that employment policy should be integrated. Whatever view one takes on these issues, it is clear that insufficient attention has been given to the importance and impact of employment policy in most accounts of the welfare state in Britain. This is especially important in the case of housing, where the state was committed to only a limited role in terms of direct public provision; without the maintenance of full employment it would have been much more difficult to boost demand for owner occupation and to manage the changing balance between public and private sector contributions to new building that occurred in the 1950s. Equally, the later abandonment of full employment policy, and the rise in unemployment, had implications for the housing wellbeing of people directly affected. In the 1980s, as will be discussed in Chapter 6, housing and employment policies worked against each other, in marked contrast to the earlier period. The rise in unemployment particularly affected workers in extractive and manufacturing industries, precisely the people who had previously been the mainstay of council housing, which was in steeply diminishing supply.

While it is necessary to have some sort of working definition if only in order, as Viet-Wilson (2000) argues, to distinguish welfare states from non-welfare states, it is also necessary to recognize that welfare states are not all the same. A good deal of research energy has gone into comparative studies, which highlight the enduring differences between the welfare states in different countries (Esping-Andersen, 1990; Huber and Stephens, 2001). Welfare states are social constructs that have to be understood in terms of specific historical and geographical contexts.

Housing and the welfare state: an analytical framework

The historical and geographical focus of this book is Britain since 1945, and therefore the analysis reflects the specificity of the British welfare state and the particular place of housing within or in relation to it. The framework for the analysis is based on two key ideas, derived from the wider academic literature: first, that the history of the welfare state since 1945 can be divided into two main periods, and second, that within each period it is possible to identify three distinct welfare state 'settlements'.

Although the origins of the British welfare state can be traced back to the early twentieth century, or even earlier (B. Harris, 2004), the importance of the reforms of the 1940s is undisputed: there was a step change in levels of public expenditure on welfare, existing services were extended and new ones introduced. Some writers have referred to these reforms as the creation of the 'classic' welfare state, which survived until the economic and fiscal crisis of the mid-1970s (Digby, 1989; Gladstone, 1999; R. Lowe, 1994). The 'classic' welfare state is often associated with the idea of a postwar consensus and a set of shared principles defining the role of the state and the rights of citizens. In this context the influence of writers such as Richard Titmuss (1958, 1968) and T. H. Marshall (1950) is frequently cited. It is important not to over-play the extent of consensus and not to give an impression of a welfare state that sprang into existence fully formed and perfect and which remained unchanged until the point of crisis. There is a risk of under-emphasizing both the contested, incremental and piecemeal character of much social policy reform in the 1940s, and the extent of change over the next thirty years.

Despite the dynamism of the welfare state in the decades after 1945, it is clear that the mid-1970s marks an important watershed, a time of crisis and turmoil in which ideas that had been more or less taken for granted for a generation came under severe attack from a number of directions. Once the long postwar boom began to falter and unemployment began to rise, it became more difficult to defend the economic and welfare policies adopted since the 1940s, and 'instead of sailing with the tide the welfare state was now battling against it' (Glennerster and Hills, 1998: 12).

Since that time the welfare state has been redefined and renegotiated. For present purposes it is argued that within the period since 1975 it is possible to distinguish two phases, either side of 1988. The first phase was characterized chiefly by crisis management and retrenchment in terms of attempts to contain and curb public expenditure. This was followed by a broader set of changes designed to re-engineer the welfare state as a whole, and 1988 stands out as the year that saw a series of major social policy measures designed to move the welfare state onto a new footing (Le Grand, 1991; see also Chapter 7 later). The process of change continues, of course, currently in the form of the New Labour project of 'modernization' of public services, but it is now possible to identify a distinctly different form of welfare state for the early twenty-first century.

The welfare state reforms of the 1940s have often been described as an aspect of the 'postwar settlement' between capital and labour, but Clarke and Newman (1997: ch. 1) have gone further and suggested that the postwar welfare state can be analysed in terms of three distinct settlements, namely the political-economic, the social and the organizational settlements. The political-economic settlement can be seen as a compromise between capitalism (based on private ownership and free markets) and socialism (based on state ownership and centrally planned economies). The political-economic settlement implied a commitment to a managed capitalist economy with full employment as a central goal, together with a series of universal services, free at the point of consumption, funded from taxes and insurance contributions. However, full employment in those days referred to male employment and the idea of the social settlement draws attention to the gendered, patriarchal and racialized nature of the postwar British welfare state. As Fiona Williams (1989) and others have pointed out, the reforms of the 1940s were largely based on assumptions about the family consisting of a male earner and dependent wife and children, whose entitlement to key benefits was grounded in the husband's contributions to the National Insurance scheme. 'This was, above all, a British welfare state, construed as serving British citizens with a known and predictable pattern of life and well understood welfare needs. This British citizen was – almost incidentally – white' (Clarke and Newman, 1997: 3).

The universalism of the welfare state was, in fact, 'deeply circumscribed' (quoted by Clarke and Newman, 1997: 4). This is a valuable corrective to generalizations about the welfare state implying that each component service somehow and unproblematically promoted social solidarity and cohesion. Finally the idea of an organizational settlement refers to the way that postwar services were delivered by large public sector organizations in which professional and bureaucratic modes of co-ordination predominated. These are usually seen as contrasting approaches, but they were combined within the developing public services organizations. The bureaucratic method provided a means of ensuring standardization and impartiality in the delivery of services, while professionalism applied expertise and encouraged progress.

Since the 1970s the three postwar settlements have been substantially renegotiated. First, the political-economic settlement has been renegotiated around a smaller role for the state in terms of both managing the economy and delivering welfare services. The consequence is acceptance of insecurity in labour markets in the face of global market forces, and greater reliance on markets as the mechanism for meeting consumer needs. The emphasis now is on preparing/disciplining the work force, managing the supply of workers rather than the demand for them. Alongside this is a marked redistribution of risk and responsibility from the state to the individual, loading financial costs onto individuals as the price of increased choice.

Second, the welfare state has had to come to terms with a changing and much more diverse pattern of households and dependency; this includes the growth in the numbers of both two-earner households (the work-rich) and also no-earner households (the work-poor). Of particular importance for both pensions policy and housing is the changing balance between households of working age and those where there is no-one under the age of 65: increasing numbers of elderly households, tending to live longer into old age, pose a challenge to established pensions arrangements, and if retirement incomes cannot be maintained at the levels that people have come to expect then this raises questions about the long term sustainability of home ownership. Old assumptions of the predominance of white nuclear families with male breadwinners and dependent wives and children have had to be revised in the light of higher levels of female employment, increasing ethnic diversity and growing numbers of one-parent households.

Finally there is a new organizational settlement based on local authorities as strategic enablers rather than service providers, relying on a range of private, voluntary and community organizations for service delivery. These are typically required to compete in provider markets or quasi-markets for the right to provide services. Not only are services now increasingly likely to be provided by non-municipal organizations but also, as a direct result, local accountability through elected representatives has been weakened. The new fragmented governance of welfare services can be seen as a challenge to the old bureaucratic and professional approaches and a shift towards managerialism, an aspect of which is an emphasis on 'letting the managers manage', but it is often accompanied by a growth of government regulation and performance monitoring (Hoggett, 1996). This has led to the growth of quasi-government by non-elected agencies directing or overseeing the spending of public money and the provision of public services (Clarke, Gewirtz and McLaughlin, 2000: 4). At the same time there is a continuing rhetorical emphasis on the notion of users as consumers with choices and options.

What does all this mean for the study of housing and the welfare state? In order to answer questions about whether housing is the wobbly pillar under the welfare state it is necessary to specify a definition of the welfare state, and to recognize that things change over time: the relationship between housing and the welfare state has to be understood historically. Narrow definitions of the welfare state in terms of public services, and definitions that employ the idea of decommodification as the key measure of welfare state solidity, lead to an analytical focus on social rented housing. On the other hand, broader definitions demand a frame of reference that includes all dimensions of state intervention in pursuit of individual and collective wellbeing. This is a more satisfactory approach, for three main reasons: first, it embraces the full range of state interventions, including measures designed to support and regulate the private and voluntary not-for-profit sectors, which would otherwise be left out of account. Second, it acknowledges that housing is an example of a basic human need that is not always satisfactorily provided by the traditional nexus of family, charity and market, but which is nevertheless difficult for the state to decommodify. In these circumstances the state can be expected to adopt a variety of forms of policy action designed to work with and through the private and voluntary sectors. Third, the broad approach implies attention to achieved welfare outcomes as well as direct service provision. The state of housing welfare in Britain is a product of much more than formal housing policy and fiscal measures directly affecting housing. Because so much housing consumption is mediated by the market mechanism, levels of housing welfare are influenced by policies affecting employment and income maintenance.

The adoption of a broader definition therefore demands that a book about housing and the welfare state addresses itself to much more than social housing. It must consider measures to supplement, complement, support and regulate the production and consumption of housing in general. It must provide a genuinely cross-tenure account, looking at local authority housing, of course, but also policies in relation to housing associations as an alternative source of new subsidized rented housing, plus issues of regulation and support for private renting and owner occupation. Whereas the narrow definition of the welfare state invites conclusions that dwell on the limited decommodification of housing and the strong residualization of the public sector, the wider definition appears to provide more scope for coming to different conclusions, but it is more difficult to interpret the evidence: for example, if, as is the case, the condition of privately owned dwellings (especially the owner occupied sector) can be shown to have improved since the late 1940s, this might be taken as evidence for the beneficial impact of the welfare state on housing in general. But it is difficult to decide how much of the measurable improvement is due to direct policy action and how much improvement would have occurred anyway, in the absence of state intervention. A good deal of private housing investment in improvement and modernization has been directly funded by government grants, but a lot more has been undertaken on the initiative of home owners whose financial resources and confidence in loan finance have been to some indefinable extent influenced, at different times, by policies of full employment or the lack of such policies.

On the question of historical perspective, the development of housing and housing policy needs to be set against the framework outlined above in relation to the welfare state. The match is by no means precise; for example, housing policy in the immediate post-1945 period did not contain the sort of reform measures associated with other key services, and it is arguable that 1954 marked a more important turning point in postwar housing policy than the mid-1970s. The analytical task in each period is to determine who was providing what for whom and on what terms. This embraces issues of differential access to services and benefits by different social groups, and changes in the types of organization delivering goods and services.

The structure of the book is that, following a discussion of approaches to thinking about housing and the welfare state in Chapter 2, the next five chapters are historical and chronological. Chapter 3 looks at themes in the development of housing and housing policy before the Second World War, partly in order to allow later chapters to indicate the continuities as well as the changes over time. Chapter 4 concentrates on the impact of the war of 1939–45 for the way housing policy was planned and implemented, suggesting that it is important to recognize both the quality and quantity of wartime planning for postwar reconstruction, and the absence of any overarching blueprint for a welfare state. Chapter 5 takes up the narrative in 1954, which is seen as a key turning point for postwar housing policy. It continues the story through to another important period, the mid-1970s. Chapter 6 deals with the period from then until 1988, by which time local authority housing was in steep decline due to the right to buy and a severe squeeze on investment. Chapter 7 provides a link between the historical narrative and the focus on contemporary issues. It reviews the wider context of change in the welfare state and suggests that a new housing policy orthodoxy had become established before the general election of 1997 brought an end to eighteen years of Conservative government.

Chapters 8–10 are broadly contemporary and are structured around the idea that the three settlements of the postwar welfare state have been renegotiated. The first of these refers to the retreat of the state in terms of both macro-economic management and regulation and service provision, and the related promotion of market based forms of consumption in largely deregulated markets. Thus Chapter 8 looks at the housing market as the predominant mode of provision today, in the context of a less regulated and more insecure labour market. The idea of a new social settlement is picked up in Chapter 9, which considers the changed role of the social rented sector, with more explicit responsibility for a diverse range of households unable to satisfy their needs in the housing market. Chapter 10 addresses the new organizational settlement, focusing in particular on two related processes: the challenge to bureau professionalism through performance management and demunicipalization through the transfer of local authority housing stock to new landlords.

Finally, Chapter 11 draws the themes of the book together and makes a number of concluding comments about change and continuity and about the housing–welfare state relationship.

Chapter 2

Perspectives on Housing

This chapter links the discussion of the welfare state in Chapter 1 with the more detailed housing focused historical narrative in subsequent chapters. It begins with a brief discussion of some of the key ideas in housing analysis, followed by a section on continuity and change as themes in the history of housing. Its main purpose, however, is to look at the way housing scholars have seen the housing–welfare state relationship, and how they have dealt with the problem of the differences between housing and the other main pro-gramme areas. This leads to a challenge to established perspectives and to a specification of the argument to be developed in the remainder of the book.

It is conventional to analyse the British housing system in terms of tenure categories, defined as the terms and conditions on which people occupy their homes. Tenure labels tell us something about the ownership of dwellings, and they enable us to distinguish different kinds of landlords and the different kinds of tenancy agreements offered to renters. For some reason there seems to be a deeply held commitment to a three tenure model of housing in Britain. For much of the twentieth century the model was owner occupation, local authority renting and private renting (the last, for most of the time, included housing associations and their forerunners: Malpass, 2000b, ch. 1). However, by the 1990s a revised three tenure model was being adopted, this time bracketing housing associations with local authority renting in a newly designated so-called social rented sector. This re-designation amply illustrates the artificial and arbitrary nature of tenures. Local authority landlords differ in significant ways from housing associations, but they are now considered together largely because of their role as the providers of housing at sub-market rents. But housing associa-tions do not confine themselves to this activity, for some are involved in the provision of care homes and nursing homes, while many provide housing on a shared equity basis. The development of shared equity illustrates the problematic nature of the three-tenure model: if someone owns half their house and rents the other half, are they owners or tenants?

Tenure is effectively both an indispensable tool of housing analysis and a potential barrier to understanding, mainly because to seek to describe the complexity of the British housing system in terms of just three broad cate-gories is to gloss over a rich variety of circumstances. Further, as Ball (1986) pointed out many years ago, tenures are merely consumption labels, based on the legalities of occupation, but they have come to be associated with distinct methods of provision. Each of the main tenure categories is generally linked with a particular mode of procurement. Thus, owner occupation in Britain is commonly associated with speculative house building, a system of financing based on loans from banks and building societies, and an exchange process mediated by estate agents and lawyers. But home ownership as a form of consumption is not necessarily linked to any particular method of organizing either the construction or the exchange process (Singapore, for example, has a very high level of home ownership, but virtually all construction work is carried out by the state: see Yuen, 2003).

Another feature of tenure labels is that they refer to dynamic phenomena, which have waxed and waned in specific ways since the First World War. In terms of their respective shares of the total housing stock it is clear that private renting has been in more or less continuous decline since 1919, while owner occupation has been growing throughout the same period. Local authority housing grew for sixty years and has been in numerical decline since 1980. Housing associations and their forerunners remained as a tiny and marginal sector until the last few years of the twentieth century. Going beyond size, each of the different tenures has changed in terms of its role in the housing system, and in the quality, affordability and desirability of what it offers to people. In this context it is relevant to mention that most privately rented houses now available were built before 1914, whereas virtually all council houses were constructed after 1919. For many years, therefore, council housing was predominantly modern by comparison, but the inevitable ageing of the stock, combined with a decline in new building by local authorities, has changed the age profile of the sector. This must have contributed to the changing popularity of council housing. Tenures therefore need to be understood historically, in the sense that generalizations that are true for one point in time may well not be true for another. As Harloe (1995: 69) has pointed out, social housing has been socially constructed and reconstructed several times.

In this context it is important to reiterate that the term social housing as a way of referring to provision by both local authorities and housing associations is a modern invention, and that historically no such unity was perceived. Indeed, in the first half of the twentieth century the plethora of charitable and limited profit housing organizations were probably more aware of the differences among themselves, and the promotion of the idea of a 'voluntary housing movement' was a conscious attempt to enhance their chances of attracting government support for a wider role. In one sense it is anachronistic to refer to social rented housing in the past because the term was not used in Britain much before 1990. But for purely analytical purposes it is helpful to think in terms of a dual social rented sector in Britain, consisting of municipal and non-municipal sub-sectors, as far back as the late nineteenth century. This then raises the question of why the two sub-sectors developed at such different rates after the First World War. It has also been suggested (Malpass, 2001) that the notion of a dual social rented sector, based on the nature of provider organizations, offers an additional dimension to the distinction between mass and residual models of social housing based on characteristics of consumers (Harloe, 1995: 71–3). Both dimensions are dynamic and need to be incorporated into historical analyses of social housing.

The dynamism of the housing system is only partly due to interventions by the state, and one of the major tasks of analysis is to disentangle the impacts of exogenous policy action from endogenous market driven change. This connects with a point made by Ball (1986), who argued that too often the British housing literature seemed to be based on a 'consumer orientation', by which he meant, among other things, that housing problems were generally conceived in terms of the difficulties faced by households in obtaining suitable accommodation at an affordable price. Furthermore, housing policy was usually conceived as the state coming to the rescue of households in difficulty. Another way of looking at the same phenomena is to see that in a capitalist economy there is a problem for house builders: how can they make profits from the supply of a commodity that is inherently expensive in relation to the regular incomes of most con-sumers? Housing policy can be understood as the state responding to the problem of the profitability of the house building industry, and variations in policy over time can be related to varying opportunities for profit in chang-ing market conditions. The precise ways in which governments intervene will depend upon the political and economic circumstances of the time and their view of the role of the state in macro-economic management. Housing is not just about the needs of consumers and builders; it is a significant part of the construction industry, which in turn is a significant part of the whole economy. The housing market as a whole includes not just the flow of newly constructed dwellings but also the much larger volume of existing houses that are offered for sale at any one time. Trying to manage the tendency of the housing market to follow a cycle of booms and slumps has become an important aspect of macro-economic management. Housing policy, then, is about much more than seeking to ensure that every household has access to a decent house at an affordable price.

The historiography of housing: issues of change and continuity

Over the years many writers have attempted to overcome the presentation of history as just one thing after another by identifying apparently distinct peri-ods or phases. Sometimes these are meant merely as descriptive labels – the dark ages, the renaissance, the industrial revolution – while in other cases there is an attempt to establish progress and causality. The best known of such approaches is Karl Marx's theory of the historical inevitability of each epoch giving way to the next. At a less ambitious level, developments in public policy have also been theorized in terms of a series of stages (MacDonagh, 1958; McGuire, 1981). In the case of housing policy there is no agreement in the literature as to the best way to periodize developments, and there is a lively debate about whether policies in different countries are tending to converge (Kemeny and Lowe, 1998; Kleinman, 1996; Priemus and Dieleman, 1999). Harloe (1995) discusses the history of social housing in terms of just four phases since 1919, while Ginsburg (1999) saw 1919–75 as one single phase. Others have suggested three distinct phases in the much shorter period of twenty-five years after 1945 (Malpass and Murie, 1999: 53–4) and four phases in the period 1970–90 (Balchin and Rhoden, 2002; Boelhouwer and van der Heijden, 1992). Obviously it all depends on how the evidence is approached and where the focus of attention lies. There is also the problem of the fuzziness of history, in the sense that it is rarely possible to define with precision the beginning and end of any particular period; changes are more likely to be gradual than sudden. In this situation some writers have fallen back on the view that there is no coherence or consistency.

A recurrent theme has been the charge that successive governments after 1945 were guilty of short-termism (P. Williams, 1997: 1–3), treating housing as a 'political football' (Yates, 1982: 204), and wilfully changing direction to reflect party political preferences (Balchin and Rhoden, 2002: xv). Other metaphors deployed in this context refer to housing policy as following a 'see-saw course' (Burnett, 1985: 291) and swinging drunkenly back and forth (Donnison and Ungerson, 1982: 285). In a statement that epitomizes the political football approach David Donnison (1989: ix) wrote:

> In every country the political movements contending for power choose particular issues as a stage on which to dramatise and symbolise their differences. If an issue is treated in that way for many years it becomes impossible to develop consistent, rational policies for dealing with it. Housing has long been one of the issues used in this way by the main political parties in Britain.

There are several objections to the political football approach. First, it betrays an implicit intolerance of the democratic process and a preference for executive dominance. Second, by suggesting that politicians are in control of policy development it seriously under-represents the importance of the constraints on governments. An alternative perspective would place more emphasis on the underlying currents driving policy, and less on the highly visible but essentially superficial activities of party politicians.

Third, if in parliamentary democracies it is in the nature of the party political struggle to be heard that different parties will seek to exaggerate the differences between their own modest/bold proposals and the puny/ outrageous proposals of their opponents, then this should inform academic analysis; rather than taking the claims of politicians at face value we should be looking at the evidence for their claims and developing our own perspective on events. This implies a need to ask questions about what drives change in the housing system and in housing policy: to what extent is change driven by party political interests, and how far do those interests reflect underlying conflicts between capital and labour? How far is change a result of deeper economic processes?

Discussion of continuity and change in housing needs to take into account the distinction between the housing system and housing policy. The latter is an overlay on the former. Policy may be, and usually is, intended to bring about change, but not all change in the system can be attributed to policy. The size of the British housing stock is such that it is very difficult to effect systemic changes with any rapidity: the number of dwellings can only grow by a very small percentage each year, and changes to the overall quality of the existing stock inevitably take time. This therefore acts as a constraint on policy, implying a need to take the long view.

One of the problems with much of the literature on public policy is a general lack of clarity or precision in relation to the key concepts of continuity and change. There is a widespread failure to recognize that the difference between them is highly dependent on the viewpoint of the observer. In general, the closer the observer the more the fine grain of policy detail will be apparent and therefore the more likely it is that a change perspective will emerge. Paradoxically, perhaps, a detailed analysis within a narrow timeframe may be more likely to produce a perception of change than a more distanced study of a longer period. A good illustration of this effect is provided by housing subsidy legislation from 1919 to 1972: in this period there were at least twelve Acts of Parliament and a focus on any one of them would highlight the detailed changes in the levels of subsidy and the criteria for payment, but on a longer term view those details fade out of sight to reveal that over the period from 1923 to 1967 all subsidy systems were based on the same model (Malpass, 1990: ch. 3).

It is true, of course, that over time changes also become clearer. In this connection it is important to distinguish between policies and outcomes: consistency of policy would be expected to produce changes in the area to which it is applied. Continuity does not necessarily imply sameness; it is often the case that governments decide to adopt new policy instruments in pursuit of continuing policy objectives. This would be likely to occur where existing instruments were found to be no longer effective in pursuit of established goals – and most policies fail eventually (Marsh and

Rhodes, 1992: 9). However, governments do not have a completely free hand in the choice of policy instruments. In a helpful rebuttal of the political football approach Kleinman (1996: 180–1) has invoked the notion of path dependence as an explanation of continuity:

> countries become locked into particular patterns of policy development at an early stage, for reasons that may be historical, deliberately chosen, or the product of accident. Once locked in, this pattern then constrains future development.

A good example of this effect would be the distinctly British form of social housing: once local authorities had become established as the main providers of new social rented housing in the inter-war period it was very difficult to envisage a different approach after 1945. This example, of course, raises the question of what happened to undermine the position of local authorities by the latter part of the twentieth century, a subject that will be taken up in a later chapter. Thus it is not that major changes can never occur, just that they are unlikely in normal circumstances. On this view changes may be frequent but contained within a dominant framework of ideas and perceived possibilities. Ginsburg (1999: 226–35) has suggested that British housing policy over a long period, 1915–75, remained within what he calls a 'liberal collectivist' framework, which had four defining features:

- rent control/regulation for private rented housing without significant fiscal incentives or cash support for landlords or tenants
- nationally regulated and subsidized provision of local authority rented housing for the 'respectable' working class
- progammes of Victorian slum clearance with replacement council housing for poor people
- fiscal and general government support for owner occupiers.

This kind of perspective is another useful antidote to political football approaches, although it is arguable that Ginsburg is rather stretching his case by claiming to perceive a policy of support for owner occupation in the inter-war years. What is clear is that inter-war governments took the view that private enterprise could and should provide for the majority of people most of the time, but they were largely indifferent as between private renting and owner occupation (indeed there is some evidence – discussed in Chapter 4 later – that by the mid-1940s the official view was that the balance of new building had tilted too much towards owner occupation). However, in support of Ginsburg, it can be seen that in the period he identifies most people did not pay the full market price for their homes: rent control in the private rented sector and subsidies in the local authority sector kept rents at sub-market levels, and income tax-paying home owners with mortgages were eligible for tax relief (at their marginal tax rate) on their mortgage interest payments. In addition, in the post-1945 era the leading building societies (who were then the main providers of mortgage finance) developed an interest rate cartel agreement, which kept the rates that they charged to borrowers and paid to lenders lower than in other parts of the market (in effect, house purchasers were subsidized by people who invested their money in building societies). Subsidy in one form or another was a pervasive feature of the British housing system throughout the liberal collectivist period.

In further support of Ginsburg's perception of long term stability in housing policy two points need to be made. First, throughout the whole of the period since the early twentieth century housing policy has been based on the same underlying assumption, namely that the market will provide for most people most of the time, and that state intervention in the form of public housing can be and should be limited. This is not only a valuable indicator of continuity but also a key influence on the nature of housing policy, in the sense that it is not just about meeting housing needs but also about maintaining profitability in the house building industry. Unlike health and education, where the public sector predominates and there is no pressure to formulate policy in relation to the interests of the private market, in housing the situation is reversed. Thus it can be said that throughout the history of housing policy a consistent theme has been the perceived importance of maintaining profitability, and so policy has been framed at least as much with producer interests in mind.

Second, following directly from the last point about the differences between housing and other mainstream welfare state services, it is significant that although Ginsburg identifies the mid-1970s as a key turning point in policy development (which is consistent with views about the welfare state as a whole), he does not attach the same importance to the immediate postwar years of social reform. Indeed, it is significant that none of the four policy continuities identified by Ginsburg dated from, or was directly related to, the postwar welfare state. To the extent that this is a correct interpretation, it suggests that in housing it was the economic convulsion of the end of the postwar boom and the collapse of Keynesian macro-economic management techniques, rather than the postwar political settlement, that was of greatest relevance. This in turn raises questions about the significance of the welfare state for an understanding of housing and housing policy.

In the period since the 1970s British housing policy has been reshaped by a new set of consistencies. Kleinman (1996: 175) has suggested that housing policy as it was previously understood (in terms of estimating needs, setting output targets, boosting house building, raising the condition of the stock, removing sub-standard dwellings and pursuing the goal of a decent home for every household) has been split into two distinct parts. For the majority of the population housing policy consists of measures designed to maintain a functioning housing market, while for the minority (those permanently or temporarily excluded from the market) there is an increasingly segregated, residualized and stigmatized social rented sector. Under the long period of Conservative government from 1979 to 1997 housing policy consistently emphasized:

- the promotion of owner occupation
- the deregulation of private renting
- acceleration of the trend away from general housing subsidy towards means-tested assistance with housing costs
- the cultivation of the idea that local authority housing was a failed solution and that it had become part of the problem to be solved.

By the 1990s, and, significantly, *before* the election of the new Labour government in 1997, a new paradigm for housing policy had been established, based on three key differences. First, whereas previously housing was subsidized in various ways, Britain is now rapidly becoming a country in which the housing system is characterized more by taxation than subsidy. Second, throughout the liberal collectivist period it was the private sector that was subject to restructuring, whereas now it is the social rented sector, through the transfer of stock from local authority ownership and control into the hands of independent or arm's length bodies. Third, the issue of the demand for housing has reappeared on the policy agenda, but in two quite different ways. In marked contrast to policy responses of the liberal collectivist period, governments in the 1990s reacted to projections indicating a need to build large numbers of houses by continuing to cut resources for social housing; it was not until 2000/01 that spending was increased. The assumption now is that not only can new building be left very largely to private enterprise but that a significant proportion of the new social housing can be secured from the private sector through the use of planning powers. The other way in which demand has become a salient policy issue has been through the emergence of the idea that, despite the overall need to build in large numbers, there are some areas where low demand is a real problem.

Approaches to housing and the welfare state

This section sets out, first, a critique of conventional approaches to housing and the welfare state in the academic literature, and, second, an alternative interpretation, which provides a guide to the argument to be developed in subsequent chapters. In an important article in *Housing Studies* in 1997, Alan Murie wrote that:

> Housing in Britain has traditionally been seen as part of the welfare state, but as the complexity of the analysis of housing has grown the relationship with the welfare state has received declining attention. The wider welfare state has been treated as a backdrop rather than a key influence or determinant of housing institutions and the development of the housing sector. It is presented as context rather than as integral or interconnected. However, a closer examination of some aspects of this relationship between housing and the wider welfare state suggests that this is a serious weakness in analysis. (Murie, 1997: 440)

This is a well made point and provides a starting point for a critical review of the literature. There are certain conventions in much academic writing about housing and housing policy. For example, since the important and influential book on state housing in Britain by Stephen Merrett (1979) historical accounts now generally attempt to set developments in housing in relation to the wider political and economic context. Interestingly, Merrett had nothing to say about housing and the welfare state as such. However, writers whose chief area of interest is British social policy normally include housing as one of the key services that constituted the bedrock of the postwar welfare state. In a wider geographical context it is interesting to note that a number of international comparative studies have neglected housing, even when housing data were collected (S. Lowe, 2004: 6–7). As mentioned in the previous chapter, the choice of services is arbitrary to some extent, although it can be seen as deriving from the responses to the five giants identified by Beveridge in 1942, and it reflects the way the welfare state was understood at the time (Tomlinson, 1995: 195–6). Most social policy texts since Penelope Hall's *The Social Services of Modern England* (1952) have adopted this approach (Alcock, 1996; Brown and Payne, 1994; Ellison and Pierson, 1998; Ginsburg, 1979; Glennerster, 1995; Glennerster and Hills, 1998; Gough, 1979; Hill, 2000; Timmins, 1996).

It is equally conventional to refer to the ways in which housing differs from the other services (Malpass and Murie, 1982: 5). Clapham, Kemp and Smith (1990: ix) wrote that: 'It is true that because of the large element of private provision and consumption in housing, this facet of social welfare does not fit easily into the model of state-provided social services followed by the health and personal social services.' In addition to the notion of housing as the wobbly pillar, it has been variously described as having 'retained an ambiguous and shifting status on the margins of the welfare state, the least decommodified and most market-determined of the conventionally accepted constituents of such states' (Harloe, 1995: 2), or 'hover[ing] awkwardly on the threshold of the status of a social service' (Townsend, 1976: 87). Housing has even been described as 'a stillborn social service lodged within a capitalist dynamic of property relations' (Cole and Furbey, 1994: 6).

The limited removal of housing consumption from the private market has been attributed to the way that housing, as a commodity, differs from health, education and pensions (Harloe, 1995: 3). According to this view, the fact that housing is property (real estate) is centrally important, because of the role of private property in capitalist societies, the power of property interests and therefore the greater strength of resistance to attempts to decommodify the provision of housing. Moreover, there has always been some form of private housing market for the majority of the population, in contrast to the situation in health and education, where, historically, markets could not be relied on to provide for large proportions of the people (Harloe, 1995: 536). This is about as far as the analysis goes; the specificity of housing within the welfare state is noted but not pursued.

Not only is housing seen as having a marginal or questionable relationship with the welfare state in the past, it is recognized to have been treated differently by governments since 1979. Observers who refer to the general resilience of the welfare state to the impact of Thatcherism in the 1980s invariably acknowledge that housing has been the exception (Le Grand, 1991). Housing, then, was always 'an insecure foundation of the welfare state' (Cole and Furbey, 1994: 7) and has become more insecure in recent decades. The idea that housing is less part of the welfare state now than it was is captured in the title of the book *Selling the Welfare State* (Forrest and Murie, 1988), and, more colourfully, in the suggestion by Cole and Furbey (1994: 2) that governments have been able to amputate its housing arm. These authors also refer to housing as 'uncertainly integrated, and then progressively detached, from the postwar infrastructure of state welfare' (ibid., 59).

There are several criticisms of existing conventional accounts. First, they are usually grounded in an implicit narrow, institutional, definition of the welfare state, leading to a focus on local authority housing to the exclusion of other forms of intervention. Second, as Murie (1997) has pointed out, connections between housing and other welfare state services are largely unexplored. Third, the origins of reforms in health, education and pensions lay in recognition of the failure and/or inappropriateness of private markets in these areas, but the basis of housing policy throughout the twentieth century was that the private market was succeeding and should be supported. This is such a fundamental difference of approach that it should give pause for thought about the validity of assumptions concerning the place of housing within the welfare state. Fourth, another fundamental problem about the place of housing within the welfare state is that it has never been either fully decommodified or simply residual – in other words, housing has never been made available as a social service, as a right for everyone, and neither has it been confined to the poor, for whom the market worked least well (Cole and Furbey, 1994: 64). Unlike any other welfare state service, for many years public housing was predominantly targeted at and used by the better off sections of the working class. Much intellectual effort has been devoted to analysing the process of residualization in recent decades, but much less attention has been given to the problem of explaining the very slow emergence of a public housing service that embraced the least well off. Fifth, some writers (notably Harloe, 1981, 1985, 1995; Malpass, 1990; Malpass and Murie, 1982, 1999) have developed ways of accounting for change in housing in the twentieth century in terms of the modernization of the private housing market, essentially arguing that the growth of public housing could be understood as a political response to tensions generated by market restructuring. This provided a way of explaining the changing character of council housing over time, but its implications for understanding the housing–welfare state relationship remained largely unexplored.

There is, in the last point, a degree of confession of personal culpability, and in a sense this book is an attempt to make good the omission. The book is also a challenge to accepted ways of looking at housing; it is an attempt to invert the conventional view, by arguing that housing policy in the postwar period is not best understood in terms of the welfare state. In relation to the more recent past and the present period, instead of seeing housing as being 'amputated' from the welfare state, it will be argued that it provides a model for the new, more limited, conditional and market-reliant form of the welfare state, increasingly delivered by non-municipal organizations. In this sense the modern housing system is more clearly delineated in terms of a large private market serving the majority, and a slimmed down social rented sector, more focused on the least well off than at any previous point in time.

The argument to be developed in subsequent chapters is that in relation to housing the postwar welfare state was a kind of rhetorical or ideological overlay on market driven processes that were already under way, and which had more impact on the content of housing policy. This is not to deny that housing was generally understood as part of the welfare state; but it is to suggest that housing policy was shaped more by market modernization than the welfare state. Looking back over the twentieth century as a whole it can be seen that state housing policy played a part in facilitating the modernization of the market, targeting different groups within the working class at different times. The capacity of the working class to press home its demands depends on the circumstances of the time. The two great wars of the first half of the twentieth century produced conditions in which radical social change became possible, and for a while working-class demands had more impact on governments than at other times. The situation at the end of each war was that houses had to be built but the market could not supply them in politically necessary quantities and at acceptable prices. In this context the state undertook the task of delivering the increased supply of houses at affordable rents. It chose to work through the agency of the local authorities as the main providers of these houses, but this was a political choice, not an inevitability. In practice the role of local authority housing was to accommodate the better off working class, while the less well off remained in the still plentiful but poorer quality private rented sector. It is very important to appreciate that local authority housing did not develop as a form of provision aimed at the least well off; on the contrary, for much of the period from the start of large scale provision by local authorities in the 1920s through to the 1960s the predominant role of this sector was to provide good quality rented housing for the better off within the working class. In the 1930s and again from the mid-1950s policy began to take on a more residual character, but overall the public sector continued to be a tenure of the better off working class. Since the 1970s, however, both housing policy and the public (or social rented) sector have become more and more residualized.

As modernization proceeded two things happened; one was that the further growth of owner occupation implied increased penetration of the better off working class, precisely the people who had become accustomed to the benefits of subsidized local authority housing. The other was that the continued decline of private renting meant that the least well off had little choice but to turn to their local authority for help. The policy problem posed in this situation was how to make local authority housing simultaneously more affordable and more accessible for low income households and less attractive to the better off. A key aspect of the strategy adopted over many years was to raise rents while extending the scope of means tested assistance for the less well off. Another key element in the process of extending home ownership down the income scale was the sale of local authority houses under the right to buy legislation of 1980. From an analytical point of view the important feature of policy towards council housing is that it started and grew as a sector mainly for the better off, but has been turned into a sector for the less well off.

The modernization thesis is not based on the view that the residualization of public housing and the emergence of owner occupation as the tenure of the majority was inevitable. These things have to be understood as historically contingent political processes. The postwar housing crisis posed problems for different groups of stakeholders: the people who needed somewhere to live, the house builders who were struggling to restart their businesses in difficult economic conditions after the dormancy imposed by wartime restrictions, and not least for the governments of the day, for whom housing was a key performance indicator. These circumstances, where houses had to be built but the market could not deliver them, were sufficient to bring about a step change in housing policy and in the level and type of state intervention, but not to challenge the underlying hegemony of the market. The response was measures designed to produce short term increases in supply rather than the sorts of systemic reform that would have threatened the market. Even in periods of acute housing crisis the debate was contained within a discourse which accepted the long term predominance of a market based housing system. When shortages were greatest and markets could not meet demand, then the state stepped in to ensure at least a politically acceptable minimum level of new building and price control in the market generally. The high quality of the council houses provided in the immediate postwar years reflected the political power of the better off working class and the subordination of the interests of the less well off. As soon as shortages eased and/or markets recovered then governments retreated from meeting 'general needs', refocusing local authorities on the needs of those who were in the worst housing (through slum clearance) and those who could not afford to pay the market rent for decent accommodation. This had the effect of removing local authorities from direct competition with private enterprise, and forcing them to concentrate on the tasks that the private sector did not or could not do effectively.

Overall, the modernization thesis provides a better account of housing and housing policy than perspectives emphasizing state intervention in terms of market failure and/or rejection. It provides a better explanation of the differences between housing and other welfare state services in terms of the degree of decommodification achieved in the post-1945 reforms, the early retreat from state housing production for general needs and the shift into slum clearance, and the long term strategy of reliance on the growth of working-class home ownership. It is strong in relation to the problem of explaining how housing is neither fully decommodified nor simply residual, and it is particularly strong in relation to the residualizing tendency in housing and housing policy since the 1970s. In this connection it is consistent with Kleinman's (1996) notion of the bifurcation of housing policy, which refers to the emergence of a distinction between state subsidized social housing provision for the least well off and a market based approach for the rest, pursued through macro-economic policy. However, the modernization thesis is not so good at explaining the emergence of local authorities, rather than housing associations, as the major providers of social rented housing throughout most of the twentieth century, or the restructuring of social renting which is seeing the belated emergence of housing associations as major players. The thesis is grounded in the modernization of the private market, but has no purchase on the restructuring of the social rented sector, for which other explanations need to be sought. It is in this context that housing and the welfare state come together. The changes currently affecting social housing, in terms of both its restricted scope and the organizational structure, are best understood as aspects of the reshaping of the welfare state, or, to use the Blairite language, the modernization of public services. Thus housing policy in the postwar period is best understood in terms of market restructuring, rather than the welfare state, but now the position is reversed.

A note on social class and social change

Frequent reference has been made above to the term 'working class' and the idea that housing policy has been aimed at different groups within that class at different times. The notion of class is problematic, but it is unavoidable in this context, if only because it was formally built into housing policy until the Housing Act, 1949. Until that time local authorities were technically restricted to providing housing for members of the working class; housing associations wishing to claim public loans and/or Exchequer subsidies were similarly constrained. Interestingly, the housing studies literature has paid more attention to the different experiences of distinct groups within the working class than to questions about, for example, the scope of the term working class and whether public housing was, in fact, restricted to members of that class. It is generally taken for granted that British public housing has always been overwhelmingly occupied by working-class households, and much has been written in the last twenty-five years about the changing social composition of social rented housing, but the question of the proportion of eligible households actually housed has not been discussed to anything like the same degree. However, it seems that even at its maximum in the late 1970s, social renting never accommodated much more than half the working class.

It is not necessary to go into great detail here about different ways of defining social classes (a subject on which there is a substantial body of sociological work), but it is important to recognize some salient features of social structure and social change that are of relevance to housing. Social classes are usually defined in relation to the occupational structure created in the economy. Conventionally, the term 'working class' has been used to embrace people employed in manual work. At the start of the twentieth century three-quarters of the employed population were in manual work of some kind (of these 30 per cent were classed as skilled, 34 per cent semi-skilled and 10 per cent unskilled). It was conventional in those days to refer to the working classes in the plural, and this was reflected in early housing legislation, which referred to artisans and labourers. Status distinctions within the working class were well understood as the self-consciously 'respectable' workers and their families strove to maintain their position in relation to the 'roughs'. Such differences were rooted in the economy and the rewards to different kinds of employment, and there was also a moral component as in, for example, the notion of the deserving and the undeserving. In this context the notion of economic core and periphery is helpful. Core workers were (and are) those who have economically valuable skills, commanding higher wages and more secure employment, yielding higher standards of living than could be expected by workers on the periphery of the economy. In the modern period rapid economic and technological change has seen formerly valued skills become obsolete, thrusting more people onto the margins of economic activity and increasing the numbers of long term unemployed. This has fuelled a debate about the notion of an underclass, cut off from the working class by more or less permanent exclusion from employment within the formal economy.

As recently as the early 1970s manual workers were still in the majority (55 per cent), but by 1991 they constituted just less than 38 per cent (Gallie, 2000: 288). There is, of course, plenty of scope to debate whether this amounts to the decline of the working class, and survey evidence suggests that more than two-thirds of people continue to see themselves as working class (Halsey, 1987: 16). Two other issues here would be, first, the question of whether the hugely increased numbers of routine clerical jobs are any less working class for being officially classified as non-manual, and second, the proportionate decline in manual work between 1911 and 1991 was greater than the numerical decline because of the very substantial growth in the number of professional and managerial jobs in the same period.

In relation to housing it is arguable that of greater significance than the relative decline in manual work are two other trends: the wider participation of women in the labour force and rising real household incomes. In the struggle to secure decent affordable housing, income is more important than social class, and the growth of female employment has helped to raise household incomes (although this has been offset to some extent by the tendency of market prices to rise as a result). The growth of female employment has been particularly marked in the postwar period; in 1951 women made up 31 per cent of the employed population (only 1 per cent more than in 1931), but by 1998 they were 46 per cent (Gallie, 2000: 293). A majority of women, including married women, now have jobs and therefore make a financial contribution to household income. The rising trend in real incomes is important and lies at the heart of improved material standards of living since the start of the twentieth century. In the period

1951–76 real disposable incomes per capita doubled (Halsey, 1987: 12), and doubled again between 1971 and 1999 (*Social Trends*, 2001: 94). Real increases, after allowing for the effect of inflation, have been central to the growth of home ownership, and in particular its expansion among the working class: by the late 1980s a majority (55 per cent) of manual workers were home owners (Abercrombie and Warde, 2000: 161).

The growth of owner occupation since the end of the First World War has contributed to a reduction in inequality in the distribution of wealth. In the early 1920s three quarters of the population owned less than £100 (A. J. P. Taylor, 1965: 171), but now more than two-thirds own their own homes (a quarter being outright owners), and houses account for around half of all net personal wealth in Britain (Hamnett and Seavers, 1996: 349). However, while the growth of home ownership may be seen as an egalitarian force, there is now good evidence of widening social inequality in Britain since the late 1970s, especially in terms of incomes (Hills, 1996). There is also evidence that a growing proportion (estimated in 2003 to be a half) of people living in poverty are now home owners (Burrows, 2003: 2).

Three further demographic indicators need to be mentioned here because of their relevance to housing. First, the total population of the United Kingdom increased by 50 per cent during the twentieth century, but the number of separate households tripled (*Social Trends*, 2002: 40). This has clearly been a major factor in the growing demand for housing, particularly from small households: in 1961 some 44 per cent of households contained only one or two people, but by 2001 the figure was 64 per cent. In partial reflection of this trend households consisting of couples with dependent children have fallen from 35 per cent to just 23 per cent of the total.

Second, trends in marriage and divorce have had an impact on the pattern of demand for housing. Many more people now live together before, or instead of, marriage and it is possible to talk of a general retreat from marriage (D. Coleman, 2000: 64). Among those who do marry, divorce is much more likely than it was in the past, partly because it has become legally easier and socially more acceptable. The absolute numbers of divorces in Britain increased from 1,000 per annum at the start of the twentieth century to over 170,000 in the early 1990s, and more marriages seem to be failing earlier (Coleman, 2000: 64). Even though a proportion of dissolving couples will sooner or later link up with new partners, this level of household breakup must lead to an increase in the demand for housing.

The final indicator of change concerns the increase in the numbers of people living in Britain who define themselves as members of minority ethnic groups. In the nineteenth century immigrants to the British mainland were mainly Irish, followed in the early 1900s by Jews from Russia and eastern Europe, and then after the Second World War immigration was mainly from former colonies in the Caribbean and the Indian sub-continent. By 1991 this postwar migration had become a group amounting to around 5.5 per cent of the total population; almost half were British born (Peach *et al.*, 2000: 128, 140). Although as a proportion of the total population the minority ethnic groups remain a small proportion, in some areas they constitute significant percentages and have certain demographic characteristics and tenure preferences that have implications for local housing markets.

Conclusion

Although the housing market has always failed to provide decent affordable accommodation for the least well off, and sometimes also a much wider section of the population, despite significant increases in real incomes, this has not led to a decommodified state-run service comparable with those associated with other main planks of the welfare state. On the contrary, it is the persistence of the market as the main mechanism for delivering housing to the majority that is striking and demanding of explanation. The main point to emerge from this chapter is that the history of housing and housing policy since the start of the twentieth century is complex, being neither wholly decommodified nor simply residual. Housing policy needs to be seen as consisting of two distinct parallel processes, given different emphasis at different times.

In this context the distinctions between different groups within the working class are important. On the one hand, there has been a gradual acceptance by the state that it has to take responsibility for the housing of the least well off, those who are least well placed to secure decent affordable accommodation in the private sector. This was slow to emerge, and for much of the last century most of the least well off remained in the declining private rented sector, but a residual social rented sector is now well established in the modern welfare state. On the other hand, key elements of housing policy need to be understood as the state facilitating the modernization of the housing market. Modernization was a process driven by market forces, including supply side changes and an increase in the demand for owner occupation, fuelled by higher living standards (which can be at least partly attributed to the welfare state). It is significant that large scale state provision of new houses was prompted by crises in the housing market, when, after the two world wars, housing shortages affected a large proportion of the working class, although the specific form of policy response tended to benefit the better off rather than the poorest. Now, however, the politics of housing have shifted, reflecting the decline of the traditional working class, rising living standards and the fact that the better off workers in the core of the economy are overwhelmingly accommodated in the owner occupied sector of the housing system.

Overall, then, the story to be recounted in the following chapters is one that shows how the role of the state in housing is essentially to support the market rather than to challenge or replace it. For much of the twentieth century this meant mainly providing good quality subsidized council houses for the better off working class and tackling the worst private housing conditions through programmes of slum clearance. More recently it has meant helping to move the better off working class into the owner occupied sector, and getting the least well off into social renting, processes that have significantly reshaped the politics of housing. With a majority of the remaining manual working class now in owner occupation it might be held that the modernization process is complete, but the state retains responsibility for a residual housing service for the poor, while for the rest seeking to ensure, as far as it can, continuing economic growth, relatively full employment and an efficient and stable housing market (Kleinman, 1996: 175).

Chapter 3

Housing Before the Welfare State

Nothing comes from nowhere, and a study of housing since the Second World War needs to take account of the fact that certain distinguishing features of the British housing system in this period have deep roots. Much has been written about the history of housing since the start of rapid urbanization in the nineteenth century and the subsequent slow development of authentic housing policy (Bowley, 1945; Burnett, 1985; Englander, 1983; Gauldie, 1974; Harloe, 1995; Malpass and Murie, 1999). The broad picture is pretty well established, and the intention here is not to go over too much familiar ground but instead to look at the antecedents of selected features of the post-Second World War housing system. These are:

- the particular character of British social rented housing, neither a wholly decommodified public service nor an entirely residual service for the poor
- the organizational form of social rented housing, dominated by local authority provision, with a very small non-municipal sector
- the growth of working-class home ownership, which has underpinned the residualization of social renting in the recent past.

All of these defining features of housing in the last half century have their origins in the period before 1945. This chapter looks at developments up to 1939, and the following chapter concentrates on the influence of history on wartime planning for postwar housing and reconstruction.

The exclusion of the poor before 1914

Before 1914 almost all housing in Britain was provided as a commodity by private enterprise responding to market forces. Private renting was the norm for all sections of the population, although many people lived as lodgers or sub-tenants in a period when sharing and overcrowding were much more common than today. There was a small amount of owner occupation, but no 'social rented sector' as we know it today, although there were the beginnings of municipal housing and there were organizations from which it is possible to trace a line of descent to modern registered social landlords (Malpass, 2000a, 2000b). The private market based housing system had a number of obvious deficiencies, which were well known and much debated at the time. The dreadful, unsanitary and overcrowded conditions endured by millions of urban residents were graphically described and analysed, and landlords who sought to profit from this situation were feared and resented by their hard pressed tenants (Englander, 1983: 5). Nevertheless, the rights of private property were deeply entrenched and well defended, and alternative approaches made very little headway before the First World War. From a modern perspective it might seem that the only opening for charitable or state provision would be if it were targeted on the poorest, the group least well served by the market. But in the context of the nineteenth century it was not so straightforward, and a combination of economic, social and political factors helped to exclude the poorest from attempts to tackle the housing problem before 1914. First, however, it is necessary to make a couple of points about the stratified working class and the nature of the 'housing problem'.

Looking back a hundred years to the early twentieth century it can be hard to imagine what life was like, so great has been the social, economic and technological change since that time. The same could be said of the previous hundred years, which had seen rapid population growth, the rise of industrial capitalism and the emergence of great towns and cities devoted to manufacturing. The nineteenth century also saw the creation of the urban industrial working class, whose labour fuelled the production of so much wealth, but whose pockets felt so little of its benefit. Britain remained a deeply unequal society, in which small numbers of very rich people absorbed hugely disproportionate amounts of income (Supple, 1981: 128). But this did not mean that everyone else was poor by contemporary standards. Pioneering research by Charles Booth in London and by Seebohm Rowntree in York in the 1890s revealed that up to 30 per cent of the whole population lived in poverty, which meant that a majority of the working class were not regarded as in poverty, according to the definitions used by these researchers.

The working class was by no means an undifferentiated mass, and the distinctions within that class are central to any understanding of the development of debate about, and remedies for, the housing situation. Reformers operated with models of a differentiated working class, and this analysis was broadly shared by members of that class themselves (although they were less likely to subscribe to the remedies specified for different groups). Then, as now, occupational differences were at the base of the status hierarchy, and skilled artisans sought to defend their wage advantage over less skilled occupations, who in turn wanted to maintain a distance from the demoralized, 'undeserving' poor, sometimes referred to as the 'destructive and criminal classes' (Octavia Hill, evidence to the Royal Commission on the Housing of the Working Classes, 1885b: 295). These distinctions were at the heart of reform strategies pursued by both top-down philanthropists and working-class political activists. Occupation based differentiation had consumption and behavioural dimensions as well: the better off were jealous of their standing as 'respectable' people, and important indicators of respectability were dwelling type and location. It is said that many of the short distance moves made by working-class families were driven by the pursuit, or defence, of respectability, through a constant search for a slightly better home in a slightly better street (Englander, 1983: 8). In high rent areas this might mean renting two rooms rather than one, but in provincial towns it might mean a house with a parlour, or where the front door did not open straight into the living room, or where there was a strip of garden between the pavement and the door. Maintaining these trappings of respectability could impose severe financial strain on a small income differential (Stedman Jones, 1971: 217).

Despite an increase in average living standards in the second half of the nineteenth century (Holmans, 1987: 32; Supple, 1981: 122–3), there was still a significant gap between the price demanded for decent quality accommodation and the amount that could be afforded by a large proportion of the working class. But this did not mean, contrary to the impression given by some writers (Robert Blatchford, 1889, quoted in Rubinstein, 1974: 140; Merrett, 1979: 4), that the working class as a whole lived in slums. Especially towards the end of the century, rising real incomes and the effect of building bylaws enabled more of the better off to acquire improved accommodation (Englander, 1983: xi). The term slum has both physical and social overtones; in the twentieth century it came to refer to neighbourhoods where the physical conditions were unfit for human habitation, but in earlier times it also carried a social connotation, referring to the homes of the poorest, lowest status, most disreputable members of society. These locations of the 'destructive and criminal classes' or the 'casual poor' (Stedman Jones, 1971) were quite distinct from the homes of the respectable poor, let alone the more prosperous artisans. In his survey of York in 1899 Rowntree divided working-class houses into three groups: class 1 comprised the 'comfortable houses of the well to do artisans', class 2 houses were 'for the most part four roomed, principally occupied by families in receipt of moderate but regular wages', while the remainder, which amounted to only a quarter of all working-class dwellings in the city, were class 3; the slums were a sub-set of this third class (Rowntree, 1901, quoted in Rubinstein, 1974: 144). Other cities may have had somewhat different rates of slum housing (Burnett, 1985: 149), and other people may have defined the categories differently, but the slums were not a way of life for the working class as a whole.

The slums were an important part of the pre-1914 housing problem in terms of their implications for public health, but they were not the whole of the problem. Equally important, especially from the consumer point of view, were the modalities of the private rental system as a whole, in particular the high rents, lack of security and the poor value for money provided by landlords, even where tenants were paying a quarter (or more) of their entire income in rent (Stedman Jones, 1971: 216–17). Rents rose by about 15 per cent between 1880 and 1900 and continued to rise in the period to 1914, absorbing increasing proportions of earnings (Englander, 1983: 5). What emerged after about 1880, and with increasing strength after 1900, was a clearly articulated demand for action to protect not only the poor but specifically the better off workers from the exploitative behaviour of landlords (Englander, 1983).

Turning now to the explanation of how the poorest were generally excluded from the benefits of attempts to tackle housing problems before 1914, the first set of reasons relate to the costs of housing and the harsh implications of the dominant economic theory, which dictated that any project had to be capable of showing a return on capital invested, and that subsidy should be avoided on the grounds that it tended to pauperize the working class:

If the State were to provide cottages at a rent which did not represent the real cost of their erection it would destroy the market for the speculative builders, and its liberality would only have the effect of driving everyone else out of the field of enterprise which would itself be incapable of entirely occupying. (Memorandum by the Marquess of Salisbury to the Royal Commission on the Housing of the Working Classses, 1885a)

In this situation the iron link between poverty and poor housing seemed to be unbreakable. However, from the 1840s onwards there were numerous attempts, concentrated in London, to develop 'model dwellings' (for a fuller account see Gauldie, 1974; Malpass, 2000b; S. Morris, 2001; Tarn, 1974; Wohl, 1977). These schemes, which were intended to 'provide both a standard and example that was worthy of imitation' (Gaskell, 1986: 3), were attempts to show that if builders and investors were restrained in their pursuit of profit, if the properties were well built and managed, and if the tenants could be persuaded to lead quiet sober lives then the housing problem might be overcome without state involvement. Both the model dwellings companies (which relied for capital on private investors who were prepared to accept limited returns) and the great charitable trusts devoted to housing (of which the Peabody Donation Fund was the most notable) struggled to resolve the difficulties inherent in trying to provide a decent standard of accommodation at rents affordable by the poor in high cost areas such as central London. There is general agreement in the literature that the model dwellings companies could not keep rents at levels affordable by the poor and that they eventually deviated from their original intention to house the poor (Stedman Jones, 1971: 184; Tarn, 1974: 102–3; Wohl, 1977: 150). This was well known at the time and they were criticized for it by the Royal Commission on the Housing of the Working Classes (1884–5). Booth's research in 1891 showed that under a quarter of the tenants of philanthropic and semi-philanthropic organizations in London were within his definition of the poor (R. Dennis, 1989: 45). Even the Peabody Fund (which was endowed specifically to aid the poor of London) generally housed members of the regularly employed and better paid, including artisans and clerks (Wohl, 1977: 156).

The standard defence to the charge of failing the poor was that providing for the better off ultimately helped the poor, who would be able to move into the houses vacated by people moving into model dwellings. This filtering theory, however, was seriously undermined by the impact of population growth, which meant that model dwellings were not even keeping up with increasing demand and therefore it was by no means clear that vacated houses would filter down to people with lower spending power. Nevertheless, filtering remained an article of faith among housing reformers into the 1890s (Stedman Jones, 1971: 199).

But it was not just economics that tended to exclude the poorest from model dwellings, which were projects with a wider social purpose, including the creation of 'a controlled environment of enforced respectability' (Wohl, 1977: 164). Rehousing people displaced by slum clearance was not necessarily seen as desirable; given the perception of slums as dens of vice, corruption and degradation there was an argument for dispersal as a desirable outcome. Through design and management the model dwellings providers sought to impose standards of behaviour that rewarded honest hard work, sobriety and respectability. The concentration on building small tenements and then prohibiting overcrowding excluded large families; others were excluded by irregular incomes, disorganized life styles or prohibition of home working in trades deemed to cause offence to neighbours (Stedman Jones, 1971: 184). Ex-service personnel were employed to impose discipline on the estates (Malpass, 1998; J. White, 1980). The authoritarian management of model dwellings was a response to the perceived need to maintain order in the face of the threat posed by the rupturing of traditional patterns of authority and deference, duty and obligation, by industrialization and urbanization. At one level this was about individual moral wellbeing and the idea that people in the teeming slums of the great cities were prey to drunkenness, prostitution and other forms of ungodly behaviour. At another level it was about the fear of social unrest, stimulated by deprivation and suffering, and unrestrained by respect for the established order. Model dwellings were therefore part of an attempt to concentrate on and work with the 'deserving poor', those who were prepared to conform to the norms and values of their social superiors. Those who were not were excluded and ignored.

Even Octavia Hill, who pioneered a system of housing management based redemptive social work aimed at a poorer group of tenants, admittedly failed to reach the truly poor: her target group was 'as low a class as have a settled abode', not the street homeless. Hill's approach, developed from 1865 onwards (Darley, 1990), was based on the view that the housing problem was largely behavioural: 'The people's homes are bad, partly because they are badly built and arranged; they are tenfold worse because the tenants' habits and lives are what they are. Transplant them tomorrow to healthy and commodious homes, and they would pollute and destroy them' (Hill, quoted in Rubinstein, 1974: 243). She set out to reach the poor by buying existing rundown houses and improving them and the tenants together by intensive management techniques that exploited the power of the landlord to influence behaviour. Her focus was on the deserving poor, who would respond to her method; those who would not were evicted. She told the Royal Commission in 1884:

> I do not say I will not have drunkards, I have quantities of drunkards; but everything depends upon whether I think the drunkard will be better for being sent away or not. It is a tremendous despotism, but it is exercised with a view to bringing out the powers of the people, and treating them as responsible for themselves within certain limits. (Royal Commission, 1885b: 297)

A different, more brutal, approach was applied to the irredeemable: simply to clear the slums and disperse the residents as part of street widening or improvement schemes, or to open up routes for new railways; in London alone it is probable that 100,000 people were displaced in this way in the fifty years to 1880 (Stedman Jones, 1971: 169). Later in the century repressive measures were still being canvassed in relation to the very poor; Charles Booth, for example, advocated in the 1890s that they should be sent to labour colonies (Waller, 1984: 43). 'It was the reformatory rather than reform which remained the dominant strain in the social thought of the period' (Englander, 1983: 102).

It used to be argued (Gauldie, 1974: 235; Merrett, 1979: 30; Owen, 1965: 393) that the manifold failings of the model dwellings companies and charitable trusts helped to make the case for state intervention and led to the rise of council housing. This position is now discredited (Daunton, 1983: 1; 1987: 40; Englander, 1983: 102) and more attention is given to the political struggle to define a housing role for local authorities and the nature of any public subsidy. 'The 1880s, it is now clear, mark a turning point that failed to turn. There was no assumption of national responsibility, no unilinear progression towards the welfare state' (Englander, 1983: xii). Some people argued that local authorities should confine themselves to housing the poorest as a way of monitoring and controlling them, others continued to oppose any kind of state provision on principle, while the organized working class began to argue that any municipal housing should be for the better off, not the poorest (Damer, 1980: 84). Property owners sitting as local councillors had a vested interest in preventing the development of a municipal sector in direct competition with their own operations (Byrne and Damer, 1980: 66).

Meanwhile, rising rents (and steeply rising rates, i.e., local property taxes) in the 1890s helped to stimulate political action around housing, articulated nationally by organizations such as the Social Democratic Federation and the Workmen's National Housing Council, and locally by numerous tenants' defence associations. A key demand at that time was for fair rents and for a mechanism to enforce them. After 1900, the newly formed Labour Representation Committee, which became the Labour Party in 1906, also saw housing as a good issue for local campaigning. It is important not to over-state the impact of working-class demands at this time, but it is also important to recognize that working-class political power and influence lay with the better off, skilled and unionized workers, not with the poor. The Labour Party set out to appeal primarily to skilled and organized labour, not the disorganized poor, and demands for subsidized municipal housing became widespread among local Labour Party branches in the early 1900s (Byrne and Damer, 1980: 67; Englander, 1983: 187). The Workmen's National Housing Council (WNHC) was explicit in 'its call for local authorities to build superior housing that would satisfy the expectations of the upper levels of the working class. It was, the WNHC stated, essential "to resist schemes that aimed at building down to the poverty standard of the ill-paid and unorganised classes"... the state should provide the financial assistance to enable local authorities to build a much higher standard of housing for the skilled man' (Swenarton, 1981: 90). In terms of the politically articulated responses of the working class to the housing problem before the First World War, the emphasis was on regulation of the private rental market and the provision of high quality subsidized council housing for the better off.

Policy developments and outcomes, 1914–39

Before 1914 British governments had relied on private enterprise to provide housing for the people, and had resisted demands for intervention to regulate rents or to subsidize new construction (even in the years after 1906 when housing production went into steep decline). In the special circumstances created by the war all that was to change, and the dramatic events of the struggle to define postwar housing policy have attracted close academic attention (Malpass, 2001; Swenarton, 1981; Wilding, 1972, 1973). First, rent control was introduced in 1915 as an emergency measure in response to a wave of rent strikes by tenants protesting against profiteering by landlords (Orbach, 1977). Rents were fixed at their August 1914 levels, despite marked inflation during the war. Second, a direct consequence of rent control was the introduction of Exchequer subsidies in 1919. Houses had to be built: there was a severe shortage, following the prewar decline and very low levels of production during the war (building had virtually stopped altogether by 1916), and housing was recognized to be a key issue for working-class voters; hence Lloyd George's famous 1918 election promise to build 'homes fit for heroes'.

A substantial house building programme was a politically inescapable commitment, but the prewar policy of relying on private enterprise would not work in the short term for two main reasons. First, investment would only be attracted to housing where there was a prospect of a competetive rate of return, which had not been available in the years immediately before 1914, and which would require rents to be set at substantially higher levels than those fixed in 1915. But as Bowley (1945: 9–10) put it: 'Increases in rents staved off in deference to public opinion during the War could scarcely be regarded as an appropriate form of peace celebration ... The opportunist introduction of rent control in 1915 had served as the key to a veritable Pandora's box of difficulties and dangers.' Second, it was expected that there would be a brief inflationary economic boom in the aftermath of the war, followed by a slump and return to lower prices; in this situation builders faced the prospect of being left with high cost products for disposal in a falling market, and therefore prudent businesses would not invest in new houses until prices had settled down. In any case, the building industry would take time to recover after the disruption and loss of manpower caused by the war. It was clear from the middle of 1916 that if houses were to be built in quantity after the war then the government would have to take responsibility. Housing had become the major domestic political issue during the war and the government was prepared to intervene in order to head off social unrest which could damage the war effort. At the end of the war there was a real fear of revolution, and concessions on the housing issue were a conscious effort to prevent this happening.

It was in these highly unusual circumstances that a step change in housing policy was achieved: government was forced to intervene in relation to prices and supply in ways that had been resisted for decades before the war. Both controls and subsidies, in different forms, were to remain in place for the rest of the century, but of course this was not intended at the time. Government intervention was seen as temporary: rent control was time limited and subject to parliamentary renewal, and the building programme under the Housing and Town Planning Act, 1919, was conceived as a plan to produce 500,000 dwellings in response to an immediate crisis, not the start of permanent state responsibility for the supply of affordable housing. Not only was government intervention temporary, it was also very limited. Despite the salience of housing as a political issue and the intense pressure on the state to respond, the market was left in place and the plan was to return to a free market once the supply bottleneck had been sorted out; the state did not accept responsibility for the housing of the whole population, the working class, or even the section of the working class most badly served by the market. In this sense, then, the primary significance of the postwar subsidized building programme can be seen as political, as well as providing assistance to the building industry, helping firms to recover by providing demand where it would not otherwise exist. This acts as a warning against the temptation to see the emergence of housing policy between the wars in terms of the subsequent establishment of the welfare state. However, it is arguable that the importance of these historically contingent measures lies in the fact that once having crossed the interventionist line it was difficult for subsequent governments to withdraw completely.

In the event, of course, local authorities built more than a million houses between 1919 and 1939, and by the end of the 1930s they were looking like a permanent presence in the housing system. After decades of resistance to the very idea of Exchequer subsidy and municipal housing (before 1914 most councils had built no houses at all), suddenly local authorities were expected and encouraged to build at scale. This sharpened debate as to what and who they were supposed to be building for, and about the allocation of subsidy to tenants on different incomes. The question of who lived in these houses is central to understanding the subsequent development and character of British social housing. In this context it is convenient to think in terms of a period from 1919 to the later 1920s, characterized by high subsidy, high rents and high quality, in contrast to the subsequent period when governments sought to bear down on subsidies, rents and the quality of new building.

A key question here is, why did the government after the war adopt a policy of high quality at a time when it was expected that prices would be high? This seems counter-intuitive, for if reducing the shortage was the priority then maximizing output within given resources would seem to be the rational option. Nevertheless, it is quite clear that the quality of 1919 Act council houses reflected government policy:

> It is the intention of the Government that the housing schemes to be carried out with State assistance should mark an advance on the building and development which has ordinarily been regarded as sufficient in the past, and that the houses to be erected should serve as a model or

standard for building by private enterprise in the future. (Local Government Board, 1919: para. 7)

Swenarton (1981: 190) has argued persuasively that the high quality of subsidized housing produced after the war was as important as the quantity, for it was through a demonstration that the future was going to be better than the past that the government hoped to manage the transition from war to peace. It was precisely because garden city standards had been too expensive for local authority housing before 1914 that they were adopted after the war, as proof of the government's commitment to producing a land fit for heroes to live in. The policy was designed to generate a flow of new houses that could be let at rents that were affordable by at least some members of the working class, and if high standards meant that rents (despite subsidy) remained beyond the reach of the less well off, then so be it. Nothing was done in the early postwar years to try to make council housing affordable by the poorest. Politically it was more important to ensure that the housing demands of the better off workers were met.

The 1919 Act was terminated in 1921, but new legislation in 1923 and 1924 continued to subsidize new building in both public and private sectors (Malpass and Murie, 1999: 41; Merrett, 1979: 310). Prices were now much lower than at their early 1920s peak, and they continued to fall until 1933–34. When prices were at their highest it was admitted that 'Rents were originally so high as to require a careful selection on financial grounds of the possible tenants, which in some cases led to the acceptance, as tenants of subsidised houses, of persons of substantial financial capacity' (Ministry of Health, 1931: 97). In this period the London County Council introduced a minimum income rule, in order to ensure that new tenants could afford the rent. However, in the later 1920s, as prices fell, the government reduced the level of subsidy per house, while urging local authorities to do more to accommodate lower paid workers. It is important to note here that the route to lower rents was lower standards rather than higher subsidy, and through to the mid-1930s Ministry advice continued to exhort local authorities to build smaller houses that could be 'let at the lowest possible rents' (Ministry of Health, 1933a: 89). Despite this:

there is really no doubt about how rent policy worked out in practice. The market for local authority houses was largely confined to a limited range of income groups, that is, in practice, the better off families, the small clerks, the artisans, the better off semi-skilled workers with small families and fairly safe jobs. Right up to the economy campaign of 1932, and even later, it was these families who absorbed most of the houses. (Bowley, 1945: 129)

The new stance on rents and standards was the first of a three-pronged approach to restructuring housing policy so as to move council housing downmarket, a change designed explicitly to respond to representations from private builders who complained they could not resume building for the working class while they faced competition from subsidized local authority programmes (Committee on Local Expenditure, 1932). The second element of the reshaped housing policy was the introduction of the first national programme of slum clearance in the Housing Act, 1930. Throughout the 1920s levels of slum clearance had been derisory, with only 15,000 dwellings removed in the whole country. The new Act required local authorities to produce estimates of slums remaining in their areas, together with five-year plans for clearance. After a slow start, which was partly due to the national economic crisis of 1931, the programme was relaunched in 1933, at which point local authority housing subsidy was confined to houses built in conjunction with slum clearance (authorities that wished to build other houses without subsidy were instructed to build small dwellings at low rents). Slum clearance needs to be seen as a responsibility given to local authorities because it was not a profitable activity for private enterprise. The subsidy for slum clearance rehousing under the 1930 Act was more generous than earlier subsidies for general needs housing, and clearance certainly provided a route into council housing for increasing numbers of poor families. But slum clearance, in the absence of a generous general needs subsidy, should be seen as a policy designed to deal with a limited number of the worst areas of housing, not as a policy designed to open up council housing to poor people as such. In the whole of the period 1930–39 only 265,000 houses were built to replace cleared slums, which looks distinctly half hearted when set against the 256,000 houses produced *annually* by private builders between 1934 and 1939 (figures refer to England and Wales: Bowley, 1945: 271).

The third strand of the new policy concerned the idea that 'Rent relief should be given only to those who need it, and only for so long as they need it' (Ministry of Health circular 1138, 1930). This message became a basic tenet of policy during the 1930s repeatedly brought to the attention of the local authorities. For example:

The essential point is that neither subsidies nor accommodation should be wasted...in so far as circumstances permit those tenants who are no longer in need of a subsidised rent should be asked to pay a higher rent or to move; and so far as practicable, accommodation should be rationed in accordance with the needs of the occupants...the houses which were built at high cost in the earlier postwar years and are let at relatively high rents, more especially those built under the Act of 1919 which cause the heaviest public burden, should be allotted, so far as possible to the better paid type of tenants. (Ministry of Health, 1934: 160)

It is hard to say how far local authorities embraced this approach, but in 1934 London County Council (which, it will be recalled, had required proof of a minimum income in the early 1920s) wrote to 300 tenants who were thought to be no longer in need of subsidized rents, inviting them to leave, and half of them apparently did so (Ministry of Health, 1934: 160). To the extent that local authorities followed Ministry guidelines it had serious implications for the future of municipal housing: encouraging the better off to move out altogether would tend to residualize the council sector as a whole, while concentrating the better off on the better quality, higher rent estates would serve to replicate the tendency of the market to segregate by income and status; herein lies the origin of some of today's problem estates.

A more sophisticated approach involved the notion of differential rents policy: that is, relating the rent paid by each tenant to their income. The principle of differential rents was introduced in the Housing Act, 1930, not as government policy at that stage but in response to a campaign by two backbench MPs, Sir Ernest Simon and Eleanor Rathbone (Malpass, 1997). There were various ways of relating rents to income – local authorities had complete freedom to decide whether to adopt the principle and to design their own schemes – but none was popular with existing tenants who found themselves being asked to pay more so that others could pay less. Successive governments in the 1930s remained lukewarm about rent rebates, although in Scotland the Health Department took a more positive line and achieved more success in establishing schemes.

To sum up this section it can be said that large scale provision of council housing after the First World War was stimulated by political demands and economic difficulties affecting the housing market, and not by a determination to help the least well off into decent dwellings at affordable rents: 'It is broadly true that the problem of providing houses at rents which the poorest members of the community could afford was not effectively solved in the period 1919–1939' (Jarmain, 1948: 1). During the inter-war period subsidies did very little to help the poor; it was mainly falling costs and standards that brought council housing within their reach. General needs housing was subject to strong residualizing pressure from the late 1920s and there is a certain amount of local empirical evidence indicating that by the late 1930s this had created a situation in which council tenants were poorer than working-class households in general (Jevons and Madge, 1946: 30). As more of the poorer sections of the population achieved access to council housing they found that what they got was a distinctly inferior product compared to what had been on offer to the better off in earlier years. By the mid-1930s local authorities were effectively confined to activities that the private sector could not or would not undertake, and by the later part of the decade council housing was being turned into a sector for the less well off. This was emphatically not a policy based on the idea that the state should provide affordable housing for the working class as a whole, or even for the poor. It was more about slum clearance and making sure that the existing stock was occupied by the poor.

The emergence of council housing

Britain differs from most other European countries in that its social rented housing was mainly built and managed directly by the multi-purpose local authorities, rather than by specialist organizations that were independent, or at arm's length from the state. Before 1914 this outcome was not predicted; councils generally displayed little or no enthusiasm for becoming housing providers, and most had built no houses at all. The total number of council houses in Britain before 1914 was probably not a lot more than 28,000 (Morton, 1991: 57), whereas the various charitable and semi-philanthropic organizations had built about 50,000 dwellings. It was not, therefore, self-evident that the postwar housing programme would rely on the local authorities, or that they would continue throughout the 1920s and 1930s to build more than 1.3 million dwellings while the voluntary organizations completed only 48,000 dwellings in the same period (Pole Report, 1944: 20). The failure of voluntary housing associations to develop on the same scale as municipal housing after the First World War is one of the more puzzling features of the British housing system (Daunton, 1987: 116). The performance of local authorities continued to be criticized and their role was questioned in different ways throughout the period, but by 1939 they owned about 10 per cent of all houses in Britain. How, then, did local authorities became established as the main providers of subsidized rental housing before the Second World War? And why did the voluntary organizations make so little impact?

The key to answering these questions lies in both the wartime debate about which agencies would be responsible for the postwar housing programme, and the implementation of that programme when the local authorities significantly out-performed the voluntary organizations, establishing a strong claim to a continued leading role. The debate, which gathered momentum from mid-1916, must have been influenced by prewar experience. In the decade up to 1914 new building by the model dwellings companies and charitable trusts had generally been in decline, while public utility societies had been increasingly active (Birchall, 1995; Skilleter, 1993) and building by local authorities had been rising steeply in the period after 1910 (Gauldie, 1974: 325). The term public utility society embraced workers' self-help organizations, known as co-partnership societies, and other bodies dedicated to the provision of working-class housing at affordable rents. Under the terms of the Housing and Town Planning Act, 1909, Public Utility Societies (PUSs) registered as industrial and provident societies were entitled to borrow up to three-quarters of the value of new schemes from the Public Works Loans Board (PWLB) on terms similar to those available to local authorities. The advantage of such loans was that they were at rates of interest below what small housing societies would have had to pay when borrowing on their own account; the PWLB passed on the benefits of its ability, as an arm of central government, to borrow at the lowest obtainable rates of interest.

The co-partnership societies, which had begun in the 1890s, flourished under this funding regime and completed some 7,000 dwellings before 1914 (Birchall, 1995: 344). These societies, based on the principle of tenants as shareholders, were an attempt to give working-class tenants some control over their housing, but of course they were only of relevance to a restricted group of workers with sufficient savings and income to become shareholders. They provided the organizational basis for working-class housing production at the first garden city (Letchworth) and the majority of the fifty or more garden suburbs developed in the Edwardian period. However, the importance of the PUSs lies not in the number of dwellings built before the war but in the fact that they provided an apparently robust model for the future, and it seems that it was this model, rather than local authorities, that was at the heart of housing policy development in the immediate prewar period (Swenarton, 1981: 45). During the war a certain amount of new building was carried out under the auspices of the Ministry of Munitions specifically to accommodate people undertaking essential war work, and the majority of these schemes were built by PUSs supported by local employers. It was expected that this sort of arrangement would continue after the war and provide a basis for at least some of the emergency housing programme.

However, from the beginning of planning for postwar housing in 1916 it was accepted that the local authorities would have to play the major role. It was taken for granted that subsidy to private enterprise was politically unacceptable (although in the event such subsidy was provided under the Housing and Town Planning (Additional Powers) Act, 1919). The Local Government Board favoured local authorities as the main providers, and received support in 1917 from the Royal Commission on Housing in Scotland. The key factor here was the need to build on a scale that could not be achieved by PUSs. The local authorities had a number of advantages: they covered the whole country; they already had housing powers; they had the organizational infrastructure, including relevant professional expertise; and they had the required financial strength (in terms of their borrowing power and their ability to draw upon the local rates if necessary). By contrast, the PUSs were few in number (there were reckoned to be only 106 active societies in the whole of England and Wales: see Malpass, 2001: 232), they were very unevenly spread across the country and they were organizationally and financially weak. Nevertheless, the PUSs and charitable trusts were very much part of the wartime debate about the post-war housing programme (Malpass, 2000c). The Local Government Board was initially dismissive of their potential contribution, but they were supported by the housing panel appointed by the Ministry of Reconstruction in 1917 (Ministry of Reconstruction, 1918a), and by a special committee set up to look at financial support for bodies other than local authorities (Ministry of Reconstruction, 1918b).

In the prolonged negotiation around the level and form of housing subsidy the local authorities had the upper hand over the Treasury: the government had to ensure that houses would be built in quantity and its reliance on the local authorities as the main developers meant that they were able to drive a hard bargain. The outcome was that the Housing and Town Planning Act, 1919, provided a subsidy system based on shared responsibility for revenue: rents would cover a proportion of costs while the balance would be covered by a contribution from local rate-payers (capped at the product of a one penny rate), with the Treasury covering the remainder. This was clearly a system that was generous to the local authorities, but unattractive to the Treasury, which has a natural dislike of uncapped commitments. The PUSs and charitable trusts, by contrast, had a much weaker bargaining position, and the subsidy offered to them was correspondingly less generous, amounting to 30 per cent of loan charges (later raised to 50 per cent up to 1927). This was ultimately the reason for the tiny number of houses built by the voluntary organizations under the Act, and for the financial difficulties that many societies later experienced (Malpass, 2000c). Altogether the local authorities in England and Wales built 170,000 houses under the 1919 Act, while PUSs and charitable trusts built just 4,545 (Ministry of Health, 1925: 52). Even private builders, who were brought into the picture very late, contributed nearly 40,000. On the one hand the local authorities showed that, given the right kind of financial incentives, they could respond and deliver, and they rapidly established themselves as providers of houses on a relatively large scale. On the other hand, the PUSs and charitable trusts patently failed to deliver, and to make matters worse they then went on to complain about their difficulties, thereby alienating themselves from senior Ministry of Health officials and damaging their long term prospects (Malpass, 2000c).

After the premature abandonment of the 1919 Act in 1921 the local authorities were criticized for alleged failures to control expenditure (Bowley 1945: 34–5; Malpass and Murie, 1999: 45), and further legislation in 1923 was designed mainly to support private builders, but the Housing Act of 1924 (passed by the short lived first ever Labour government) provided a more secure basis for the growth of local authority housing. John Wheatley, the Minister of Health in the Labour government of 1924, is credited with a long term vision of a growing municipal housing sector, and under his Act more than half a million council houses were built before its termination in 1933. At this point the only financial assistance for new housing production was the slum clearance subsidy, and general needs housing was effectively left to private enterprise: 'the Government had gone as near to rejecting responsibility for working class housing as it could' (Bowley, 1945: 140). The 1930 slum clearance programme had stalled badly in the wake of the national economic crisis of 1931 and the government appeared to have no policy for tackling the huge number of ageing, neglected working-class houses lacking in modern amenities but not technically due for clearance as slums.

Criticism of the government's stance on housing led to the appointment of the Moyne Committee in March 1933 (Ministry of Health, 1933b). This was a committee of Members of Parliament chaired by Lord Moyne (a former Conservative MP), briefed to report on the problem of rundown working-class housing in areas not suitable for clearance, and to consider what might be done to promote the supply of houses for the working class 'without public charge' by PUSs or similar bodies. The local authorities had proved that they could build suburban estates on greenfield sites, but the 'reconditioning' of existing dwellings was not their strength. It was, however, an area of work that a growing number of small voluntary housing associations were interested in, but their expansion was hampered by problems in raising capital and the general reluctance of local authorities to co-operate and assist them. Throughout the period from 1923 to 1939 PUSs were entitled to the same Exchequer subsidy as the local authorities, but there was no obligation on local councils to make a rate fund contribution and most chose not to. Critics of the performance of local authorities argued for the creation of some kind of national housing finance board, which would be responsible for promoting and lending to PUSs (National Housing Committee, 1934).

The Moyne Committee provided a platform for opponents and critics of local housing authorities, and the committee's report represented a real challenge to the continued ascendancy of municipal housing. The committee did not accept the idea of a housing finance board, which had been opposed by representatives of private builders as well as local government; but it did make recommendations that were broadly favourable towards the PUSs in relation to reconditioning. The committee accepted the view that local authorities were not best suited to, or interested in, the improvement and management of scattered properties in working-class neighbourhoods. The way forward would be for local authorities to have compulsory purchase powers to acquire such dwellings, which they would then pass on the approved PUSs. The committee proposed that the Ministry of Health should have powers to finance this work, and that there should be a Central Public Utility Council which would be responsible for approving both societies and individual projects. The council would stimulate the formation of new societies and supervise their activities. The similarities between these proposals and the Housing Corporation (established in 1964) are striking.

The response to the Moyne proposals was generally favourable (Garside, 1995: 110) and it seemed for a while that the PUSs were on the brink of breaking through to a significant role in housing policy. However, the report did not settle the issue and over the next two years there was a prolonged debate, in the course of which the local authorities defended their position as the established instruments of housing policy implementation. They worked on and cultivated the scepticism of senior civil servants, who regarded PUSs as 'bodies neither efficient nor easy to deal with, as their members were not normally men of affairs' (Sir Arthur Robinson, senior Ministry of Health civil servant, Public Record Office (PRO), HLG 29/213). No doubt influenced by the experience of dealing with PUSs in the implementation of the 1919 Act, ministerial advisers backed away from endorsing the notion of a Central Council, or any other measure that would both promote PUSs and alienate the local authorities. The outcome of the post-Moyne debate was that the local authorities consolidated their position in relation to housing policy, while the housing associations (as PUSs came to be known from then on) were kept on the margins.

The triumph of the local authorities, and the thwarting of housing association ambitions, was also a setback for the millions of working-class families living in the areas that would have been tackled under a policy of reconditioning (it was not until 1949 that grants were introduced to support the improvement of older houses). More generally, the mid-1930s has been seen as marking the high point of municipal growth and power (Laski, Jennings and Robson, 1935), and the way in which the local authorities were able to see off the challenge to their role in housing is consistent with this interpretation. By the end of the 1930s local authorities owned well over 1 million houses, and although many of the smaller councils, especially in the south, had built very few, the large urban councils were landlords of thousands, sometimes tens of thousands, of houses. Nevertheless, Bowley (1945: ch. vi) has raised the question of why they failed to build more, especially in the relatively favourable market conditions in the period 1929–33, when the 1924 Act subsidy for general needs housing was still available and the need for affordable rented housing was still acute. Although the total output of local authorities was impressive, it was dwarfed by that of private enterprise, which outbuilt the municipalities every year from 1924 onwards.

The growth of working-class home ownership

Of the 4 million new houses built in Britain between the wars, over 70 per cent were constructed by private enterprise, and, in marked contrast to pre-1914 practice, the majority were sold for owner occupation. Individual home ownership was the emergent tenure of this period, although precise figures are not available. Conventional estimates put owner occupation at no more than 10 per cent in 1914, but there is no firm basis for this and it is known that some places had much higher levels (Speight, 2000; Swenarton and Taylor, 1985). There is also debate about the 1939 level, but it was probably about a third (for a discussion of the derivation of this figure see Swenarton and Taylor, 1985: 376–8). Unlike the local authority sector, the growth of owner occupation was swelled by the sale of around a million existing private rented houses (mostly in the 1920s).

That private enterprise was capable of producing very large numbers of dwellings, especially in the boom years of 1933–38, is not in doubt. The social distribution of those houses, however, is not so well understood, and the issue to be explored here is: who were the direct beneficiaries from the growth of home ownership between the wars? The question of how far the owner occupier market was able to meet the demand from working-class households is important for two reasons: first, at the point in 1933 when local authorities were told to stop building for general needs there was still a significant shortage of working-class houses (variously estimated by Bowley (1945: 52, 94) to be between half and three-quarters of a million). According to Bowley's analysis, private sector output between 1919 and 1934 over-supplied the need for houses of higher rateable values, and so the builders needed to widen their market by pressing the government to withdraw local authorities from the field, leaving the working-class market to them. But could they supply houses at affordable prices? Second, if it can be shown that owner occupation was indeed catering for a significant proportion of working-class demand by 1939 this has implications for the modernization thesis, suggesting that the market had adjusted to owner occupation as the major form of consumption for new production, and that local authority housing was already settling into a residual role. This in turn has implications for the historiography of housing and the welfare state, reinforcing the view that progress was not by any means linear, and that before the Second World War there was no expectation of a large, broadly based state sector.

There is general agreement that house prices and interest rates put home ownership beyond the reach of working-class families as a whole during the 1920s. Even a majority of the houses built for owner occupation with the aid of the 1923 Act subsidy were considered to be non-working class (Bowley, 1945: 80). But in the 1930s market conditions were quite different and much more favourable (Pole Report, 1944: 10). Not only were prices continuing to fall up to 1935 but mortgage interest rates fell too, and building societies developed ways of widening access by raising the proportion of the purchase price covered by mortgage (thereby lowering the amount of deposit required) and by extending loan repayment periods (lowering the monthly payment). Intense competition among both builders and building societies led them to seek ways of expanding the market for new houses and persuading more people to buy. Even in high-priced London there was a good selection of houses for sale in the new suburbs in the range £550 to £1,000, with some astonishingly low priced houses, at less than £350, offered for sale in the mid-1930s (Jackson, 1973: 188–9). If it was high prices that helped to establish municipal housing in the 1920s it was low prices that fuelled the owner occupier boom in the next decade; indeed, Merrett (1982) has argued that without the economic slump there would have been no housing boom.

There is little doubt that between the wars owner occupation took off first and grew fastest among middle-class salaried white collar workers and professionals, whose incomes tended to rise in real terms during the 1930s. Bowley (1945: 177) quotes evidence from a sample of budgets of civil servants, local government officers and teachers in 1938–9, showing that virtually two-thirds were home owners. She thought it was 'perfectly obvious' that home ownership was far more general among the middle class than the working class. It also seems inevitable that the huge increases in the supply of houses sold for owner occupation must have drawn in households from a wider range of incomes. However, later research concluded that despite the impressive scale of the housing boom in the 1930s relatively few working-class families were able to become home owners: 'By 1939 owner occupation had become more, not less, middle class; less, not more, working class' (Swenarton and Taylor, 1985: 392). This position has been challenged by Speight (2000), first on methodological and analytical grounds and then on the basis of his own research evidence. He argues that 'not only *could* many "working class" households, broadly construed afford to buy new houses from 1932–3 onwards, but many actually *did* so' (Speight, 2000: 2, emphasis in the original). Speight's use of a broadly construed definition of the working class should be noted here; he argues that the key difference was income based rather than the traditional manual/non-manual divide, and so he includes lower paid non-manual workers.

In the absence of good contemporary survey evidence a standard technique for investigating who could afford to buy is to look at the weekly cost of buying at a typical price and then comparing that with information about wages. In this context a key datum is that in the inter-war years 'it was generally considered that a gross rent of 10/- [10 shillings] inclusive of rates was the *maximum* that the families of ordinary unskilled labourers, or even in many cases of semi-skilled labourers, could afford' (Bowley, 1945: 96). With the rates burden generally at three to four shillings per week it was clear that for this group of lower paid workers net rent or mortgage costs could not exceed six or seven shillings. Earnings for this group of workers averaged around £2–10 shillings per week in the mid-1930s. However, most male skilled workers earned in excess of £3 per week in 1935 and Speight (2000: 22) argues that, with extended loan periods and maximum percentage loans, houses priced at less than £600, of which there were very large numbers, especially away from London, were within reach of workers on £3 to £4 per week.

This kind of deductive reasoning involves a lot of ifs and buts – it assumes both a willingness and ability to devote a quarter of income to housing, which must have been different for households of different sizes and for workers in different industries: secure, regular earnings were implicit, uninterrupted by sickness or unemployment. It requires to be supported by evidence of what actually happened. Speight brings together evidence from a range of contemporary sources and more recent research to show that working-class households bought a significant proportion of the new houses. For example, he quotes figures from the Abbey Road Building Society to show that by 1938 half of its new loans were awarded to wage earners (as distinct from salaried workers), and quotes the general manager of the Society saying that, 'Of those who made the [housing] boom possible I should judge that about half the purchasers were black-coated workers and the other half better paid artisans' (Speight, 2000: 12). It is important to be clear about what is being argued here: in terms of purchasers of new houses, working-class households represented a significant proportion, but the proportion of the working class as a whole who were home owners at the end of the 1930s remained low, especially in comparison with the middle class. Survey evidence from 1938 shows that fewer than 18 per cent of urban working-class households were home owners (Speight, 2000: 13). Whether the growth of working-class home ownership was a result of reasoned preference or constrained choice is a matter for debate, but, looking back to the inter-war period, the committee on the role to be played by private enterprise after the Second World War argued that what was needed was a lot more rented housing, apparently accepting the criticism 'That in order to obtain a house young married couples had no alternative owing to the scarcity of houses for letting, but to undertake the purchase of houses on mortgage at a cost which imposed an undue strain on their means' (Pole Report, 1944: 25).

Conclusion

As stated in the introduction, this chapter set out to review a limited set of issues to indicate that while much has changed in relation to housing and housing policy there are also some important continuities over long periods of time. In particular it has been shown that key features of housing in Britain since 1945 had their roots deep in the previous period. Housing policy was slow to develop in the nineteenth century, despite the poor living conditions endured by substantial proportions of the working class, a powerful reminder that neither the existence of suffering nor its revelation to the public at large is sufficient to call forth a policy response. Self-help organizations, charitable trusts and model dwellings companies failed to make any real impression on the problems of overcrowding, poor quality and affordability, while most local authorities remained reluctant to commit rate-payers to supporting municipal housing. And even when there was debate about what role the local authorities might play there was disagreement about whether they should provide a minimal form of housing for the least well off or subsidized high quality housing for the better off skilled and politically organized workers. In practice most of the people who benefited from the limited amount of what would now be called social housing were drawn from among the rather better off and more securely employed workers. Although housing was established as a political issue before 1914, nothing much had been achieved in terms of policy development and implementation; the forces of reaction remained entrenched and market forces continued virtually unfettered.

However, the impact of the Great War was to intensify the housing problem and to raise its political salience to the point where previous barriers to policy change were breached. Suddenly rents were subject to control and the Exchequer was providing subsidy for house building. It was in the period immediately after the war that the municipal dominance of British social housing was established, setting a pattern for the rest of the century. Local authorities had their critics, of course, but they proved to be powerful enough to consolidate their position and to see off a challenge in the mid-1930s from advocates of a more technocratic, centralized and non-municipal approach. As a result the motley collection of voluntary organizations then operating in the shadow of local government continued to be marginalized for another forty years.

The years immediately after 1918 also saw council housing established as a high quality form of provision for those who could afford to pay rents that, although subsidized, remained higher than the rents in the controlled private sector. It was only later, when prices fell, and especially after local authorities began to concentrate on slum clearance in the 1930s, that the poor began to obtain access to council houses in significant numbers.

But what they got was generally of poorer quality than the general needs housing built in the 1920s. At the same time the boom in private house building, stimulated by falling prices for land, labour and capital, brought house purchase within the reach of a widening section of the population, including the better off working class. The boom in house building by private enterprise in the second half of the 1930s, and the re-positioning of local authorities in terms of slum clearance, supporting not competing with private builders, were to prove highly influential in the next decade when policy makers thought about the sort of long term policies they wanted to put in place after another long and damaging war.

Chapter 4

Housing and the Second World War

The Second World War, from September 1939 to the summer of 1945, was front page news every day for six years; it was an all-encompassing, inescapable event, touching the lives of all who lived through it and having a lasting effect on key areas of social, economic and political life. British military casualties were fewer than in the war of 1914–18, but in many other ways the impact was more far reaching. In the First World War the aeroplane had still been something of a novelty and a marginal factor in the conflict, but by the 1940s the warring nations were able to bomb each other's military bases, naval ports, mines, factories and residential areas, bringing civilian populations into the front line for the first time in the history of warfare – in the first half of the war there were more British civilian casualties than military (Titmuss, 1958: 82). Within days of the start of the war a million and a half women and children were evacuated from London and other large cities where air raids were most likely. The billeting of people from poor inner-city areas on middle-class families in the reception areas revealed much that had previously been hidden about the extent and persistence of poverty, inequality and class differences in Britain. On the basis of his work on the evacuation Richard Titmuss (1958: 82) argued that the increasing intensity of warfare, embracing a wider proportion of the population, led to increased state involvement in social policy and fuelled demands for the creation of a better postwar society.

Demands for a statement of war aims emerged very soon after the crisis of the retreat of the British army from Dunkirk in June 1940, and grew into a full scale public debate about postwar reconstruction (Addison, 1977; Calder, 1969). The outcome was a series of social reforms from the Education Act, 1944, to the National Assistance Act, 1948, which together were later defined as creating the welfare state. The task of this chapter is to focus on housing in this context of war and social reform, taking in the fourteen years from 1939 to 1953, in a conscious attempt to give more attention than is common in accounts of postwar housing policy to the importance of policy planning during the war itself. If the narrative is constructed from 1941 or 1942 then a different light is cast on subsequent events, revealing more continuity than is generally recognized. The decision to continue the chapter to 1953 is based on the view that the publication of the Conservatives' White Paper, *Houses – the Next Step*, signalled the end of the extended transitional period and the beginning of the reshaping of housing policy in a deliberate reversion to the stance adopted in the 1930s (Merrett, 1979: 246).

Assessing the impact of the Second World War on housing and housing policy is not straightforward, most obviously because we can never know what would have happened in the absence of the war. However, it is reasonable to assume that things would not have gone on exactly as they were; all the historical evidence suggests that housing market booms are temporary phenomena, and in fact the output of new houses by private enterprise was falling in the two years before the war (Holmans, 1987: 66). It should not be assumed, therefore, that private house building would have continued at the sorts of levels reached in the late 1930s, or that the outbreak of the war was the sole cause of the end on the boom. But it is also clear that the balance between supply and demand was dramatically different in 1945, and that the war had helped to create circumstances in which high output would dominate policy debates for the next twenty years. In the absence of the war, policy would probably have continued on broadly the lines established in the 1930s, and the balance between private and public sectors would have remained essentially the same, with private builders continuing to build for a broad spectrum of general needs, while local authorities pressed ahead with slum clearance and urban renewal (Garside, 1995).

As shown in Chapter 3, enough progress had been made in shifting demand into owner occupation for it to be arguable that the war interrupted an active and successful process of market modernization, and without the war the residualization of public housing (already under way before 1939) would have become more pronounced sooner, and the local authorities would never have become collectively the owners of nearly a third of the total housing stock. On this view, the impact of the war was to create the conditions without which the great expansion of local authority housing would never have occurred. In a kind of re-run of events in and after the First World War, the social and economic disruption of war required that houses be built, but disabled private enterprise from meeting demand. This time, however, the war was followed by a longer period of sustained building by local authorities: in the twenty years after 1945 they built 60 per cent of all new houses, and out-built the private sector every year until 1959. Getting on for half of all the council houses ever built were constructed in this twenty-year period. The impact of the war on housing policy is still being felt, for without the large amount of local authority building in the early postwar period issues such as the right to buy and more recently the large scale transfer of council houses clearly would not have been so important or contentious.

However, there is an alternative view, based on the idea that the war had very little impact on the long established and deeply held belief within government circles as to the proper form of housing policy. This places the emphasis on the persistence of the underlying faith in the ability of the private market to provide for most people most of the time. Appreciation of this point depends upon constructing the narrative from the early part of the war, not from the election of the Labour government in July 1945.

Wartime planning for housing

The Second World War has not attracted the same attention from housing academics as the First. This may be attributable to fact that there is nothing to compare with the dramatic nature of the rent strikes of 1915 or the ground breaking changes that followed from them, in terms of rent control and state subsidies for postwar construction. In that brief interlude the mundane history of housing, hitherto largely concerned with slums, building bylaws and the absurdly inflated reputations of conservative moral entrepreneurs such as Octavia Hill, suddenly became associated with high politics and establishment fears of revolution. No such dramatic turn of events took place during the Second World War, and there was no change in policy equivalent to the steps taken in 1915 and 1919. Instead, writers looking for a story have focused almost entirely on the struggle of the post-1945 government to build sufficient houses to meet demand in very difficult circumstances. Events during the war itself tend to be summarized in a standard formula, which notes that blanket rent control (which had been eased in the 1930s) was re-introduced right at the start of hostilities; house building slowed rapidly as resources of materials, capital and labour were diverted for the war effort, with the result that fewer than 200,000 permanent houses were completed in the six years of the war; meanwhile, the impact of bombing was that some 450,000 dwellings were destroyed or rendered uninhabitable, with a further 4 million damaged to a lesser extent; a quarter of the total housing stock had been affected (War Office, 1944); this took place alongside a population increase of about a million. The housing shortage had to be tackled in a postwar period in which the country was victorious but exhausted, and with an economy that was effectively bankrupt.

In fact a good deal of detailed policy planning had been going on since quite early in the war. The great public debate about postwar reconstruction contained much of relevance to housing, not least in terms of the growth of interest in planning the redevelopment of blitzed city centres and densely populated urban areas, together with popular support for the containment of the sort of suburban sprawl that had been much criticized in the 1930s; the preparation of master plans for London and other major cities presented a vision of a brighter, cleaner future (Ward, 1994). Professional journals and conferences buzzed with idealistic schemes for a better Britain, but the key policy making arena lay within central government departments, largely behind closed doors, in the work of committees of ministers and officials. Throughout the reconstruction debate, which gathered momentum after the publication of the Beveridge Report in November 1942, housing was generally recognized to be a problem of the first magnitude. As the end of the war approached so ministers became more focused on the urgency and importance of the housing question; thus Lord Woolton, Minister of Reconstruction, echoed concerns expressed at the end of the First World War:

> Of all the problems facing us on the Home Front, housing is the most urgent and one of the most important from the point of view of future stability and public contentment. (PRO CAB 87/9, R(44)153, memo by Minister of Reconstruction on Housing Policy, 5 September 1944)

Despite the importance attached to housing throughout the war, some commentators have pointed to what they see as the lack of a thorough-going policy review in the style of the Beveridge investigation into social security (Cole and Furbey, 1994: 60; Donnison, 1967: 166; Murie, 1994: 126). However, there were three sub-committees of the Central Housing Advisory Committee looking at key issues: temporary dwellings (chaired by Lewis Silkin, no report published), design standards for postwar construction (Dudley Report, 1944) and the role of private enterprise in the postwar period (Pole Report, 1944). These committees were additional to the important work being undertaken by civil servants, principally those in the Ministry of Health, which continued to have responsibility for housing despite the ambitions of the newly created Ministry of Works (rivalry between the Ministries of Health and Works continued to be an obstacle to progress in planning throughout the war).

Attitudes within Whitehall need to be set in the context of officials' awareness of the prewar situation. On the one hand, the post-1918 experience led to expectations of a severe postwar housing shortage, which would require state intervention, given the equally firm expectation that after the war there would again be a brief economic boom followed by slump and unemployment. On the other hand, civil servants in the Ministry of Health looked back at the 1930s and consoled themselves with the belief that their housing policy had been working pretty well: the private market boom had done much to ease the housing shortage, while at the same time bringing home ownership within the reach of a growing proportion of the population, and the local authorities had begun to make inroads into the problems of slum clearance and overcrowding. Within the Ministry this was seen to be the right policy, with the right division of responsibilities for the long term, although it was understood that in the short term there would be urgent problems calling for special measures – which came to mean a leading role for local authorities (PRO HLG 101/316, paper by Sir J. Wrigley, June 1941).

Postwar housing policy began to take shape at a time when the military side of the war was still going badly and peace was a distant prospect. Towards the end of 1941 the Official Committee on Postwar Internal Economic Problems commissioned a paper from the Ministry of Health on long term housing policy, together with an analysis of short term problems associated with evacuation and the accommodation of demobilized people. Drafts of these papers were circulated within Whitehall in the autumn of 1942 and incorporated into the main wartime policy document, *Postwar Housing Policy*, submitted to the war cabinet in May 1943 (PRO CAB 117/125). A number of key assumptions and proposals later included in the policies of both the wartime coalition and postwar Labour governments derive from this early work. The starting point for all discussion of housing at that time was the question of the number of houses that would need to be built. Given the impact of the war, in terms of both the numbers of dwellings destroyed or damaged by bombing, and the virtual cessation of new building, this is not surprising. What is surprising in the circumstances of an economically draining war is the enthusiasm with which both civil servants and their ministers embraced very ambitious postwar building targets. Echoing the 1919 slogan of 'homes for heroes' the Ministry of Health paper on long term policy (1942) set out a bold position:

It is certain that the country will expect an even more vigorous policy after this war. The next four million dwellings must be built more quickly than the last [which took twenty years], and the work must be carried out, not haphazardly, but to a planned programme which must take account of the work of repairing war damage and of overtaking the heavy arrears of maintenance which have accumulated during the war. Every family who so desires should be able to live in a separate dwelling possessing all the amenities necessary to family life in the fullest sense, and special provision must be made for old people and single women. (PRO CAB 117/125 Post War Housing Policy, appendix iv, para. 3)

This represented not only a commitment to a much increased rate of building but also indicated a step change in policy, possibly constituting the earliest official reference to the policy objective of a separate dwelling of adequate standard for every family; this was later incorporated into the coalition government's housing White Paper of March 1945, and has become, in slightly different forms, a fixture in statements of housing policy. In terms of numbers, the 1942 estimate by the Ministry of Health suggested that, assuming the war ended in 1944, there would need to be a building programme of 1,350,000 dwellings in the first postwar decade (ibid., paras 44–7). 'It is obvious, however, that something on a much bigger scale must be visualised' (ibid., para. 48), and so the estimate was cranked up by a further 1.5–2.5 million, to allow for replacement of unfit and obsolete houses. This gave a grand total of 3–4 million houses needed in England and Wales in the first postwar decade (ibid., para. 50). In addition there was an existing deficit of 435,000 dwellings in Scotland, and it was stated that the postwar programme should be at least 50,000 houses each year (ibid., para. 62). The figure of 3–4 million dwellings in ten years became the officially proclaimed target of the coalition government. The scale of ambition involved can be appreciated by noting that the target implied 300–400,000 new houses per year, whereas even in the boom years of the mid-1930s the rate never climbed above 350,000, and in the event total annual completions remained below 300,000 every year until 1953.

Some people, including the prime minister, doubted the need for so many new houses, given that they expected the population to fall (Churchill, 1952: 114). Others argued that in the economic conditions likely to prevail after the war the country could not afford to commit so many resources to replacing houses that were still capable of being lived in (PRO T 230/256, paper by Mr Harcourt Johnstone, November 1943). Supporting the case for a large building programme was the formidable figure of Ernest Bevin (Minister of Labour and National Service). As early as May 1942 he was arguing that if large scale unemployment was to be prevented it would be necessary to absorb as much as a quarter of the insurable population into the construction industry (PRO CAB 117/125, memo to Jowitt, chair of the Reconstruction Problems Committee). Housing was central to Bevin's strategy, which was approved by the cabinet in 1943 (this rare example of joined-up thinking was well in advance of the publication of the much better known 1944 White Paper on employment policy: see Ministry of Reconstruction, May 1944).

In contrast to the ambitious scale of the house building programme the dominant approach to implementation was distinctly conservative. The theme repeatedly expressed by ministers and civil servants was that in the long run the private sector should provide the bulk of new housing for sale or rent:

The field for local authority house building after the war will, in my view, as was the case before the war, depend to a large degree on the extent to which the housing needs are met by the erection by private enterprise of houses for sale and letting ... the policy of the government for several years before the war was that local authorities ... should build houses for the replacement of slums and the abatement of over-crowding and also for meeting general housing needs for houses for the working classes in so far as they are not being met by private enterprise. (PRO 117/125, parliamentary answer by Ernest Brown, Minister of Health, 15 July 1943)

Proposals for delivery mechanisms other than the private market and municipal action received little support. In the mid-1930s there had been a serious debate around proposals to establish a National Housing Corporation, an idea supported by some distinguished housing specialists, but such ideas made no progress, largely because of local authority opposition (Malpass, 2000b: ch. 5). The Committee on Internal Economic Problems considered the idea a non-starter, because of local authority opposition and the likely impact on private enterprise, although it did see potential for such independent bodies in relation to new towns (PRO CAB 117/125 Postwar Housing Policy, July 1943).

So much for the longer term, but what was to be done in the immediate aftermath of the war? Here, too, a considerable amount of groundwork was undertaken by the coalition government. Right from the start of planning, in 1941, it had been assumed that there would need to be an emergency programme to deal with the transitional period at the end of the war. Working from the precedent set by the First World War, it was accepted that, for a while at least, after the war it would be necessary to rely on the local authorities to provide the majority of new houses (PRO CAB 117/125, Postwar Housing Policy, July 1943, para. 28).

In December 1943 the Minister of Health proposed a target of 100,000 houses built or under construction after the first year of peace, and 200,000 by the end of the second year; at the same time he reiterated the view that for the transitional period (which came to be synonymous with the two year programme) the local authorities should be the main providers of new houses (PRO CAB 124/446, memo by the Minister of Health, December 1943). The target of 300,000 permanent houses, plus 200,000 temporary 'prefabs' was approved by the war cabinet, and became the benchmark for the transitional period (the coalition's White Paper of March 1945 referred to 300,000 permanent houses built or under construction within two years, of which 200,000 should be completed: see Ministry of Health, 1945, para. 14). In an important paper in January 1944 the Minister of Reconstruction set out detailed plans for housing in the transitional period (PRO CAB 87/7, Postwar Housing, 22 January 1944). The paper repeated the long term target of 3–4 million dwellings, but adopted a new figure of 750,000 necessary to meet urgent postwar needs (ibid., para. 2). It also repeated the familiar mantra about the importance of private enterprise in the long term, and reliance on local authorities during the first two years. The paper concluded with a series of recommendations about measures that needed to be put in place to allow an early start on the permanent housing programme. The list included references to legislation needed to extend the scope of subsidy to enable local authorities to build for general needs, and the importance of encouraging local authorities to start buying land ahead of the relaunch of building.

The process of negotiating a postwar subsidy regime, to enable local authorities to expand building for general needs, was initiated in December 1943 (PRO, T 227/804, letter from George to Hale), and in early 1944 not only was it noted that local authorities already had sites for up to 135,000 new houses, but plans were under discussion for the preparation of these sites by a switch of contractors from the airfields construction programme (PRO, T 227/804, Advance Preparation of Housing Sites). One important requirement for an orderly restart of house building was a control framework to ensure that labour and materials were available for housing and not drawn away into other types of construction work (something that had been missing in 1919); in March 1944 the Reconstruction Committee was recommended to propose the continuation of Defence Regulation 56A (control of civil building) and its extension so as to limit annual unlicensed expenditure (PRO CAB 87/7 R(44)49). This effectively gave local authorities complete control over the allocation of building materials and labour.

In addition to the concerns, mentioned above, about the commitment to a large long term postwar housing programme, there were two issues specific to the short term programme that provoked controversy. First, the idea of a programme of temporary houses had been considered by a sub-committee of the Central Housing Advisory Committee (CHAC), which had deprecated the principle of temporary housing (PRO HLG 36/18 note to Mr Hearder, 14 December 1943). But Churchill became personally very committed to the idea and insisted that better progress be made (PRO CAB 124/447, personal note from Churchill to Sir E. Bridges, 2 September 1944). The temporary houses programme was the responsibility of the Ministry of Works, which was not supported by the Ministry of Health in this matter.

The second controversial issue around the programme for the transitional period was the role of private enterprise and the possible provision of subsidy. Having been initially excluded from, but then brought into, the subsidized programme after the First World War, private builders were keen to establish that they should be involved in the immediate postwar programme, and that 'where private enterprise and local authorities were meeting the same needs, private enterprise should be eligible for the same

Exchequer subsidy' (PRO HLG 36/18, minutes of CHAC, 21 April 1944). When this proposal was put to the Reconstruction Committee it was also suggested that private enterprise might account for about 50,000 dwellings in the transitional period, leaving the local authorities to build more than 80 per cent of the total programme. Despite this modest amount an important principle was at stake and both Attlee and Bevin recorded 'grave misgivings' about subsidy for private enterprise (PRO CAB 87/6, meeting of 10 July 1944). Nevertheless, subsidy for private builders was included in the housing White Paper of March 1945 (Ministry of Health, 1945, para. 26). Two months later the coalition broke up and Churchill became prime minister in a caretaker government, pending a general election.

Labour in power: the eclipse of private enterprise?

The Labour Party secured a historic election victory in July 1945, for the first time winning an overall majority (of 146) in the House of Commons, but the new government took office at a point when the country faced huge difficulties in terms of managing the return to peace and rebuilding the economy. Cairncross (1985) constructed his account of the period 1945–51 around a series of crises and turning points: the coal shortage of early 1947, the crisis over the convertability of sterling in the summer of 1947, the devaluation of the pound in 1949 and the impact of rearmament due to the war in Korea in 1951. Sympathetic accounts of the postwar government's construction of the welfare state refer to the considerable achievement that this represented, given the circumstances. Others, notably C. Barnett (1986), have deplored what they see as the profligate pursuit of social objectives at the expense of investment in economic recovery. From a different direction writers such as R. Lowe (1993, 1994) have pointed to the conservative and backward looking approach of the Attlee government, and the failure to implement the Beveridge proposals in full. In other areas, too, the government has been criticized, for compromises in the health service and for not pressing ahead with comprehensive education. Although Labour created the welfare state it did so on the basis of extensive preparatory work carried out during the war by and under the coalition government, and the continuities are obvious. Meanwhile, the private sector continued to flourish in each of the main social services (Marwick, 1982: 184). What does the evidence on housing contribute to this kind of debate?

It has been shown above that the new government inherited a clear, coherent and detailed housing policy for both the immediate postwar recovery period and for the longer term, covering the next ten to twelve years. The coalition government's White Paper had been based on an ambitious objective, which has continued to underpin housing policy ever since:

> The Government's first objective is to afford a separate dwelling for every family which desires to have one ... [and] to secure a progressive improvement in the conditions of housing in respect of both standards of accommodation and of equipment. (Ministry of Reconstruction, 1945: paras 4–6)

It was a policy based on years of work and negotiation around the scale of the problem and how best to tackle it. The most striking feature of housing policy at the end of the war was not, then, the lack of preparation but the continuity with prewar policy and the confidence that this was still the best way forward for the long term.

From Labour's point of view, housing had historically been a good issue for the Party, which in the early years of the twentieth century had been able to mobilize support around tenants' resentment towards private landlords. Labour had subsequently lent its support, both nationally and locally where it gained control of local councils, to the growth of municipal housing. In the 1930s Labour accused private enterprise of having failed to provide decent housing for the mass of the people and of being unable to meet the need for ordinary decent housing to let: 'Only the public authorities can do the job in the way it must be done – comprehensively, speedily and efficiently' (Labour Party, 1934: 17). At the same time the Party expressed support for a National Housing Commission with responsibility for ensuring that the housing programme was carried out, and for acting in default of local authorities where necessary (ibid.: 18).

Labour was an explicitly socialist party, committed to the nationalization of core industries. Its manifesto for the 1945 general election was derived from *Labour's Immediate Programme* (1937) (Durbin, 1985: 243–8), and wartime publications such as *The Old World and the New Society* (1942). Its position on housing was never very clearly stated, however. In the late 1930s the Party was committed to the nationalization of land, but this was dropped in favour of the public ownership of development rights, and state acquisition of ownership at the point of development, as proposed in the report of the Uthwatt Committee in 1942 but never actually implemented (A. Cox, 1984: 77–80; Ward, 1994: 90–1). Despite the political importance of housing, both in wartime reconstruction debates and at the 1945 general election (Fielding *et al.*, 1995: 36; Morgan, 1984: 44), it was given little attention in either *The Old World and the New Society* or the 1945 manifesto, *Let Us Face the Future*. The former referred to the importance of planning (in the widest sense) and 'planned production for community use', but its discussion of a 'social service state' concentrated on health, education and social security, making no mention of housing. The manifesto avoided specifics:

> Housing will be one of the greatest and one of the earliest tests of the Government's real determination to put the nation first. Labour's pledge is firm and direct – it will proceed with a housing programme with the maximum practical speed until every family in this island has a good standard of accommodation. That may well mean centralised purchasing and pooling of building materials and components by the State, together with price control. (Craig, 1975: 129)

Opinion polling was in its infancy at the 1945 general election, but the evidence suggests that housing was easily the most important issue for voters (Hennessy, 1993: 85) and a good issue for Labour candidates to emphasize (Morgan, 1999: 40). Nevertheless, Labour's position on housing was curiously weak, saying nothing about how the development programme was to be delivered; interestingly there was no reference in the manifesto to the programme of new towns that, in fact, proved to be one of the Attlee government's most successful postwar innovations, demonstrating Labour's willingness, under certain circumstances, to resort to non-municipal special purpose bodies to deliver substantial numbers of new houses. 'In 1945–51 Labour used the label "socialist" to describe its policies without either embarrassment or apology' (Francis, 1995: 223), and as a socialist party committed to full employment and a programme of nationalization, the absence from the manifesto of proposals for the public ownership of the construction industry is striking, especially given the importance of construction in the pursuit of full employment, as mentioned earlier.

The commitment to a massively increased construction industry labour force might have been used by Labour as a justification for public ownership of at least the large contracting firms. Nationalization had been Labour policy for a decade, although the list of industries to be brought into public ownership varied over time; construction seems not to have been a target at any time, despite frequent criticism of speculative builders (Durbin, 1985: 214–18; Middlemass, 1986; Morgan, 1984: ch. 3). However, in 1944 the Labour Party Conference had passed an amendment, against the wishes of the leadership, calling for transfer to public ownership of a list of industries, including large scale building. This defeat for the National Executive was welcomed by left wingers including Aneurin Bevan (Brooke, 1992: 104). But instead of a socialist housing policy based on the public ownership of the means of production, the Labour government opted for a municipal development programme, relying to a large extent on privately owned building firms to deliver production. A socialist housing policy, firmly located in the context of a coherent view of a 'social service state', might have been expected to refer to a universal right to decent affordable housing and to include proposals to municipalize the failing, declining private rental sector, but this was not part of Labour's policy in 1945. Indeed, later, in 1949, when proposals for municipalizing private renting were put forward they were forcefully dismissed by Bevan (Donnison, 1967: 165).

What Labour actually brought to housing policy in 1945 was a definition of the situation, shared with the coalition government, that demanded a focus on output rather than radical reform. Indeed, resistance to changes in the established ways of working became a feature of Labour's housing policy in the second half of the 1940s. Commitment to local authorities as the main instruments of housing policy, at least in the transitional period, was common ground, but with Aneurin Bevan at the Ministry of Health this became an article of faith. Bevan's stance on housing is remembered chiefly for his commitment to building by local authorities and for his defence of high space standards in new council houses (Malpass, 1990: 76–7). His enthusiasm for local authority housing was matched by his antipathy for private enterprise; rejecting the coalition's proposal for post-war subsidy for private builders, Bevan memorably remarked that, 'The only remedy the Tories have for every problem is to enable private enterprise to suck at the teats of the State' (quoted in Foot, 1973: 74). The official position was that local authorities should license only one new private house for every four council houses (which was actually a higher proportion of private housing than had been discussed under the previous government), but, initially at least, Bevan was understood by his officials to incline to the view that obstacles should be placed in the way of private housing (PRO CAB 124/450 Progress report on Housing, November 1945). He also urged young couples to avoid the burden of a mortgage and to wait, if they could, for a council house (House of Commons Debates, 17 October 1945, vol. 414, col. 1,222). It was matter of cross-party agreement at that time that in the 1930s many young people had opted for home ownership because they had no real choice, and that what was needed after the war was a big increase in the supply of houses for rent (Pole Report, 1944: 25). In the circumstances this meant local authority houses.

Bevan is credited with support for a wider social base within public housing and for wanting to break down the spatial segregation of different social classes. He also refused to countenance the construction of council houses aimed at 'managers' (Morgan, 1984: 184) yet it is interesting that the simple legislative amendment needed to remove the words 'working class' from the subsidy legislation did not come until 1949, and initially Bevan proclaimed what seems very like a class bias in housing policy:

> Before the war the housing problems of the middle classes were, roughly, solved. The higher income groups had their houses; the lower income groups had not. Speculative builders, supported enthusiastically, even voraciously, by the money lending organisations, solved the problem of the higher income groups in the matter of housing. We propose to start at the other end. We propose to start to solve, first, the housing of the lower income groups. In other words, we propose to lay the emphasis of our programme upon the building of houses to let. This means that we shall ask the local authorities to be the main instruments for the housing programme ... It is ... a principle of the first importance that the local authorities must be looked to as the organisations and source for the building of the main bulk of the housing programme. The local authorities are admirably suited for this purpose. (*House of Commons Debates*, 17 October 1945, vol. 414, col. 1,222)

This rhetoric is a long way from the inclusiveness of policies being developed for health, education and social security, providing further evidence of the way that housing differed from the other key areas of social policy.

Bevan's enthusiasm for the local authorities was not shared by all his officials and colleagues. The inter-war housing record of the local authorities was open to criticism (Bowley, 1945), and Marwick (1968: 277–8) has suggested that the impact of the war exposed the more general weaknesses of local councils, especially the smaller ones. There had been experiments before 1939 with the establishment of government sponsored housing associations to build houses in the north east of England and in Scotland (Malpass and Jones, 1996), which might have provided the basis for further organizational innovation after the war; but Bevan would have none of it. There are references in the literature to Bevan's resistance to the establishment of a housing corporation to act in default of local authorities. Foot (1973: 72–3) refers to it as an attempt by the Ministry of Works to create a huge organization, which, among other things, would greatly strengthen the position of that ministry in its struggle with the Ministry of Health for pre-eminence in relation to housing (see also Hennessy, 1993: 170; Morgan, 1984: 165–6). In fact the proposal was quite modest in scope, with planned output scaled down to 1,000 dwellings per year. A key problem that was never overcome was that the financial viability of the project was always open to question – the costs of houses built by the corporation were expected always to be higher than where a local authority undertook the work itself. The Minister of Works, George Tomlinson, pressed ahead with trying to set up the corporation in the face of scepticism from the Treasury, the Ministry of Health and the National Federation of Building Trade Employers, but in August 1946 he caved in to Bevan's continued opposition (PRO T 161/1249, letter from Tomlinson to Bevan, 10 August 1946, T 227/804, National Building Corporation).

A final point to make here, before turning to the implementation of Labour's housing policy, concerns Attlee's failure to move swiftly to implement the manifesto commitment to establish a Ministry of Housing and Planning, combining the housing powers of the Ministry of Health and the planning powers of the Ministry of Town and Country Planning (Craig, 1975: 129). The fragmented responsibility for different aspects of planning, housing and the building process were well known before the end of the war, and clearly Bevan had a massive task on his hands in setting up the NHS at the same time as tackling the housing shortage. Leaving housing within the Ministry of Health until 1951 has come to be seen as Attlee's greatest administrative error (Morgan, 1984: 163; Timmins, 1996: 141). The fragmentation of responsibilities around a number of Whitehall departments had been recognized as an issue in relation to the prefabs programme. The Ministry of Health had overall responsibility for housing policy generally, but the Ministry of Works was responsible for the building industry and for advice on design and building techniques. The Ministry of Supply planned production and placed orders for steel houses, while the Ministry of Production made sure that the production of prefabs did not interfere with war production. The Ministry of Labour and National Service supplied the workers, and, finally, the Ministry of Town and Country Planning insisted on being consulted about the layout of estates (PRO CAB 124/449, Ministry of Reconstruction, 1945). The opportunities for confusion, conflict and delay were obvious, and Attlee's failure to act left him open to press criticism for having 'too many cooks' (*Picture Post*, 28 September 1946, quoted in Hennessy, 1993: 170).

The housing problem in 1945 was so severe and so widespread that everyone agreed that building up the construction programme as quickly as possible was the priority. In this context Treasury resistance to increases in subsidy finally yielded to Bevan's insistence (Timmins, 1996: 142). The legislative basis of the postwar housing programme was the Housing (Financial and Miscellaneous Provisions) Act, 1946, which trebled the money value of Exchequer subsidy for local authority houses, extended the subsidy period to sixty years and altered the balance between Exchequer subsidy and local rate fund contribution from the prewar ratio of 2:1 to 3:1. Even with this generous level of support, to approach completion of the task of dealing in one parliament with existing shortage and removal of houses already condemned as unfit for human habitation would mean building a total of 1.25 million houses, or 250,000 per year

Table 4.1   *Permanent dwellings completed in Great Britain, 1945–51*

Year	Local authorities	Private	Other	Total
1945	1,936	1,078	–	3,014
1946	25,013	30,219	168	55,400
1947	97,340	40,980	1,370	139,690
1948	190,368	32,751	4,497	227,616
1949	165,946	25,790	5,891	197,627
1950	163,670	27,358	7,143	198,171
1951	162,584	22,551	9,696	194,831
Total	806,857	180,727	28,765	1,016,349

Source: *Annual Abstract of Statistics* (1962).

but, as Table 4.1 indicates, this was never achieved and the total fell well short of expectations.

To the total of permanent houses must be added the 160,000 prefabs completed between 1945 and 1948 – this was also well short of initial expectations, but reflected Labour's strong opposition to the principle of temporary dwellings, despite their popularity with the public (Gay, 1987; Vale, 1995). The story of Labour's struggle to build in line with both need and popular demand has been recounted in some detail elsewhere (Foot, 1973; Merrett, 1979; Morgan, 1984). It was a battle against the odds: despite the wartime preparations, the new government struggled to inject momentum into the programme in the face of continuing shortages of labour and materials, neither of which was helped by the administrative complexity of the central government bureaucratic apparatus (mentioned above) and the commitment to working through local authorities (many of which were small and had not built many houses in the past). Things only became worse during the dreadful winter of early 1947, followed by financial crisis in the summer of that year. The housing programme represented a major call on scarce resources, in competition with demands for investment in the reconstruction of a competitive exporting economy, and political commitment to the maintenance of Britain's position as a leading military power as the Cold War with the Soviet Union developed. The economic situation was such that from 1947 'Bevan's instrument for house building had to be used in reverse; instead of stimulating laggard authorities into action, it became a main function of the Ministry to stop local authorities building too much' (Foot, 1973: 95). (The chief mechanism used for this purpose was a system of controls that enabled the Ministry of Works to set earliest starting dates for building projects.)

Thus, even before the inauguration of the National Health Service and the reformed social security system, in July 1948, the housing programme was already going into reverse.

Assessments of Labour's housing policy between 1945 and 1951 have tended to focus on quantitative performance indicators; at the time there was much criticism, and the failure to meet expectations was said to have played badly with voters. Later academic commentaries are more generous in recognizing the scale of the achievement of a million dwellings in such difficult circumstances, and approvingly note Bevan's defence of high space standards in new council houses (Malpass, 1990: 77; Merrett, 1979). However, Power (1987) argued that too much emphasis had been placed on new building to the neglect of management, and there is certainly an argument for saying that the failure to invest in developing the management infrastructure to support the growth of public housing was a serious error. Just why this happened is difficult to explain, for it stands in sharp contrast to the stance taken in relation to town and country planning at that time; here there was official encouragement for the appointment of professional planners and for the establishment of new university courses (Cullingworth, 1975).

In the present context two further questions arise: how far did Labour depart from established policy trajectories, and what, if anything, did housing policy have to do with the welfare state? The problem of answering the first of these questions is that we cannot know exactly what a different government would have done in the same circumstances. We can be confident that whoever was in power after 1945 the local authorities would have played a leading role in reducing the housing shortage, although there remain the imponderable questions of the degree and duration of their dominance. It seems unlikely that a government of a different political stripe would have given much prominence to housing associations in the postwar building programme. As the previous chapter described, housing associations in the 1930s had failed to convince a Conservative dominated government that they had much to offer, and although they tried to talk up their potential contribution at the end of the war there was never a realistic possibility of them being given much to do (Malpass, 2000b: 116). Similarly, rent control in the private sector would have remained in place under a different government; no relaxation of control could be envisaged in conditions of such severe shortage of supply or, as one leading Conservative later put it, the houses had to go up before the rents (Macmillan, 1969: 407).

Labour departed from coalition housing policy in two important ways: it failed to undertake any slum clearance throughout its period in office, in marked contrast to the policy indicated since at least 1943. However, whether, in practice, another government would have been able to restart slum clearance any earlier is very much open to doubt. The other area was Labour's refusal to countenance subsidy for private builders, and here we can be more confident that a Conservative government would have followed the recommendations of the Pole Report. Although Labour's stance was criticized by the Opposition as an indication of Bevan's doctrinaire approach, the coalition's own proposals had given the local authorities the leading role during the transitional period. One way of looking at housing policy after the war is to interpret the first decade as an extended transitional period. And who is to say that a different government would not have found it expedient to carry on with local authorities in the lead for longer than the arbitrarily defined two-year transitional period?

On the question of the relationship between Labour's housing policy and the welfare state the widely held view has been that, 'Housing ... deserves its honoured role in the saga of Labour's welfare state' (Morgan, 1984: 170). This conclusion rests on the fact that not only were a large number of houses built after 1945 but the great majority of them were let at subsidized rents, and were allocated by publicly accountable local authorities on some kind of needs basis, rather than being distributed through the market on the basis of ability to pay. To the extent that these dwellings helped to ease the housing shortage and improved the overall average quality of accommodation they contributed to the wellbeing of the nation, and because they were part of the public sector they were consistent with a dominant (big government) theme of the period; in that sense housing policy can be seen as consistent with the welfare state.

However, 'The drive to meet production targets completely overshadowed any attempt to reconsider the state's responsibilities for meeting a basic social need or achieving a more equitable housing system' (Cole and Furbey, 1994: 60). The concentration on house building should not obscure the lack of reform agenda. Building a lot of council houses was not the same as reform on welfare state lines. First, Labour's housing policy left the private rented and owner occupied sectors untouched and unreformed, in marked contrast to the institutional reorganizations that were characteristic of the welfare state reforms in health, education and social security in the same period. Second, while the touchstone of reform in other programme areas was universalism, Labour's housing policy was quite different. Universalism meant opening up access to public services as a right of citizenship, which in practice meant removing barriers to working-class participation in services such as health and education, and extending the benefit system to cover a wider range of contingencies. But universalism also meant providing the middle class with free services for which they had previously paid. Housing policy did not conform: there was no sustained attempt to make council housing more affordable for the least well off, and there was certainly no attempt to attract the middle class (who, in general, showed no enthusiasm for becoming council tenants).

In 1945 the government adopted a guideline rent policy of 10 shillings per week in the public sector, considerably less in real terms than many tenants had been paying between the wars. Rents at that level were probably well within reach of the majority of working households in postwar Britain, but they were above the levels found in the poorer quality parts of the controlled private rented sector. Moreover, the government did nothing to stick to the 10 shilling norm in the face of strongly rising construction costs: the subsidy levels set in 1946 were not raised at all during the remainder of the life of the Labour government, resulting in inevitable upward pressure on rents. Meanwhile rent rebate schemes, which had made little impact before 1939, actually went into decline after 1945 (Malpass, 1990: 83–5). As a consequence of the decision to build high quality council houses, but with no means of targeting them to the least well off, the majority of new houses seem to have been allocated to people who were in relatively well paid manual work – precisely the people who were both essential to the recovery of the British economy (as well as the bedrock of Labour's electoral support) and the very people for whom the private builders had been building in such large numbers in the 1930s.

Postwar housing policy was not shaped around welfare state notions of universalism or citizenship rights, but was driven by twin imperatives: a need to respond to the demands and interests of a politically and economically powerful section of the working class (specifically *not* the poor), and the need to rebuild the construction industry. Labour's postwar housing policy, then, like the policies of its inter-war predecessors, gave most to the better off, and in difficult circumstances excluded the poor from the frame of reference. From the point of view of the builders, Labour's stance could not have been much more helpful: it gave them a substantial flow of work which could not have been guaranteed by unfettered market forces in the immediate postwar years. The fact that private builders were responsible for the construction of the great majority of postwar council houses indicates that private enterprise was not eclipsed in the way that the size of the local authority programme might suggest (Malpass, 2003). One might almost say that it was the poor who were eclipsed by policy to a much greater extent than the private builders. A final point to make in this context is that it was only towards the end of Labour's first term that the label 'welfare state' came to be applied to the postwar reforms, and therefore it is important to remember that the policy planning and implementation process since 1942 was not conducted within a coherent project called the welfare state. Housing policy was following its own, different, logic; its subsequent annexation by or to the welfare state should be seen for what it is: an understandable piece of political rhetoric, which has misled scholars for half a century.

Conservatives in a hurry

Labour won a general election in 1950, but lost seats to the Conservatives while piling up a larger overall share of the vote. With its majority reduced to just six a second term Labour government was always likely to struggle, and in this case it is depicted in the literature as tired and divided; Morgan (1999: 85), for example, describes the government as 'an ageing team intent on grim, bunker-like survival and little else'. Bevan left the Ministry of Health in early 1951, to be replaced by Hugh Dalton in a newly separated Ministry of Local Government and Planning. With the economy in some trouble, Attlee called a surprise election in October 1951, resulting in a Conservative majority of 17, large enough to sustain them through a full parliament. Labour again won more votes, and continued to do well in the postelection opinion polls, giving them reason to expect to return to power when the electoral pendulum swung their way. No-one foresaw then that it would be 13 years before another Labour government was returned.

At the Conservative Party conference of 1950, when, allegedly, the chairman momentarily lost control of proceedings (Morgan, 1984: 485), the Party pushed the leadership into a commitment to build 300,000 houses per year. This represented a 50 per cent increase on the output achieved in 1951, but it was a target that had been consistently exceeded, in very different circumstances, in the 1930s. Housing 'was a plank of Labour's platform which was not sufficiently nailed down by the Attlee government, thus giving the Conservatives an opportunity to prise it away from their opponents' (P. Clarke, 1996: 240). The Tory manifesto for the 1951 election defined housing as 'the first social service' and promised that it would be given priority second only to national defence (Craig, 1970: 146).

The man given the post of Minister of Housing and Local Government was Harold Macmillan, a Conservative with decidedly liberal tendencies. It is an indicator of the political salience of housing at that time that although Macmillan had hitherto not been a front rank political figure the housing portfolio enabled him to establish his credentials for further preferment (Clarke, 1996: 241); within less than three years of moving on from housing Macmillan was prime minister – it is difficult to imagine such a sequence of events today. Macmillan had the advantage of taking over after Attlee's belated organizational restructuring that had finally separated housing from health in 1951, and at a time when local authorities were really getting into their constructional stride. It is usually said that in these circumstances any short term expansion of the programme had to rely mainly on the local authorities. What also needs to be recognized is that the government saw the need in terms of new houses to let, and they had no expectation that, given the continuation of rent control, the private sector would produce the right kind of houses (PRO, CAB 129/58, C(53)23, 22 January 1953). In order to increase the number of new council houses Macmillan encouraged local authorities to reduce standards (taking further a process begun in the last months of the Labour government: see Malpass, 1990: 82–3), but he also put through an increase in the level of subsidy for each new council house (the Housing Act, 1952, raised Exchequer subsidy from £16 10s. to £26 14s., with a similar proportionate increase in rate fund contribution: Malpass, 1990: 82). He sought to popularize his housing drive in terms of the 'People's House', despite a 'brutal' lowering of standards (Merrett, 1979: 246). At the same time Macmillan announced that private builders would henceforth be permitted to build up to a half of all new houses, and they would no longer need building licences for houses of less than 1,000 square feet.

Economic difficulties, the demands made by the war in Korea and the continuing debate over the allocation of scarce resources for home consumption or industrial export all raised questions over how quickly the target could be achieved. The Treasury wanted to work towards 300,000 by 1954, but Macmillan, backed by Churchill, proved to be adroit in securing more than his share of resources and pressed ahead with the housing programme at such a pace that the target was achieved a year early (see Table 4.2). Macmillan consistently under-estimated likely output, showed little willingness to rein in the local authorities, and was not trusted by the Treasury: 'it was exasperating when Macmillan would agree amiably in Cabinet to make vague cuts, but would completely ignore Cabinet instructions in issuing orders to his civil servants' (Jones, 1991: 36). Throughout 1953 the Treasury was concerned about the lack of control over the housing programme, with its worrying implications for

Table 4.2 *Permanent dwellings completed in Great Britain, 1952–54*

Year	Local authorities	Private	Other	Total
1952	193,260	34,320	12,342	239,922
1953	238,883	62,891	16,975	318,749
1954	234,973	90,636	22,196	347,805

Source: *Annual Abstract of Statistics* (1962).

expensive imports of materials, and in the autumn Macmillan seems to have broken an undertaking to his cabinet colleagues and committed the Exchequer to as much as £100 million extra for housing on the basis of approvals issued to local authorities for house building (PRO, T 230/256, note from Hall to Strath, 11 November 1953, and T 227/806). This led to the target being significantly exceeded in 1954 and to the Treasury pressing the cabinet for a decision to make 300,000 no longer a target but the upper limit for housing production in future. It is clear that relations between the Ministry of Housing and Local Government (MoHLG) and the Treasury were generally strained at this time, and that the Treasury did not trust a word Macmillan said, on housing or other issues (Cullingworth, 1980: 111–21).

In the context of the early 1950s it was judged by the Conservative government to be more important to achieve quantitative output figures than that new houses should be of this or that tenure. Only once the 300,000 target had been demonstrably passed did they begin a major reorientation programme, which is the subject of the next chapter.

Conclusion

Existing accounts tend to underplay the differences between housing and the other key social policy areas in the early postwar years. The key difference was that in the case of housing the government had to respond as quickly and effectively as possible to a most pressing social and political problem. To do so it made use of the local authorities as the most efficient policy instruments available, rather than as part of a long term plan to reform the housing system as a whole. In other policy areas there was not the same overwhelming urgency demanding immediate action, but there was in each case a clearly articulated commitment to progressive reform. The lack of a reform agenda in housing is striking, and at least as worthy of comment as the achievement of large numbers of new houses. Thus although the Labour government recognized the social and political importance of housing, and although it built lots of good quality and relatively affordable dwellings, it left housing as the least decommodified and most market determined of the welfare state services. The imperatives of production and an ideological commitment to municipal provision dominated the government's approach, squeezing out consideration of long term systemic reform. The lack of housing rights, the retention of user charges and the persistence of a predominant market sector all contributed to the distinctive position of housing in relation to the welfare state and subsequently made the public sector vulnerable to attack from governments less committed to public provision.

In contrast to those commentators, such as Donnison (1967) and Glennerster (1995), who have implied that the Labour government had little to build on, the preparatory work from 1942 onwards had laid out a vision of an extensive programme of new building and replacement over a ten-year period, and detailed plans for the immediate postwar years. Housing policy in the late 1940s can be seen as essentially the coalition's policy, modified by the pressure of events and given a Labour spin, in the sense that the emphasis on local authority house building was extended beyond the planned transitional period. As such, policy was informed by the thinking of the 1930s, to the extent that it assumed a need to emphasize new housing for rent (Pole Report, 1944: 26). The strong growth of demand for home ownership that was later to dominate housing policy was not foreseen. Labour's policy had a distinctly anti-private enterprise edge, especially during Bevan's time as Minister of Health, but in the longer run this was bound to lead to growing tensions between housing and labour market policy. The point here is that the success of the postwar policy of full employment, and the rising living standards that were produced by the long boom, strengthened demand for market based housing solutions, especially home ownership, thereby threatening the popularity of local authority housing, irrespective of the ideological stance of the government in power. There is no evidence that the housing implications of postwar labour market policy were foreseen or theorized at the time.

Chapter 5

Reshaping Housing Policy

Two useful opening generalizations about the period covered by this chapter (1954–74) are that, first, it formed a large part of the long post-war economic boom – the longest period of economic growth and rising prosperity since the industrial revolution (Harloe, 1995: 210) – and second, as the period progressed it became clear that the welfare state would survive the election, and re-election, of a Conservative government. However, both of these generalizations require qualification: although the boom years were a period of full employment and rising living standards, there were also times of financial and economic difficulty, which became associated with the notion of 'stop–go' policy ('an oscillation of government policy between expansion in the interests of reducing unemployment and con-traction once expansion tilted the balance of payments into deficit': Cairncross, 1992: 14). And alongside rising individual living standards there emerged growing concern about Britain's relative economic decline and slower rates of growth than in other industrialized countries. These two developments were both threats to the welfare state, to the extent that macro-economic concerns led governments (or at least Chancellors of the Exchequer) to try to constrain the growth of public expenditure on welfare services, while rising household spending power in expanding markets for consumer goods highlighted the limitations of public services and fuelled people's ability and willingness to opt for private solutions (such as home ownership).

Housing retained a high political salience, and high levels of new build-ing were maintained, at least until the late 1960s. A combination of rising living standards and developments in housing policy meant that by the end of the period more than half of all households owned (or were buying) their own homes, and local authority housing was coming under increas-ing criticism from both left and right. The long boom and the welfare state policies associated with it were undoubtedly very good for housing (in the sense that the overall quantity and average quality of dwellings improved significantly), but it has also been suggested that housing was one of the factors that helped to sustain the boom itself:

Public and private investment in housing and infrastructure, with its pow-erful multiplier effects on consumer and producer industries, generated

76

and fed on rising levels of employment and real income. (Harloe, 1995: 211; see also Cairncross, 1992: 38)

On the question of the Conservatives' attitude to the welfare state, while it is clear that they did not dismantle it neither did they meekly accept it on the terms established under the Attlee government (Glennerster, 1995: 73). R. Lowe (1989: 508) suggests that although the mid-1950s has often been seen as barren and dull in terms of social policy, it actually witnessed a major battle over the future shape of the welfare state. Churchill had never been enthusiastic about the proposals in the Beveridge Report, and according to Jones (1991: 40) when they returned to power in 1951 the Conservatives were determined to limit the growth of the welfare state. Their position was built around criticism of lack of individual choice, the wastefulness of universalism and the heavy burden of welfare on the economy – ideas that were to echo down the decades. Whiteside (1996) has argued that the Conservatives significantly departed from the Attlee government's welfare state – indeed, that they effectively redefined the welfare state – by moving away from the complex and extensive economic interventions aimed at reconciling economic inefficiency and social justice. Under Labour in the late 1940s, she argues, there was a closer connection between social welfare measures and policies of economic management; in this context the provision of subsidies and benefits was seen as grounds for wage restraint by the trade unions which, as a result of full employment, were in a relatively powerful position to demand pay increases.

The stance of the Conservative governments weakened central planning and management of the economy, and helped to narrow the definition of the welfare state, focusing more closely on the basic services of health, social security, education and housing. Spending on these services continued to rise during the Tories' first term – by 28 per cent (Whiteside, 1996: 95) – and this trend stimulated the Treasury into repeated demands for restraint by spending ministers. Reference has already been made (in Chapter 4) to the pressure put on the housing programme, and in 1952 substantial cuts were imposed in school building; in 1954 an independent inquiry was set up to look at the costs of the NHS, with the intention that it should produce proposals for savings, and in 1955 the Treasury pressed for the establishment of a ministerial committee to review social services spending (R. Lowe, 1989). The NHS inquiry backfired on the Treasury, producing recommendations for increased expenditure (especially on capital projects – not one new hospital had been built since the war), and rejecting the extension of direct user charges (Timmins, 1996: 206–7). Equally bad from the Treasury point of view was the experience of the Social Services Committee, which resulted in spending ministers mounting an effective defence against demands for cuts and charges. The housing minister

(Duncan Sandys) simply refused to attend the committee, and his officials displayed extreme reluctance to submit information (R. Lowe, 1989: 512). The Treasury emerges very badly from this episode, according to Lowe's analysis: 'The "Treasury point of view" was ... concerned neither with good government nor with value for money, let alone with the wider economic, social or political benefits of public expenditure, but with short term savings' (Lowe, 1989: 522). He goes on to suggest that the mid-1950s was a period when long term reforms should have been implemented but the chance was missed.

Housing, however, was the exception, despite the stand taken by Sandys in relation to the Social Services Committee. Far from being a dull and barren period, the mid-1950s saw a package of far reaching policy changes, which set housing on a course that it maintained for many years, and in some respects still maintains into the twenty-first century. In particular, the changes implemented in this period marked the beginning of unequivocal bipartisan support for owner occupation and set local authority housing on course for residualization. The first task of this chapter, therefore, is to spell out the package of housing policy changes and to establish their long term importance. A question to be borne in mind here is the extent to which the redirection of housing policy in the 1950s should be understood in terms of change or continuity: was it a sign of a distinctively Conservative alternative to Labour's welfarism, or was it, in fact, a reversion, after an extended postwar transitional period, to the principles laid out in the paper on *Postwar Housing Policy* in 1943 (see Chapter 4 earlier)?

'A grand design for housing'

Reference was made in Chapter 3 to the way that some housing scholars have depicted the course of housing policy as lacking coherence and consistency. Others have seen the mid-1950s policy changes as evidence of Treasury cuts in welfare spending. In fact there was considerable internal coherence and momentum in the way housing policy developed at this time. In January 1953 Macmillan set out for his cabinet colleagues a series of measures that he described as a grand design for housing (PRO, CAB 129/58, C(53)23). Characteristically, his starting point was the success of the house building programme, but, he argued, they must move on to tackle the problem of the maintenance and repair of older houses, and this meant grasping the nettle of rent control. On the one hand, he saw that the unresolved housing shortage required continuation of control, but, on the other hand, there needed to be some way of allowing landlords to increase rents in order to finance investment in repair and maintenance work. One of the problems with the way that rent control had been operated since 1915 was that there were wide variations in the rents paid for similar properties, and rents did not necessarily reflect differences in quality. Macmillan favoured an approach based on allowing landlords to increase rents according to a formula determined by rateable value, and subject to the requirement that the houses were in 'good tenantable repair'. Long term reform required a new valuations Bill (following flaws in the Act of 1948), but in the meantime Macmillan wanted an interim measure to stimulate landlords to increase repairs expenditure.

The next part of the strategy focused on what Macmillan called 'operation rescue', designed to relaunch slum clearance and to give local authorities powers either to insist that landlords carry out work necessary to make houses habitable or to acquire such properties at site value and to carry out the work themselves, pending demolition. On owner occupation, Macmillan's submission to cabinet is particularly interesting and revealing, given that the White Paper published later that year is remembered mainly for the following quotation:

> One object of future housing policy will be to continue to promote, by all possible means, the building of houses for owner occupation. Of all forms of saving, this is one of the best. Of all forms of ownership this is one of the most satisfying for the individual and the most beneficial for the nation. (MoHLG, 1953: para. 7)

However, at that time a large majority of people still rented, and Macmillan clearly expected that they would continue to do so: 'however much we may be able to encourage the owner occupier, a great proportion – probably the great majority – of ordinary folk will require houses to rent' (PRO, CAB 129/58, C(53)23, para 39). (Research published in 1958 concurred with this view, suggesting that 60 per cent of individual incomes could not support mortgaged house purchase: see United Nations, 1958: 6.) Macmillan went on to say that 'private enterprise cannot, in my view, do the job in the future. Whatever we may do about rents will only help to keep existing houses in repair. I doubt if it will encourage genuine private building to let on any great scale' (ibid., para. 40). This is revealing both in terms of the modest expectations of owner occupation entertained by policy makers in the early 1950s, and their recognition that decontrol of rents was essentially about stimulating investment in the repair of the existing stock; they had, in effect, written off the private landlord as a source of new building long before this was admitted publicly. This (as it turned out) realistic view of private landlords helps to explain why the Conservative governments of the 1950s and early 1960s were prepared to allow the construction of so many council houses. In a letter to the Chancellor (R.A. Butler), setting out his thoughts on housing, Macmillan wrote:

> We are allowing for 80,000 private enterprise houses (mostly for sale) in 1954. At present, signs are quite good; but it may be merely a damned-up demand and we may have difficulty in keeping it up or expanding it ... *But it is clear that there will be a limit to unsubsidised private enterprise in respect of houses to sell.* For not everyone can afford to buy or ought to be his own landlord. (PRO, T 227/806, letter from Macmillan to Butler, 11 June 1953; emphasis added)

Even more surprising is the revelation, in the same letter, that he was concerned that the provision of new rented housing should not be left to the local authorities in the long term, and that he had already (in January 1953) set up a committee to study alternatives, which he referred to as 'co-ownership and co-partnership': 'a new form of Association, different from the present Housing Association and conceived on a more popular basis' (ibid.). This interest in new forms of landlord did not surface in the White Paper and it was not until 1961 that there was public discussion of the idea. The argument that it was somehow undesirable for local authorities to become the main providers of rented housing became a theme developed by successive governments and it is important to note both this early statement of the idea and the fact that the government took no further action. The Conservatives' vision of housing in the welfare state did not, at that time, include a major role for housing associations, and the existing associations were not only kept very much on the margins but were also channelled into specialist areas (such as provision for elderly people) rather than being given a role in meeting the pressing general housing shortage.

Macmillan's grand design was supported by the Treasury, especially in relation to rent decontrol, which they linked to the problem of the rising burden of housing subsidies: 'A realistic rents policy for all houses is a condition of reducing the housing subsidies, and we can only attack the subsidies if we first break the iron ring of rent restriction' (PRO, T 227/806, paper by Owen, 14 April 1953). The argument here was that low private sector rents held down local authority rents, thereby requiring the latter to be subsidized by the Exchequer. From the Treasury point of view the over-riding problem was the cost of subsidies, and tackling it required three steps:

- the lifting of private sector rent control
- the development of a more economically coherent rents policy for the public sector
- a shift in construction from subsidized council to unsubsidized private enterprise.

All this was broadly consistent with Macmillan's plans, and with the thrust of policy laid down in 1943. Of these three steps, the third proved to be the easiest to carry out in the short term, and most successful. Rent decontrol was much less successful, and moving to a local authority rents policy based on current values and incomes took almost twenty years to implement (and even then it failed in practice: see Malpass, 1990: ch. 6).

Although the Treasury was keen to support Macmillan's proposals on rent control it was also determined to contain the scale of the housing programme, demanding that total resources should be pegged to the equivalent of 300,000 new houses per year, and that the new emphasis on older houses should not be allowed to increase overall expenditure. By the time the strategy was unveiled to the public, in November 1953, the claims to a grand design had been removed and the White Paper was prosaically titled: *Houses – the Next Step* (MoHLG, 1953). Given the political sensitivity of rent decontrol the government sought to put a positive spin on its proposals, expressing its support for owner occupation without prejudicing continued building for rent. It announced the re-launch of slum clearance, and the introduction of deferred demolition, but stated explicitly that the intention was not that local authorities should confine their new building activity to the demands of clearance. In a statement that neatly reflected the policy of 1943 and contemporary Treasury concerns, the White Paper said:

> Private enterprise must play an ever increasing part in the provision of houses for general needs, and will continue to be given every encouragement that circumstances from time to time permit. Any increase in private enterprise house building, whether for letting or for sale, would in some measure lighten the ever-growing burden of housing subsidies, which, in the interest of the general body of taxpayers, cannot continue indefinitely at the present rate. (MoHLG, 1953: para. 91)

The reshaping of housing policy in the mid-1950s was, then, not simply, or even mainly, that housing was the service most vulnerable to Treasury pressure, but it was driven by internally coherent thinking. And the minister's refusal to co-operate with the Social Services Committee was not a reflection of an unwillingness to change, but quite the opposite in fact; the ministry was motivated by a commitment to change, although on its own terms, not at the behest of a cuts-based Treasury agenda. The discourse was constructed around promotion of private enterprise and the need to tackle the condition of the existing housing stock as a way to avoid having to build yet more subsidized council houses. That this had serious long term implications for the role of the public sector within the overall housing system was not discussed. Nevertheless, the residualization of local authority housing can be traced back to the grand design and its implementation.

The housing situation

Before looking at the implementation of the emergent strategy it is
appropriate to pause to consider the housing situation at that time. In 1951,
despite the construction of a million postwar houses, plus 160,000 prefabs,
the crude housing shortage (comparing the numbers of dwellings and households) was still 800,000, and there were nearly 10 million households (in
England and Wales alone) living in conditions that were either unfit for
human habitation, lacking in basic amenities (bathrooms, piped hot water,
inside WC), overcrowded or shared (DoE, 1977a: 10). This represented
nearly three-quarters of the population; in Scotland the situation was worse.
Figures for 1958 suggest that council tenants were more likely than both
owner occupiers and private tenants to have exclusive use of a fixed bath, a
flush toilet and a hot water supply (Donnison, Cockburn and Corlett, 1961).

By 1953 there were twice as many council houses in Britain as there
had been in 1939, making up almost 20 per cent of the total supply
(owner occupiers were approaching 30 per cent and private tenants were
still a little over 50 per cent). As the fastest growing tenure category of the
postwar decade, with the most modern houses and subsidized affordable
rents, the social composition of the tenants of council housing is of interest, partly because of the contrast with the trend of the 1930s, but more
importantly because the early 1950s provide the benchmark against which
to measure subsequent changes as the process of residualization gathered
pace. As the previous chapter demonstrated, the postwar Labour government concentrated on quantitative housing targets, and with need so
pervasive there was little attempt to target new houses on those with
the lowest incomes. What limited evidence there is suggests that council
housing in 1953 was overwhelmingly a broadly based working-class
tenure, not skewed towards the least well off. Figures from the Family
Expenditure Survey show that only 16 per cent of families in the bottom
quarter of the income distribution were council tenants, which, at a time
when council housing made up 18 per cent of the stock, was a slight
under-representation of this group (Gray, 1979: 201). Another analysis
showed that in 1953 council tenants had average incomes only a little
below the median, and that under half of council tenants had incomes in
the two lower quartiles (Bentham, 1986). The fact that people on middle
incomes were to be found living on council estates was a mixed blessing;
on the one hand it helped to avoid the social polarization that was to
become the bane of social housing in later years, while on the other hand
it gave ammunition to right-wing critics who accused such people of occupying subsidized housing that they did not need, thereby depriving poorer
and more needy families (for an example see Malpass, 1990: 86; also
Tucker, 1966).

On the whole we can say that council housing in 1953 was a tenure of working families, with at least one member in full time manual work, benefiting not only from the state's investment in public housing but also full employment, which was helping to spread affluence and rising living standards. Moreover, a new council house was something to prized; the postwar estates consisted mainly of good quality, two-storey cottage style houses, let at rents that were subsidized, affordable and attractive to better off workers. For the less well off there remained the still extensive, poorer quality private sector, with lower, controlled, rents. The new estates had physical and social characteristics that made them desirable places to live (the very same characteristics that later made them places where the right to buy was most successful). Modernity in all its forms was valued over the past and there was a widespread preference for new houses and modern design; enthusiasm for Victorian houses and 'period features' was to come much later. As a result, people moving into new council houses in the early 1950s saw this sector very differently from the way it is generally perceived today; they were likely to be moving from old, rundown, private rented accommodation, probably shared with their in-laws. Having their own kitchen and bathroom, with constant hot water, in a house on an estate with none of the negative stereotyping that was later to develop, was a genuinely positive experience.

Implementing the strategy

In the event, the implementation of the strategy differed in three main ways from the plans outlined by Macmillan in 1953: for five years local authorities lost their role as providers of general needs housing; the strategy came to rely more heavily than had been anticipated on private building for owner occupation, and the idea of developing new style housing associations lay in abeyance for eight years. Encouragement of private enterprise had begun even before the White Paper, in the sense that restrictions on materials and building licences had been eased, and were finally removed at the end of 1954. In addition, in 1953 the Conservatives repealed the contentious development charge (a measure introduced by Labour in 1947 to divert to the community the benefits of development: see Cullingworth, 1980: ch. 4; Ward, 1994: 108). As a result of this positive approach to private builders, and the parallel negative stance in relation to local authorities, new building by the private sector increased in both absolute and proportionate terms in almost every year from 1953 to 1964 (see Table 5.1).

Embedded within the 'other' column are the very low levels of building achieved by housing associations in this period. Apart from a small burst of activity between 1953 and 1956, housing associations never managed

Table 5.1   *Permanent houses completed in Great Britain, 1953–64*

Year	Local authorities	Private	Other	Total
1953	238,883	62,891	16,975	318,749
1954	234,973	90,636	22,196	347,805
1955	191,803	113,457	12,135	317,395
1956	166,267	124,161	10,197	300,625
1957	165,910	126,455	8,725	301,090
1958	140,519	128,148	5,028	273,695
1959	122,165	150,708	3,801	276,674
1960	124,738	168,629	4,451	297,818
1961	112,421	177,513	6,128	296,062
1962	124,090	174,800	6,538	305,428
1963	118,179	174,864	5,829	298,872
1964	148,624	218,809	6,958	374,391

Source: Annual Abstract of Statistics (1962, 1981).

to build more than 2,000 dwellings per year until 1964 (Malpass, 2000b: 120, 151). Having peaked in 1953, output by local authorities was very nearly halved over the next six years, and over the same period new council houses fell from 75 per cent to 44 per cent of the total. Nevertheless, council housing was still growing at a significant rate throughout the period, but the form and quality of new housing were different, reflecting its changing role in the housing system.

First, in terms of size the 1950s as a whole saw a marked decline in overall standards of new building. The average new three-bedroom council house (and this type of house comprised well over 80 per cent of all new building in 1945–48: see MoHLG, 1955: 9) fell from 98 square metres in 1949 to 83 square metres by 1959 (Malpass, 1987: 147). Not only did the average for three-bedroom houses get smaller but these became a shrinking proportion of total output as more two-bedroom houses, and, more importantly, flats, began to be built. Moreover, as the slum clearance campaign gathered pace after 1955 the proportion of flats in high rise blocks also began to increase, reaching a quarter of public sector new building by the mid-1960s (Gittus, 1976: 132). The benchmark for high rise design was set by early schemes such as the London County Council's Alton estate at Roehampton, set in a parkland environment, but later estates lacked the same quality and refinement and contributed to what Dunleavy (1981: 354) referred to as the delegitimization of public housing as a whole, despite the fact that most authorities never built any at all, and high rise flats never constituted as much as 10 per cent of the sector. Whereas previously most council housing had taken the form of traditionally constructed, two-storey houses on low rise, low density estates, slum clearance estates created a new set of images: high density, high rise flats, constructed in non-traditional ways, using industrialized systems. The fact that these estates were expensive to build, unattractive to live in, especially for families with children, and that one high rise block (Ronan Point) actually fell down undoubtedly helped to shift demand into the private sector, where builders were still sticking overwhelmingly to traditional methods and styles.

Changes in the design and layout of new council estates were not, of course, intended to undermine the sector (they can probably be explained in terms of continuing Treasury pressure on unit costs and overall expenditure), but the more local authorities were urged to concentrate on slum clearance and the housing of the less well off, the smaller and less attractive were the dwellings that they able to offer. This echoed the experience of the inter-war period discussed in Chapter 3. In terms of policies intended to change the character of public housing, it is necessary to refer to the impact of slum clearance and rents and subsidies. Taking slum clearance first, the Housing Repairs and Rents Act, 1954, introduced a new definition of unfitness, and required local authorities to prepare and submit to the minister estimates of the numbers of slums remaining in their area, and their plans for removing them. The Act also introduced a subsidy to assist local authorities to carry out patch-up repairs on acquired properties that could not be immediately demolished.

The slum clearance campaign attracted criticism at the time for a number of reasons. First, there were wide and often counter-intuitive variations in the numbers and proportions of unfit houses identified by the authorities. Second, of the 847,000 unfit dwellings identified in England and Wales only 375,000 were scheduled for demolition within the next five years, and in places such as Liverpool and Manchester the local plans implied that slum clearance would take an unacceptably long time (English, Madigan and Norman, 1976: 26). Third, in the event, although some authorities started early and energetically, overall progress was very slow. Later, of course, further criticism of clearance developed around its impact on established communities and the quality of the estates built to rehouse people (A. Coleman, 1985).

The re-launch of slum clearance and the constraints on general needs housing inevitably had an effect on the social composition of the public sector and perceptions of its role and purpose. Slum clearance rehousing was bound to draw in increasing numbers of people on low incomes and people previously associated with the least desirable neighbourhoods. Although there later developed a good deal of romanticism around the remembered warmth and strength of working-class communities allegedly destroyed by clearance, at the time there was, for some people at least, a perception that breaking up these neighbourhoods was a civic duty. For example, Wilfred Burns, who was to become chief planner at the Department of the Environment, argued that:

> In a huge city, it is a fairly common observation that the dwellers in a slum are almost a separate race of people, with different values, aspirations and ways of living … Most people who live in slum areas have no views on their environment at all … One result of slum clearance is that a considerable movement of people takes place over long distances, with devastating effects on the social groupings built up over the years. But one might argue, this is a good thing when we are dealing with people who have no initiative or civic pride. The task, surely, is to break up such groupings even though the people seem to be satisfied with their miserable environment and seem to enjoy an extrovert social life in their own locality. (Burns, 1963: 93–4)

In practice, slum clearance often resulted in whole estates being stigmatized, with enduring implications for the subtle differentiation within the local authority stock. More generally, the more that local authorities were directed to concentrate on slum clearance the less chance there was for anyone not living in a clearance area to obtain a council tenancy, and therefore the more likely they were to seek private sector solutions, especially if they had the financial resources to do so, thereby contributing to the long term process of changing the social composition of council housing.

Changes in the subsidy system added to the rhetorical pressure on local authorities to turn away from general needs provision and to concentrate instead on rehousing people from clearance areas. What happened in the mid-1950s was the development of a rents policy designed to make council housing simultaneously more expensive for people on higher incomes and more affordable for people on low incomes. The strategy was to try to get councils to raise rents by redistributing subsidy away from general price reductions and into means-tested rent rebates targeted at low income tenants. Official files reveal that from the early 1950s the Treasury was aware of the need, at some stage, to move to a public sector rents policy based on current values rather than historic costs (PRO, T 227/806, Owen to Playfair, 1 July 1953, and T 230/256, paper by Grieve Smith, 11 February 1954). This meant abandoning rent setting based on the costs of provision (debt charges plus management and maintenance) and moving to an approach based on the current value of the house in relation to current wage levels.

The barrier standing in the way of this change was political rather than technical. To move to a current value rents policy would have involved reducing or removing subsidies awarded by previous governments for periods of up to sixty years, and it was regarded as politically unfeasible to renege on these commitments, given the predictably outraged response from the local authorities. But there was a need to do something. By the mid-1950s most local authorities had stocks of houses that had been built up over a period of more than thirty years, many of which had been built at very low prices in the 1930s, which meant low debt charges, made even lower by the effects of inflation during and after the war. Nevertheless, these cheap houses continued to attract Exchequer subsidy, which meant they could be let at very low rents, especially when compared to the cash value of wages in the prosperous 1950s.

Another aspect of the situation was the potential for widening differences in rents charged for older and newer houses in ways that did not reflect differences in quality or utility. The strategy adopted throughout the period after 1955 was to allow the value of subsidies paid on new houses to fall in real terms, and to encourage local authorities to pool this income with subsidies still being paid on older houses. In other words the benefit of subsidy was to be withdrawn from older, cheaper houses with low debt charges, and used to compensate the tenants of newer, higher cost houses. This would have the effect of raising the average rent in areas where the local authorities carried on building, but where the local authority chose not to build, or to build relatively little, then there would be much less upward pressure on rents. Accompanying this was a stream of advice and exhortations to local authorities to introduce rent rebate schemes.

Rent and subsidy pooling had been legally possible since 1935, but only in 1955 did the government adopt it as a device through which it could exert leverage on average council rents. From April 1955 the level of Exchequer subsidy for houses completed after that date was lowered by 17 per cent, and by the end of 1956 the subsidy for general needs housing had been removed altogether, leaving in place only assistance with houses built to replace cleared slums, and one-bedroom dwellings (assumed to be for elderly people: see Malpass, 1990: 90–2). This sent an unmistakable signal to local authorities that they should no longer engage in building to meet general needs – a reversal of what had been stated in the White Paper only three years earlier. At the same time, under the Housing Subsidies Act, 1956, local authorities were relieved of any responsibility to make a rate fund contribution in support of their housing activities. Hitherto it had been seen as a basic principle of local authority housing finance that the cost of subsidy should be shared between the Exchequer and the local rate-payers. Relieving local authorities of the obligation to subsidize their housing revenue accounts was explicitly about encouraging them to raise rents (i.e., to shift more of the cost of council housing onto tenants themselves, which was also what the government was doing by lowering the level of Exchequer subsidy). In practice, it seems that rents did rise after 1957 and rebate schemes became more widespread, but even in the late 1960s, after more than a decade of pressure to extend rebating, around 85 per cent of Exchequer subsidy continued to be distributed via general price reductions and fewer than 10 per cent of tenants were benefiting from rebates (Malpass, 1990: 111). To some extent this illustrates the differing perspectives of central and local government: while the centre wanted to residualize council housing for wider housing and economic policy reasons, there was little attraction in this for the local authorities responsible for managing the service.

Turning to the reform of rent control, the Housing Repairs and Rents Act, 1954, was judged to have failed: it gave rise to too many disputes, and discouraged landlords from either repairing their houses or increasing rents (M. J. Barnett, 1969: 44). However, it was always seen as merely an interim measure. The passage of a new Valuation Act, 1956, opened the way for a more thorough-going Rent Act, which duly followed in 1957. Barnett (1969) argues that there was a wide political and professional consensus about the need to reform rent control, although he suggests that the public were ill-informed. Other writers, however, have emphasized that the approach adopted in the Act was highly controversial (e.g., Holmans, 1987: 412), and that it 'Provoked a longer and more acrimonious debate than any other Bill introduced since the war' (Donnison, 1967: 174). But Donnison and Barnett agree that the Act was based on flawed data, no proper research and a misunderstanding of the housing market. The 1957 Act introduced immediate decontrol of rents of higher value dwellings (above a specified rateable value); dwellings of lower rateable value were decontrolled at the next change of tenant, and where control remained in place landlords were permitted to increase rents to twice the gross value for rating purposes (i.e., twice the 1939 market rents).

Looking back at the Act with the benefit of hindsight, an obvious omission was some sort of means-tested assistance to compensate the least well off tenants facing rent increases that were high relative to income. The implementation of the Act, in terms of both rent increases and loss of security of tenure, aroused considerable controversy, and although increases were not dramatic in relation to earnings the overall effect of the Act was to raise decontrolled rents above those charged for similar council houses. Given the marked differences in quality this might be seen as creating an incentive to join the queue for a council house. However, the impact of the Act is usually seen in terms of the growth of owner occupation, as sitting tenants preferred to buy the houses they occupied, rather than accepting higher rents and less security, while other properties were transferred by landlords taking advantage of the opportunity to obtain vacant possession before selling (Donnison, 1967: 229). One thing that is abundantly clear about the 1957 Act is that it did not result in an increase in private investment in new housing to let, confirming Macmillan's prediction in 1953.

Alongside the decontrol of private renting the government moved ahead with a series of measures designed to expand demand for home ownership. It will be recalled that Macmillan had entertained modest expectations of future demand, and therefore he was to construct a supportive policy environment. Cullingworth (1979: 100) has described policy towards owner occupation in the 1950s as 'benignly passive rather than forcefully active' although other writers have identified a series of measures designed to encourage expansion (Boddy, 1980: 18). The abolition of the development charge, for example, reduced the cost of new building, as did the ending of building controls in 1954; from 1954 to 1957 the government operated a scheme for guaranteeing excess advances, and in 1958 it removed Stamp Duty on houses purchased for less than £3,000. In 1959 the government passed the House Purchase and Housing Act, which made available a loan of £100 million to the building societies to encourage them to lend on older houses (built before 1919 and valued at less than £2,500). At the same time the government encouraged local authorities to increase their mortgage lending activity at the lower end of the market (where building societies were reluctant to go). A further measure designed to boost the market was the abolition of Schedule A tax on owner occupied properties from April 1963; this was a tax on the imputed investment income derived from owner occupation, and in principle it sought to tax the rent that owners were deemed to be charging themselves (the theory was that housing was an investment good and should be taxed accordingly – after all, landlords were taxed on their rental income, and owner occupiers could be regarded as investors in the same way).

All this needs to be set alongside the development of the system of grants for owners of older properties lacking in basic modern amenities. The grant system had been introduced in 1949, but had not made much impact. It was extended by the Acts of 1954 and 1959, making it easier for purchasers of older properties to obtain financial assistance with the installation of basic amenities and other improvements (Thomas, 1986: 61–2). It has to be said, though, that the growth of owner occupation during the period covered by this discussion was mainly due to the effects of full employment and rising living standards. It was the rise of 'affluence' and confidence about security of employment that enabled more people to afford the higher costs of mortgaged home ownership and made the risks seem manageable.

By the early 1960s it was becoming clear that even though owner occupation was growing faster than had been expected, the supply of rented housing was not keeping up with need and demand. With private investors showing no interest in new building, local authorities effectively confined to building for slum clearance and the housing associations idea having made no progress there was a need for new ideas. A White Paper, published in February 1961, indicated both a return to general needs building by local authorities and a more residualist rents policy:

> The government's aim is to secure that there will be houses for rent in sufficient numbers to keep pace with the rising demand of a prosperous society. As real incomes go up, more and more of this need, both for sale and to rent, should be met by private enterprise. For those who can neither afford to buy their own homes nor to pay economic rents there will be the 3.5 million publicly owned houses – increasing in number as local authorities continue to build for *the needs which only they can meet*. The taxpayer already subsidises the houses to the extent of £61 million a year, but at present, many council houses and flats which ought to be available to those who really need them are still occupied by people who, whatever their situation when they first became local authority tenants, have since become well able to make their own arrangements without need of subsidy. Increasingly, however, such tenants are making their own arrangements as councils adopt more realist rents policies. (MoHLG, 1961: 3; emphasis added)

This was a pretty unequivocal statement about the future of council housing: new building would not be confined to slum clearance, but it would deal only with those needs that the market could not meet. As the Rent Act had driven some people out of private renting into the arms of the local authorities, so realistic rents policies would drive the affluent workers out of council housing and into the market (Merrett, 1979: 252). Significantly, the White Paper announced that in future subsidies would not be committed for long periods and future governments would be able to reduce or cancel them. Two years later another White Paper, just before the Conservatives lost power, revealed that the government had in mind a radical overhaul of housing subsidies, signalling a move to current value pricing (MoHLG, 1963). However, this reform had to wait until the Tories were back in office.

The one new idea launched by the Conservative government in 1961 and carried on by Labour after 1964 was the promotion of cost rent and co-ownership as forms of provision that would stimulate a revival of investment in private renting (Malpass, 2000b: 134–7). The new organizations were modelled on Scandinavian precedents and were intended to prevent the emergence of local authorities as monopoly landlords. Lack of enthusiasm among lenders and builders led to the involvement of the existing housing associations, and their National Federation was given the task of distributing the £25 million of public money made available as loans (not subsidy) to start off what was expected to become a substantial permanent feature of the British housing system. Central government had been providing an annual subvention to the Federation since 1935 but seized this opportunity to intervene to try to strengthen the organization (PRO HLG 118/177 Reconstitution of the NFHS). This was the first time that the Federation and its members had been given a specific role in pursuit of housing policy, and unfortunately they failed to impress. Not one existing association built any houses under the 1961 Act (although a small number did set up new societies), and the Federation itself was sidelined in 1964 by the creation of the Housing Corporation as a body dedicated to the promotion of the expanded scheme (Malpass, 2000b: 137–41).

Housing investment increased in the early 1960s and completions of new council houses rose in 1962 for the first time after eight years of decline. This was part of wider increases in expenditure on key public services. At the same time the government published its hospitals plan, which launched the first major round of new hospitals since the war, and agreed to implement the recommendations of the Robbins Report (1963), which led to a massive increase in higher education spending, including the establishment of new universities and the expansion of others. But by 1963 the Conservatives had been in power for a dozen years and were approaching the end of their third term tired and increasingly out of touch with a rapidly changing society. Macmillan had shone as housing minister a decade earlier, and his first couple of years as prime minister earned him the label 'Supermac', but by 1963 the youth cult was gathering pace, and in the era of the Beatles he was seen as an elderly, grouse shooting prime minister tainted by a high profile sexual scandal involving a government minister (the Profumo affair). He retired, handing over to the even more out of touch Earl Home. Even so, Labour, now led by the ebullient former grammar-school boy, Harold Wilson, only just managed to win the election of October 1964, creeping into office with an overall Commons majority of just four.

Housing under Labour: consensus consolidated

In many ways the 1960s turned out to be good decade for the welfare state. As just mentioned, the Conservatives had begun to increase expenditure in key areas, and the return of a Labour government augured well for the future. Although later judgements of Labour's time in office have tended to be critical of the lack of progress on issues such as poverty (Townsend and Bosanquet, 1972), the new government started off by abolishing prescription charges and raising pensions by the largest ever amount (Timmins, 1996: ch. 12). Later achievements included the reform of means-tested social security (with the old National Assistance Board being replaced by the Supplementary Benefits Commission), the encouragement of comprehensive schools and the launch of the polytechnics and the Open University. The welfare record of the Labour government needs to be seen in the context of continuing economic difficulties, which included inheriting from the Conservatives 'the most dangerous sterling crisis since ... 1951' (Bogdanor and Skidelsky, 1970: 51) and the devaluation crisis of November 1967, which led to further pressure on public expenditure.

How did housing fare in this period? Glennerster (1995: 95) has suggested that 'The framework of ideas that was driving the 1964 government's social policies can be traced back in a fairly unbroken line to the 1920s and 1930s.' In housing policy, however, Labour had moved a long way from its position when last in office, and it rapidly abandoned some commitments entered into while in opposition in the 1950s. The most important and obvious change was that the Labour leadership had come to accept the growth of owner occupation as inevitable and desirable. There would be no going back to the days when local authorities built 80 per cent of all new houses and couples were advised to avoid the blandishments of mortgage lenders. Nevertheless, Merrett (1979: 254) cautions against seeing the housing policies of the Labour government of 1964–70 as a replication of those of their Conservative predecessors. Housing was still a high-profile political issue, and with such a small parliamentary majority an early general election was a real possibility; housing was therefore an area in which the new government sought to make its mark quickly. The minister given the housing portfolio was Richard Crossman, who had not shadowed the post in opposition and who was not therefore expecting it. Crossman's priorities were to resolve the acknowledged problems in the wake of the Rent Act, 1957, and to crank up the house building programme.

It has been claimed that whichever party had won the election something would have been done to restore a degree of rent control (Banting, 1979: 30). During its long period in opposition the Labour Party had become committed to a policy of municipalization of all remaining private rented houses, but the idea was dropped before the party returned to office (M.J. Barnett, 1969: ch. 11). Crossman, working with a small group of advisers, produced a durable solution to the apparently intractable problem of regulating private renting. It was, in essence, a compromise between control and freedom, based on regulated tenancies and 'fair rents': tenants and landlords would in future be able to apply to a newly created cadre of independent rent officers for the establishment of a regulated (secure) tenancy and the determination of a fair rent. The definition of fair rent was one that was fair to both the tenant and the landlord, and which was set in relation to the size, quality and location of the dwelling, assuming a balanced market (i.e., fair rents excluded any scarcity premium). The scheme overcame the rigidity of rent control by allowing for periodic reviews of fair rents, and for increases to be phased in over a run of years. This amounted to a system of moderated market rents, but allowed prices to move more or less in line with inflation and incomes. The fair rent system was introduced in the Rent Act, 1965, but it spread only slowly through the sector at a rate dependent upon applications from tenants and landlords. Again the opportunity was not recognized, or not taken, to introduce a matching system of rent allowances for low income tenants subject to regularly rising rents. Nevertheless, the concept of fair rents survived as a cornerstone of policy in relation to private renting until 1989, and in the meantime it provided the basis for a major expansion of the housing associations (see Chapter 6 later).

On the size of the housing programme, Labour became embroiled in an unseemly and damaging numbers game. It had hinted at a target of 400,000 dwellings per year, but in the White Paper of 1965 the total was raised to a promise of 500,000 per annum by 1970, 'and more thereafter' (MoHLG, 1965: para. 1). At the 1966 general election (at which Labour won a larger majority) the Conservatives raised the stakes to 500,000 by 1968. In fact, as Table 5.2 shows, the target of 400,000 was only reached twice, and, given the criticism that is now heaped on so much of the housing built in the 1960s, this is probably something to be thankful for.

On the question of the size of the housing programme, the only party political difference concerned who could build the most. And on the respective long term roles of owner occupation and council housing there was by now a high degree of agreement, as the 1965 White Paper revealed. It referred to the possibility of local authorities building as many

Table 5.2 *Permanent houses completed in Great Britain, 1965–70*

Year	Local authorities	Housing associations	Private	Total
1965	151,305	3,991	213,799	369,095
1966	161,435	4,558	205,372	371,365
1967	181,467	4,984	200,438	386,889
1968	170,214	6,291	221,993	398,498
1969	162,910	7,336	181,703	351,949
1970	157,067	8,493	170,304	335,864

Sources: Malpass (2000b); Merrett (1979).

as 250,000 houses per year by 1970, but this would only be 50 per cent of the target, and the increase was seen as a temporary expedient:

> once the country has overcome its huge social problem of slumdom and obsolescence, and met the need of the great cities for more houses let at moderate rents, the programme of subsidised council housing should decrease. The expansion of the public programme now proposed is to meet exceptional needs; it is born partly of a short term necessity, partly of the conditions inherent in modern urban life. The expansion of building for owner occupation on the other hand is normal; it reflects a long term social advance which should gradually pervade every region. (MoHLG, 1965: para. 15)

Local authorities were encouraged to press ahead with large urban redevelopment schemes, which often went beyond the strict definition of slum clearance. As they did so they tended to provoke a backlash from people who did not see themselves living in slums, or even in areas that should be redeveloped (N. Dennis, 1972). At the same time the relative advantages of new local authority dwellings began to decline as more high rise blocks were built in inner city areas, increasingly using industrialized building systems of dubious merit (McCutcheon, 1975). The government pressed local authorities to adopt non-traditional factory based methods of construction (in a vain hope that this would reduce costs), and at the same time it urged them to adopt the higher space and heating standards for individual dwellings set out in the Parker Morris Report (MoHLG, 1961); these standards did not become mandatory until 1969 when they were a condition of eligibility for the higher rates of subsidy offered by the Housing Subsidies Act, 1967. The combination of ambitious output targets, untried building techniques, higher dwelling standards and tight cost constraints was a potent mixture, which led to some estates that were badly designed, poorly built and hard to live in from the start. In the longer run this has proved to be a crucial factor in the declining appeal of council housing as the problems of these schemes have tended to catch the headlines more than the millions of successful traditionally built houses (A. Coleman, 1985).

In the late 1960s a number of factors came together to bring about an end to the long period of high output policy. Growing public disquiet about the impact of large scale redevelopment was only one of these, and not necessarily the most significant, although, together with the recognition that redevelopment was embracing more areas with relatively high levels of owner occupation, it provided a justification for re-thinking the approach and moving to greater emphasis on the rehabilitation of existing dwellings.

The most immediate imperative was the economic crisis of 1967, culminating in the devaluation of the pound sterling in November (Cairncross, 1992: 163–71). This was accompanied by an appeal to the International Monetary Fund, whose assistance always comes with strings attached, usually in the form of demands for cuts in public expenditure. These duly followed in early 1968, proposing a cut of £500 million in 1968–9 and more thereafter; included in the package was a cut in local authority housing production and, although it was not apparent at the time, this marked the end of both high levels of building by local authorities and the abandonment of the numbers game. Ever since the war the main political parties had competed with each other in terms of quantitative housing targets, but after 1968 this sort of posturing disappeared from public debate, apparently for good. In fact, even before the devaluation crisis ministers had been preparing the ground for a change of housing policy, referring to the approaching end of the overall shortage and implying the possibility of scaling down public investment in new building (Gibson and Langstaff, 1982: 63). Instead, as a White Paper revealed in March 1968 (MoHLG, 1968), there was to be an expansion of rehabilitation and improvement, including the designation of general improvement areas. This was both a response to public opposition to large scale clearance and an attempt to shift the thrust of policy from public to private sector, for the intention was that the majority of rehabilitated houses would remain in private ownership. And this, in turn, represented a redistribution of responsibility for tackling the quality of older inner-city housing away from the state and onto the shoulders of individual owners, a move initially underpinned by the availability of state funded improvement grants. Nevertheless, it can be seen as signalling a partial retreat from the welfare state.

The shift into rehabilitation provided a boost for housing associations, which had been quietly modernizing themselves, partly as a result of an infusion of youthful enthusiasm from activists reacting to the perceived damage done to local communities by large scale redevelopment (Malpass, 2000b: 141–8). They were also aided by injections of money from some local authorities (principally the Greater London Council) and the homelessness charity Shelter (which was founded in 1966, partly to raise and distribute money for housing associations). In addition, the Housing Subsidies Act, 1967, gave associations a subsidy in relation to costs incurred in the acquisition and conversion of existing properties (previously the only assistance available for this sort of work came through the improvement grant system).

Nevertheless, 1968 marked the end of high output policy. In the wake of devaluation and the 1968 White Paper the production of new council houses fell away steeply, a process helped by the fact that by 1968 and 1969 the Conservatives were in control of most of the large urban local authorities (including cities such as Sheffield and Newcastle). Private sector output also fell, and the government's target of half a million dwellings per year was abandoned without ever looking seriously achievable, despite the government's strongly supportive stance on owner occupation. The apologetic tone of the 1965 White Paper's explanation for the planned increase in council house building contrasts with positive references to owner occupation. For example, it was said that the government must go beyond meeting existing demand for home ownership, to take account of an even larger 'suppressed demand' from people currently unable to afford it. Thus it was that in 1968 a Labour government introduced a device known as the option mortgage, which was a subsidy paid to mortgage lenders in respect of borrowers whose incomes were too low for them to benefit from mortgage interest tax relief; the subsidy enabled lenders to charge such borrowers a lower interest rate, giving them the equivalent of tax relief at the basic rate of income tax (Boleat, 1982: 42).

It will be recalled that in the 1950s the Treasury had argued for more building by private enterprise and less by local authorities, on the grounds that the latter was subsidized while the former was not. By the late 1960s this position was being challenged, partly because it was beginning to be realized that the abolition of Schedule A tax had increased the net value of tax relief on mortgage interest (up to 1963 they had more or less cancelled each other out). The privileged position of mortgaged home owners became even more apparent in 1969 when the government announced the withdrawal of tax relief on most personal loans other than for house purchase or improvement (this did not take effect until 1974). The Treasury continued to argue that tax relief was not a subsidy, merely income forgone, but it was undeniably the case that for a given level of expenditure income forgone in one area had to be raised from another. The cost of mortgage interest tax relief across the whole UK in 1968–69 was £195 million, while the combined cost of Exchequer housing subsidy and rate fund contributions in England was little more than £140 million (*House of Commons Debates*, vol. 781, 3 April 1969, written answers, col. 181).

Fair deal for housing?

The year 1970 is an important one in the history of housing in Britain, for it marks the point when owner occupation became the majority tenure. In future no political party with pretensions to office would be able to ignore the electoral implications of this development. The general election of June 1970 saw the return of a Conservative government, headed by Edward Heath, who remained in office until February 1974. These were difficult years, with rising unemployment, rising inflation, bitterly fought trade union legislation, major strikes and a worsening international economic situation. In forming his administration Heath created the Department of the Environment (DoE), which combined the old Ministries of Housing and Local Government, Transport and Public Building and Works. At the head of this super-department was Peter Walker, a rich, confident and combative former property developer (a sharp contrast to his predecessor, Anthony Greenwood, a Labour traditionalist whose father had been Minister of Health in the government of 1929–31). With housing production no longer a ministerial virility symbol, Walker turned his attention to issues of housing finance that the previous government had baulked at.

In the inflationary decade of the 1970s finance was to dominate housing policy debate, and in a sense the housing problem was turned on its head: for decades the argument had been that housing was both expensive and in short supply, necessitating subsidized production. Now the debate shifted on to the argument that there was no longer an overall shortage and that people (especially local authority tenants) were not paying enough for their houses. Meanwhile, strongly rising house prices in the early 1970s only served to highlight the differences between the costs and benefits of the two main sectors. During 1971–3 Britain experienced an unprecedented increase in houses prices (37 per cent in 1972 and 32 per cent in 1973), initiating the first of what has become a series of boom–slump cycles in the housing market (Boleat, 1982: 103–4; Hamnett, 1999: 24–7). The rapid rise in house prices raised questions about the role of mortgage lenders in fuelling the spiral and about the way that higher prices dragged up the cost of tax relief. This was an important debating point, given that the government was arguing at the same time that subsidies to local authorities were too high and had to be contained. Ministers sought to escape their critics by repeating the assertion that mortgage interest tax relief was not a subsidy, while maintaining that local authority subsidies should be measured not just in cash terms but in relation to the difference between actual and market rents (Julian Amery, *House of Commons Debates*, Standing Committees, Session 1971–72, vol. vi, cols 118, 121).

In June 1971 the government published a White Paper (DoE, 1971) in which it finally confronted the problem of moving local authority rents onto a current value pricing basis, almost twenty years after it had been identified as a logical step. The proposals were undeniably radical and confrontational, prompting the Labour spokesman, Antony Crosland, to describe the subsequent Bill as 'the most reactionary and socially divisive measure that is likely to be introduced in the lifetime of this parliament – and that is saying a good deal' (*House of Commons Debates*, November 1971, vol. 826, col. 48).

The government planned to:

- break with the convention that no government ever withdrew subsidies promised by its predecessors
- remove the freedom of local councillors to set rents at reasonable levels
- require all local authorities to set fair rents for all their houses, in most cases well above existing reasonable rents
- abandon the no-profit rule on local authority housing revenue accounts
- introduce a mandatory rent rebate scheme for the public sector
- introduce a means-tested rent allowance scheme for private tenants
- make fair rents the basis for receipt of subsidy in the housing association sector.

This amounted to a thorough-going reform of housing finance in the rented sectors, effectively moving to a standard, cross-sector pricing policy (except that in private renting fair rents were not mandatory), which had much to recommend it in terms of tenure neutrality. But, of course, it intentionally left unreformed the tax privileges of owner occupation. There was probably never going to be a good time to remove the cherished freedom of councillors to set rents, but to combine this with inflationary rent increases at a time of rapidly rising prices and relatively high unemployment was asking for a fight. Even more contentious was the proposal to allow the revenue from rents to exceed what was needed to cover the costs of the service, and to use surpluses for the benefit of tax-payers at large and to cover the costs of rebates to the least well off (this was opposed on the grounds that rebates were really a form of poor relief and should be paid out of general taxation, not as a transfer from people only slightly better off). The Housing Finance Act, 1972, duly became the most bitterly contested piece of housing legislation in the whole post-1945 period. The details of the Act and the political struggle that it precipitated need not detain us here (for a fuller account see Malpass, 1990: ch. 6). For present purposes it is sufficient to note that although the Act shattered the conventions that had guided local authority housing finance for fifty years, and in that sense it was a watershed, it was nevertheless about the introduction of new instruments with which to pursue long established policy objectives.

The Housing Finance Act was at one level a technical measure designed to deal more effectively with the distribution of subsidy amongst both authorities and tenants (it had been argued, convincingly, that hitherto some authorities and some tenants had been receiving more subsidy than they needed, while others had been getting less). It was also about re-equipping central government with effective tools for making sure that local authority rents kept pace with inflation. In addition it introduced the long-overdue rent allowance system for private tenants, and attempted, unsuccessfully as it turned out, to provide a separate subsidy system that would encourage housing associations to build more. But at another level the Act was a highly political measure, designed to hasten the residualization of the local authority sector, making receipt of rent assistance conditional on a means test, and encouraging better off tenants to opt for owner occupation – in 1980 this was achieved through the massive incentive of the right to buy at heavily discounted prices, but in 1971 the minister was only able to offer to pay removal and legal costs (P. Walker, *House of Commons Debates*, November 1971, vol. 826, col. 43). In fact there was a short lived boom in the sale of council (and new town) houses in 1971 and 1972.

The Housing Finance Act was technically flawed and too confrontational to survive. It had been conceived in an era of low inflation but was implemented in high inflation; as a result it was inflexible and would have needed amendment in any case. It also relied on legal and administrative means to ensure local compliance, which made implementation much more difficult than the financial mechanisms used hitherto (and subsequently). But, most of all, the Act was doomed by the opposition to it from councillors and tenants, who persuaded the Labour leadership to promise to repeal the contentious parts when they returned to office.

Conclusion

Throughout the period covered by this chapter housing was never far from the forefront of domestic political debate, although, as has been described, the issues changed from time to time, ranging from the sheer volume of new building, to slum clearance, rent control, rehabilitation and rents policy. But the thesis underlying this book is that to understand public policy we need to look beneath the surface of political controversy to deeper currents and longer running continuities. That is not to say that politics are unimportant, but they are not enough. Politicians are constrained in all sorts of ways, not least by the pressure of events, which helps to explain the apparent consensus on social and economic policy during much of the period. Far from housing policy swinging around as governments changed, this chapter has drawn out the consistencies, particularly in relation to the growth of owner occupation and the impending residualization of local authority housing, and the way that these trends can be related back to the broad objectives for postwar policy set out in 1943. Of course, this is not to argue that housing ministers never took a decision without consulting the wartime plan, or that the plan was based on accurate predictions of the postwar situation. On the contrary, the 1943 plan was wrong about population growth and housing demand, and it was wrong about the levels of replacement that could be achieved in the first postwar decade. It was also wrong about the pattern of supply and demand in the private sector, failing to foresee the strong growth of owner occupation. Nevertheless, the course of housing policy from 1954 to 1974 was consistent with the central idea that private enterprise could and should provide for most people most of the time. From 1954 onwards policy was driven by a partitioning of roles, with the public sector concentrating on slum clearance and the needs that the private sector could not meet, while private enterprise was encouraged to expand the volume of its output and to widen the appeal of home ownership.

In the context of a chapter concerned with the so-called 'classic welfare state' the conclusion has to be drawn that whereas other services were growing and expanding in ways broadly consistent with what are seen as welfare state principles, housing was not. Although the council sector continued to grow it did so at a much slower rate than owner occupation, and all the while it was becoming more narrowly focused on supporting, rather than competing with, the market. This leads to two final related points. First, it is important to remember that housing benefited enormously from the classic welfare state, especially from the commitment to economic growth and full employment, which helped to create a golden age for owner occupation. Second, policy was not just supporting the market but was actively shaping it in a number of ways, helping to shift demand from renting into owner occupation. In this connection, Macmillan's concern about the sustainability of demand for new private houses is a powerful reminder that housing policy was about much more than building council houses for some and letting the free market deal with the rest.

Chapter 6

Housing and Welfare State Restructuring

The period covered by this chapter, from the mid-1970s to the late 1980s, is relatively short, but action packed. It begins with the economic crisis that killed off the long postwar boom, and which had profound implications for the confidence of governments in their ability to manage their economies for the benefit of their people; this in turn had implications for the development of welfare states. The collapse of the Bretton Woods agreement of 1944 (Skidelsky, 2000: 337–72) governing international exchange rates in 1971 was followed by a fourfold increase in world oil prices in 1973, imposed by OPEC (the cartel of oil producing countries) and the world economy entered a new period. The postwar ascendancy of liberal and social democratic ideas began to be effectively challenged by a resurgent conservative ideology, epitomized in the 1980s by the presidency of Ronald Reagan in the United States and the dominance of British politics by Margaret Thatcher. Renewed faith in markets and scorn for services provided directly by public bureaucracies has continued to eat away at the role of the state in general and the welfare state in particular.

In Britain the period began with the government confronting difficulties from a number of directions, including the unwelcome combination of rising unemployment and rising inflation, mounting industrial unrest, and resurgent nationalism in Scotland and Wales. In Northern Ireland the Troubles, which had started with housing based civil rights protests in the late 1960s, spilled over to the mainland in the form of a series of bombings that killed more than fifty people. In the course of an ineptly handled industrial dispute with the miners (who, until 1972, had not staged a national strike since 1926) the government put the whole country on a three-day working week in early 1974 and the Prime Minister, Edward Heath, called a general election at the end of February on the issue of 'Who governs Britain?' The result was indecisive but Heath eventually resigned and Harold Wilson formed a minority Labour government, which won a tiny overall majority at a second election in the October. The economy, in common with those of other advanced capitalist countries, was badly affected by the impact of the huge increase in oil prices, and inflation continued to rise towards a twentieth-century peak of 25 per cent in 1975. The British economy seemed to be particularly hard hit, however, leading to a humiliating rescue operation by the International Monetary Fund, which demanded cuts in public expenditure in return for substantial loans (Cairncross, 1992: ch. 5).

By 1977 Labour had lost its overall majority in the House of Commons and was kept in power by a pact with the Liberals. The government struggled on, through the public sector workers' strikes during the infamous so-called 'winter of discontent' of 1978–79, until it was finally defeated in the Commons on the issue of Scottish devolution. The subsequent general election, in May 1979, brought in a radical right wing Conservative administration led by Margaret Thatcher, a self-proclaimed conviction politician who openly despised what she saw as the consensual approach of previous years. The outcome was an intensification of the sorts of policies that had been reluctantly adopted by Labour: inflation and public expenditure were identified as key problems. But far from seeking reconciliation with the trade unions Thatcher set out to curb their powers and restrict the rights of workers to take strike action. This can be seen as a prerequisite for more radical measures to reduce the scope and scale of the welfare state. In relation to both the unions and the welfare state the aim of the new right was to regain ground ceded by capital to labour in the postwar settlement. A great set piece battle took place between the miners and British Coal (with the government standing right behind it) in 1984–85, and this time the miners did not win. As for the welfare state, it was housing that bore the brunt of the attack, although inequality, which had been declining until about 1977, began to widen still further as tax cuts rewarded the better off, while social security entitlements were cut back and long term unemployment rose, chiefly among former industrial workers. The first half of the 1980s were years of recession and high unemployment, especially in certain areas where older industries were worst affected. About 20 per cent of national manufacturing capacity was lost in a couple of years in the early 1980s, as unemployment trebled between 1979 and 1983, when it reached 12 per cent (Glynn, 1999: 189–90).

There had been economic downturns before but the world recession of the mid-1970s was on a different scale, and because existing techniques of economic management were seen no longer to work the situation precipitated a paradigm shift in government thinking and in the terms of public debate. An alternative to the demand management techniques associated with Keynesianism was offered by monetarism, an approach that shifted attention to the control of the money supply. This became popular with some governments, particularly in Britain, as a way to reduce inflation. Whereas hitherto the welfare state had been generally accepted as having positive political and economic effects it now came to be depicted as a burden on the economy, no longer part of the solution but part of the problem to be tackled. The welfare state, 'the almost universally accepted model for creating a measure of social peace and harmony in European postwar societies has itself become the source of new contradictions and political divisions in the 1970s' (Offe, 1982: 8). The abandonment of a policy commitment to full employment, a decision taken under Labour in 1975 but fully endorsed and continued by subsequent Conservative governments, was not only a departure from postwar Keynesian economic orthodoxy but also a move of great importance for the welfare state. Full employment underpinned the welfare state in general and housing in particular. It both maximized tax revenues and minimized demands on the social security budget. In relation to housing, full employment underpinned demand in the market, especially the owner occupier market where future expectations of security of employment were crucial in generating the confidence needed by both lenders and borrowers in the mortgage market. The abandonment of full employment, and the subsequent rise in unemployment, depleted tax revenues while driving up the cost of income maintenance. This necessarily meant either increasing taxes or reducing expenditure in other programme areas.

For the Labour government of 1974–79 it is reasonable to interpret their cuts in welfare spending in terms of a pragmatic response to a crisis; it was only with the election of a radical right wing Conservative government in 1979 that the welfare state was attacked in principle (Robinson, 1986). At the heart of the Conservatives' assault on the welfare state was a two-pronged strategy: first, the level of public expenditure, and the burden of taxation on which it depended, was identified as a problem that had to be tackled, and, second, the delivery of welfare state services was identified as paternalistic, bureaucratic, inefficient and generally unsatisfactory, thereby justifying the promotion of alternatives, including markets, with their much-vaunted virtues of consumer power and choice. These strands combined in the form of the argument that public provision was bad, private good.

It has been argued (e.g., by Kerr, 1981: 11) that Labour's stance on housing, in particular its promise to repeal the most contentious parts of the Housing Finance Act, 1972, was one of the main reasons that it won the two general elections of 1974. To the extent that this is true it was surely the last time housing, especially council housing, would help Labour into office. By 1979 the Tories were making council housing into an election-winning issue by promising tenants a right to buy their houses at deeply discounted prices. Housing had always been seen by Labour as an issue that worked well for the Party, and it was often perceived as the party of council tenants, but by 1979 the tables were dramatically turned and the confusion at the centre of Labour's position was exposed. The newly elected Tory Prime Minister, Margaret Thatcher, claimed that thousands of people had voted Conservative for the first time precisely because of the offer of the right to buy (quoted in Malpass and Murie, 1990: 88). On this view dismantling the welfare state, or at least part of it, had become a popular vote winner.

The main developments in housing policy between 1974 and 1988 have been set out in a number of accounts covering some or all of the period (Forrest and Murie, 1988; Harloe, 1995; Hills, 1998; Malpass, 1993, 2000b; Malpass and Murie, 1999). They can be summarized as follows:

1   The incoming Labour government repealed the contentious parts of the Housing Finance Act, 1972, and substituted a temporary subsidy system for local authority housing.
2   The Housing Act, 1974, reconstituted the Housing Corporation and introduced a new subsidy system for housing associations, giving them a significant boost (at least until the 1980s).
3   A housing finance review was set up in 1975, and later broadened into a review of housing policy as a whole, but in the end radical reform was rejected.
4   The Housing (Homeless Persons) Act, 1977, introduced new rights for certain categories of homeless people.
5   From 1979 the over-riding policy objective was the expansion of owner occupation.
6   The Housing Act, 1980, introduced the right for council tenants to buy their homes at discounted prices, and a new system allowing central government to drive up council rents by the rapid removal of Exchequer subsidy.
7   In 1982/83 a new Housing Benefit system was introduced to rationalize existing forms of means-tested assistance with housing costs.

It is arguable that despite the intensity of the political debate housing policy was shaped at least as much by economic exigencies as by ideology. But while public expenditure as a whole was coming under increasing pressure, the cuts in the housing budget were exceptional. From the mid-1970s onwards housing was the chief target for cuts in public expenditure, and from 1979 it was at the leading edge of the Conservative government's attempts to reduce and remodel the welfare state in line with 'what the country can afford'. While other public services were seen to have been generally resilient in the face of the Thatcherite onslaught housing was regarded as the exception, at least until the late 1980s (Le Grand, 1991). In fact, as this chapter seeks to show, other important changes were taking place, with implications for housing which have not been fully explicated in the existing literature.

While much attention has been paid to the cuts in investment in council housing and the virtual cessation of new building by local authorities, less has been written, from the point of view of an interest in the restructuring of the welfare state, about the housing implications of the growth in unemployment, the cuts in social security benefits and the deregulation of finance markets. The key points to be brought out concern the way in which, on the one hand, more people were being thrust into the housing market at a time when rising unemployment and the instability consequent upon deregulation were making it an increasingly uncongenial place for those on low and moderate incomes to be seeking solutions to their personal housing problems while, on the other hand, public housing was subject to resource cuts at exactly the point when they were most likely to benefit the poorest sections of the community (Forrest and Murie, 1988: 14). This was an old story, for as has been mentioned in earlier chapters, the poor tended to miss out on improved housing opportunities before 1914; in the 1930s they found that when they were given some priority in the allocation of council housing the new dwellings then being built were distinctly inferior to those of the 1920s; and again after 1945 the poor missed out on the early period of high quality new dwellings, only to be given improved access once the quality had been reduced.

Housing and the expenditure cuts agenda

In the midst of the economic crisis of the mid-1970s attention focused on the rapid rise in public expenditure generally, fuelled by spiralling inflation and confronted by a government lacking effective means to control the situation. For the rest of the decade the discourse continued to be built around attempts to cut expenditure, and the incoming Conservative government cited public expenditure as being at the heart of Britain's economic difficulties. Accounts of expenditure trends in the 1970s show that although social security spending rose year by year, driven inexorably upwards by increasing numbers of people with no income from employment, in the wake of the crisis even the NHS suffered cuts in 1977–78, but otherwise health spending continued on a generally upward curve; education spending, however, fell in real terms in the second half of the decade, and remained static for most of the 1980s; cuts in capital expenditure were particularly severe in education, but in the context of falling numbers of children in schools (Glennerster and Hills, 1998). Between 1975 and 1988 education spending fell as a proportion of gross domestic product. 'No such previous reduction in education's share of the nation's resources had occurred [in the twentieth century], even following the Geddes "cuts" of the 1920s or the retrenchment of the 1930s. It is not to be found in the experience of any other leading nation' (Glennerster and Hills, 1998: 36). Nevertheless, the cuts in housing were on an altogether different scale.

Defining and measuring public expenditure on housing is a complex and difficult subject, involving 'much adding together of apples and pears' (Hills, 1998: 132). However, at the level of overall expenditure there is no doubt both that deep cuts were made and that the housing budget was cut far more than other welfare programmes, especially in the early 1980s, when housing accounted for three-quarters of all planned cuts (House of Commons, 1980: v). It is important to look beyond the headline figures because in addition to the cuts in aggregate spending a major restructuring process was in hand. Public expenditure on housing can be analysed in terms of four main components:

- net capital investment (the creation or substantial enhancement of fixed assets)
- net current expenditure (mainly Exchequer subsidies and local authority rate fund contributions)
- means-tested assistance with housing costs attributable to the social security budget (housing benefit from 1982 to 1983)
- mortgage interest tax relief and other subsidies to home owners.

Public investment expenditure in housing peaked in 1974–75 and then fell in nearly every year for the rest of the period under review; it is important, when assessing the cuts in housing spending in the second half of the 1970s, to relate them to the unusually high levels of 1974–75. Nevertheless, by 1978–79 spending was 19 per cent below the peak, and the planned cuts for the early 1980s accelerated the trend of the late 1970s, amounting to 48 per cent (House of Commons, 1980: viii). Net capital expenditure in Great Britain (at 1995–96 prices) fell from a peak of over £12 billion in 1974–75 to just under £4 billion in 1988/89 (Hills, 1998: 182). This translated into a steep decline in the number of new public sector houses being completed (see Table 6.1). Housing associations also suffered a decline, though of less severe proportions.

Two further points to be made here are that a greater proportion of local authority capital expenditure was devoted to improving existing council houses (although critics argued that the level of investment remained inadequate to maintain the quality of the stock: Cantle, 1986), and a growing proportion of the whole programme came to be funded by capital receipts from the sale of council houses. This meant that gross expenditure was larger than implied by the net figures, but that the programme was dependent on the unpredictable flow of capital receipts.

The cuts in housing spending in the 1970s were focused on local authority capital budgets, and at that time were mainly driven by a perceived need to reduce the overall level of public expenditure; later cuts were part of a dual strategy that included a planned shift to a more market based housing

Table 6.1   *Dwellings completed in Great Britain, 1974–88*

Year	Local authorities new towns and govt depts	Housing associations	Private sector	Total
1974	118,724	9,920	140,865	269,509
1975	147,571	14,693	150,752	313,016
1976	147,232	15,770	152,181	315,183
1977	137,384	25,127	140,820	303,331
1978	107,968	22,771	149,021	279,760
1979	86,188	17,835	140,481	244,504
1980	86,027	21,097	128,406	235,530
1981	65,506	19,306	114,923	199,735
1982	37,233	13,118	125,431	175,782
1983	35,097	16,092	147,797	198,986
1984	33,984	16,642	159,090	209,716
1985	27,227	13,073	156,351	196,651
1986	22,794	12,464	169,838	205,096
1987	20,043	12,047	179,397	211,487
1988	19,717	11,944	193,465	225,126

Source: *Housing and Construction Statistics.*

system. In the case of current expenditure the trend in the 1970s was strongly upwards, but in the 1980s there was also a dual focus, designed to lighten the burden of subsidies, while at the same time moving from general subsidy to means-tested assistance with housing costs. A feature of housing finance in the second half of the 1970s was that council rents were drifting downwards in real terms, while Exchequer subsidies to local housing revenue accounts were rising. By 1979 council rents stood at a historically low level in relation to both wages and costs, a development that can be explained more in terms of counter-inflation policy than commitment to a low rents policy. The growth in subsidy expenditure in this period was, arguably, an accident of relatively high investment in 1975–77 at a time of high inflation (DoE, 1977b: 192–3).

After the election of the first Thatcher government in 1979 local authority capital spending continued to be squeezed, especially in terms of new building, but attention now turned to rents and subsidies. Whereas the Labour government had struggled and prevaricated over the introduction of a new subsidy system the Conservatives pressed ahead, slipping it onto the statute book almost unnoticed amidst the controversy around the introduction, in the same Bill, of the right to buy (Malpass, 1990: ch. 7).

The new system was exceptionally powerful, enabling the government to withdraw subsidy on the assumption of specified levels of rent increase. In its first year of operation, 1981/82, rents rose (on average) by 48 per cent. By the third year, 1983/84, the aggregate subsidy bill for England and Wales had fallen by 84 per cent in real terms, leaving a majority of local authorities with no Exchequer subsidy at all (Malpass, 1990: 141). This was a change of historic proportions, but it was only half of the story, for higher basic rents meant more people would have to claim means-tested assistance. Official figures suggest that in 1985 some 66 per cent of council tenants claimed housing benefit, compared with 44 per cent in 1976 (Malpass, 1990: 145). Lower general subsidies were, therefore, to some extent matched by increases in targeted benefits, aimed at the least well off.

To accommodate rising numbers of claimants the government introduced a reformed and rationalized system of means-tested assistance with housing costs. The Social Security and Housing Benefits Act, 1982, set out to simplify the existing system and to make it easier for both claimants and staff to work out entitlement in individual cases. One important feature of the new housing benefit was that administrative responsibility was to lie with the local authorities, rather than with the Department of Social Security, although at the same time the government acknowledged that housing benefit was properly regarded as a social security benefit and not a housing subsidy. Part of the reason for reform had been that means-tested assistance with housing costs was becoming increasingly important, helping a growing proportion of tenants and absorbing significant proportions of administrative staff time (Donnison, 1982). Another argument that had been put forward, but rejected, was that since the poorest home owners received no help with housing costs (apart from rates rebates), reform proposals should be drawn widely enough to embrace mortgage interest tax relief, making it possible to extend the new housing benefit to all low income households, regardless of their tenure status. The cost of including low income home owners was memorably described by David Donnison as 'no more than the small change to be shaken out' from the reform of tax relief (Donnison, 1982: 188).

Reform of mortgage interest tax relief had been advocated for some years, but always rejected by governments. The official review of housing finance, set up in 1975, had initially been about tackling the 'dog's breakfast' of different and inequitable arrangements in different tenures, and it had been expected that proposals would emerge to reform the tax privileges enjoyed by home owners (especially the better off), but by its publication in 1977 views had changed and the case for radical reform was now dismissed as 'academic dogma' (DoE, 1977a: iv). The complexities of the debate about how to measure the tax position of home owners need not be explored in detail here (see National Federation of Housing Association, or NFHA, 1985; Hills, 1991), and it is sufficient to note that the conventional indicator of assistance to home owners, mortgage interest tax relief, rose from £1,450 million in 1979/80 to £5,400 million by 1988/89 (Wilcox, 1993: 165). The cost of tax relief was boosted by inflation and rapidly growing numbers of mortgaged home owners, but, nevertheless, the contrast with the steep decline in subsidies to local authority housing is striking, and reflected the main emphasis within housing policy at that time.

Promoting the market

Successive governments since the early 1950s had supported the growth of home ownership, and the Labour government's housing Green Paper of 1977 had been lyrical in its enthusiasm, referring to it as a 'basic and natural desire' (DoE, 1977a: 50). But under Margaret Thatcher the promotion of home ownership moved up several levels, and became the dominant theme of housing policy throughout the 1980s. By this stage the continued expansion of home ownership effectively meant encouraging more and more lower income households to buy. In opposition during the late 1970s the Conservatives had developed an approach to housing that seized upon and amplified two currents of opinion: dissatisfaction with the performance of local housing authorities and the widespread aspiration to home ownership. In a sense the sale of council houses was a policy whose time had come: the growth of owner occupation had hitherto been fuelled in roughly equal proportions by both new building and transfers from private renting (Holmans, 2000: 488), but the latter represented a rapidly diminishing source of supply, rising living standards had made it possible for more council tenants to consider buying, the growth of local authority housing departments had created some very large and unwieldy bureaucracies and some of the high rise/high density estates produced by local authorities in the 1960s and 1970s were already undermining the reputation of council housing as a whole. It was also true, of course, that Tory housing policy was riddled with contradictions: the success of the policy of council house sales would depend upon the earlier achievements of local authorities in producing houses that tenants actually wanted to buy in neighbourhoods where they were content to carry on living; existing home owners had done well out of inflation, but the government was committed to reducing inflation; at the same time as promoting home ownership the government adopted economic and labour market policies that were inimical to it; and while promoting home ownership among low income purchasers the government both reduced social security benefits and introduced a means-tested housing benefit that excluded home owners.

Housing policy in the early 1980s was pursued with scant regard for subtleties of this kind. The message was quite clear, and significantly different from earlier years: local authorities were no longer to be regarded as contributing to the solution to housing problems – they had become part of the problem. Henceforth housing was to be treated as a commodity and policy was to be framed accordingly. Of course, it has been argued throughout this book that policy has always been based on the idea that the market will be the main provider, but the position adopted by the Conservatives after 1979 represented a particularly aggressive intensification of this view and an explicit rejection of the idea of housing as a social service for a wide spectrum of the population. This translated into the idea that housing policy was to be developed in relation to demand and the market's assessment of how, and how far, to meet it. Government ministers were scornful of arguments for planned levels of output based on need, and dismissive of the pleas of lobbying organizations and academics who pointed to rising numbers of homeless people and other indicators of a system under stress. Above all, perhaps, the Thatcher governments were hostile to local government as such, depicting it as bureaucratic, inefficient and self-serving.

The right to buy was a flagship policy at the 1979 general election and the government pressed ahead with its introduction in the Housing Act, 1980 (and the Tenants' Rights, Etc. (Scotland) Act, 1980). Tenants of more than three years' standing were given the right to buy at a discount from the open market value starting at 33 per cent and rising to 50 per cent for people who had been tenants for 20 years or more (the discounts were later extended, starting at 32 per cent after two years and rising to 60 per cent, and for tenants in flats the discount reached 70 per cent after just 15 years: see Forrest and Murie, 1988: 55–63). In this context the sale of council houses emerged as a quintessentially Thatcherite policy, the most successful of the early privatization measures; indeed, in the period 1980–86 it was more successful in terms of receipts than all the others put together (Forrest and Murie, 1988: 10). Moreover, for several years in the early 1980s the sale of council houses was the major source of growth of home ownership, outstripping growth due to new building. From its introduction in October 1980 to 1988 around 1 million council houses were sold under the right to buy in Great Britain as a whole (Wilcox, 1993: 64). We should not forget that tenants of non-charitable housing associations were also given a right to buy at reduced prices and, although the numbers eligible were much smaller, more than 17,000 right to buy sales took place between 1981 and 1988 (Wilcox, 1993: 64).

The right to buy was not the only policy for expanding low income home ownership, but it was certainly the most successful. A series of other initiatives was introduced, including shared equity, and building and improving for sale (Booth and Crook, 1986; Forrest, Lansley and Murie, 1984). These had very limited impact. Much more difficult to assess is the effect of other, unquantifiable, factors such as the constant rhetorical emphasis given to the virtues of home ownership by ministers, and the matching denigration of public renting. From the middle of the 1980s the economic recovery following the early 1980s recession, together with favourable housing market conditions, almost certainly had much more impact on demand than specific initiatives, including the right to buy. In this context of accelerating house prices and quickening market activity the government steadfastly refused to reform mortgage interest tax relief, although it did hold the ceiling for entitlement at £30,000 from 1983. In inflationary conditions this meant that tax relief was available on a falling proportion of the average mortgage. Tax relief was also confined to the standard rate of tax, which was itself tending to fall, so that despite Margaret Thatcher's very personal commitment to the retention of the benefit it was actually of diminishing significance as the decade wore on.

Towards a residual public sector

The other side of the privatization coin was, of course, the increasing residualization of public housing. It was during the late 1970s that the idea of public housing becoming a residual sector began to be discussed. Probably the earliest published reference was Alan Murie's (1977: 49) claim that the policy of council house sales being developed by the Conservative opposition would leave the poor with no real choice within a 'residual welfare council sector'. There are arguments for believing that the residualization process had, in fact, already been under way for some years, and it is significant that another early discussion came in the context of a review of the Labour government's housing Green Paper (Harloe, 1978). Harloe suggested that council housing might become a sort of 'ambulance service concentrating its effort on the remaining areas of housing stress and dealing with a variety of "special needs" such as the poor, the homeless, one-parent families, battered wives and blacks'. This idea took root and soon the term 'residualization' entered the academic housing discourse. It was derived from the social policy literature, in which Richard Titmuss had outlined what he called the residual model as the antithesis of the welfare state model of provision (or in Titmuss's terms, the institutional redistributive model of social policy: Titmuss, 1976).

The residualization of social rented housing can be analysed in terms of three dimensions:

- reduction of the stock of dwellings as a result of sales outstripping new building
- changing social composition of the tenants, with increasing proportions of the poor and economically marginal
- changes in housing policy designed to make social renting into a more residual sector, a safety net for those who cannot gain access to market based forms of provision (see also Forrest and Murie, 1983, 1988).

Although councils had sold houses for many years the numbers involved had never been great, and new building had always resulted in continued growth of the sector as a whole. But from 1980 onwards this ceased to be the case, and in every year since then the supply of council houses has gone down. Housing associations managed to build more than they sold, but they were unable to stem the overall numerical and proportionate decline of social rented housing. At the outset no-one really knew how many tenants would take up their right to buy, and it is safe to assume that a million sales in eight years exceeded even the government's hopes and expectations. Once it became clear that sales would result in a significant reduction in the supply of the local authority houses, debate began to focus on the question of how far the process would go, how small the sector would become and what would be the characteristics of the residue (English, 1982). In this context interest focused on the questions of which dwellings would be sold, and would councils be left with just the least desirable dwellings on the least popular estates? Research evidence soon confirmed that houses were selling much faster than flats, and the government passed further legislation in 1986 to extend the inducements to tenants of flats to take up their right to buy. But the picture that emerged was one of much more than a simple difference between rates of sales by dwelling type. Forrest and Murie (1988) were able to show that sales were not only heavily concentrated among houses as opposed to flats, but that they were also concentrated on some estates rather than others. There were also significant differences in the rates of sales at the regional and district levels, with sales tending to be more common in English regions where home ownership was already higher, especially the south east (Forrest and Murie, 1988: 111–14). At the local level variation was more marked. In the period 1979–85 the stock of council houses fell by about 12 per cent overall, but the highest selling authorities disposed of more than a quarter of their houses, while the lowest sellers lost less than 2 per cent (Forrest and Murie, 1988: 118–19).

Unsurprisingly, tenants choosing to exercise their right to buy were not a uniform cross-section. The propensity to buy reflected both ability, and willingness, to sustain the costs of ownership, and the type and location of dwelling occupied. The people who were best placed when the right to buy was introduced were those who were then in middle age, giving them entitlement to maximum discounts, and who were lucky enough to occupy houses on estates built in the 1940s and 1950s, before the concentration on the building of blocks of flats. These people constituted a privileged cohort of tenants, whose experience of council housing was distinct from that of younger, later entrants. Research in a number of localities showed that the typical purchaser under the right to buy in the early 1980s was a male skilled manual worker in his mid to late forties, with a grown up family (Forrest and Murie, 1988: 173).

Thus the impact of the right to buy can be measured in different ways. It reduced the overall supply of affordable rented houses, more markedly in some regions and districts than others, and it tended to strip out the better off tenants in the best houses. This had significant neighbourhood effects, based on the pre-existing social and physical differentiation within the council sector. For example, writing about Birmingham (the largest municipal landlord in England at that time), Forrest and Murie said that:

> In certain areas, and particularly in the outer wards with attractive houses with gardens, council estates have changed significantly and have become mixed tenure estates... But in other areas, and particularly in inner city estates with high numbers of flats and maisonettes, the picture is very different. They remain largely one tenure estates. Those on the social and economic margins such as the homeless and unemployed have been increasingly funnelled into these estates. (Forrest and Murie, 1988: 160)

It is important to note the date of this comment, for it shows that some of the seeds of twenty-first century concerns about social exclusion were sown in the 1980s, and were recognized by at least some analysts at the time. The impact of the right to buy helped to focus academic research and debate on the subject of the changing social composition of local authority housing, and a number of authors published evidence to show both that increasing proportions of the least well off were now to be found in the municipal sector, and increasing proportions of council tenants were drawn from the lowest income groups (Bentham, 1986; Forrest and Murie, 1983; Hamnett, 1984; Robinson and O'Sullivan, 1983). It was not just a question of income: people from lower socio-economic groups, elderly people and very young households were becoming more heavily represented, while people in middle age were a declining proportion; single parents were over-represented by comparison with their share of all households, as were Afro-Caribbean households. The evidence for the 1980s stood in marked contrast to earlier years: in 1962 only 11 per cent of council tenant households had no earned income, but by 1982 the

figure was 44 per cent, a much faster rate of increase than in the population as a whole (in the same period the proportion of all households with
no earned income rose from 16 to 30 per cent: Holmans, 2000: 491).

A slightly different angle suggests that by 1984 approximately 53 per cent of
households in council housing were headed by an economically inactive
person, and that overall nearly two-thirds of council housing heads of households were not working (Forrest and Murie, 1988: 69). At the same time it
was shown that two-thirds of the long term unemployed (continuously out
of work for more than one year) were to be found in the council sector
(M. White, 1983: 38). Reactions to this emerging picture varied. Some (e.g.,
Clapham and Maclennan, 1983) suggested that the concentration of the
least well off in council housing was a good thing, in the sense that for too
long these people, who were most in need of subsidized housing, had been
excluded. The majority of academic comment, however, took a different line,
pointing to the problems of tenurial and spatial polarization.

Despite the warnings from academics and others, government policy
continued to be made and changed in ways that were designed to intensify
the residualization of the local authority and housing association sectors.
It has been argued in earlier chapters that this trend can be traced back to
the mid-1950s, from which point, for example, local authorities were
encouraged to raise basic rent levels and to adopt rent rebate schemes to
cushion the impact on the least well off. This marked the beginning of the
shift from general subsidy to means-tested assistance, a measure designed
precisely to bring about a change in the social composition of council tenants. By the period under review here a mandatory rent rebate scheme was
in place, and as has already been mentioned this was developed into the
housing benefit scheme in 1982–83. This was a change made necessary by
the growing proportion of tenants depending on means-tested assistance,
and by the planned, accelerated withdrawal of general subsidy under the
Housing Act, 1980. The right to buy, the new rents and subsidy policy and
housing benefit were part of a package of carrot and stick policies
intended to encourage better off tenants to buy or move out, while at the
same time making it easier for people on lower incomes to afford higher
rents. Another policy innovation, the effect of which was to strengthen the
tide of residualization, was the Housing (Homeless Persons) Act, 1977.
This gave local housing authorities statutory duties towards people who
were homeless within the meaning of the Act, and who were members of
specified priority groups.

Finally in this context it is appropriate to mention that under the
Labour government from 1974 to 1979 the basic stance, and the message
communicated to the general public, was that the market should be
encouraged. Under the Conservatives after 1979 this was reinforced in the
clearest possible terms. The combined effect of reduced levels of new

building, burgeoning levels of sales after 1980, and the waxing of rhetorical vilification and denigration of council housing by ministers – who were, at the same time, promoting the advantages of owner occupation – were all sending the same message: owner occupation good, council renting bad. It is hard to quantify the effect, but the message coming from the government and its supporters could not have been clearer.

The non-municipal alternative to council housing

In relation to housing associations, however, the stance of both Labour and Conservative governments was not so clear-cut. The Housing Act, 1974, gave the appearance of consensus and the prospect of a step change in the level of activity achievable by associations after the difficulties of the short-lived Housing Finance Act, 1972. The 1974 Act was indeed a watershed for housing associations, for it introduced Housing Association Grant (HAG), a tailor-made form of capital grant covering typically 80 per cent of the costs of development schemes, both new build and rehabilitation. The new system created a virtually risk-free operating environment for housing associations: the whole of their development costs was covered by public funds, either in the form of HAG or the residual loan, which was determined by calculating the debt that could be serviced by fair rents set by the Rent Officer service, and since fair rents could be relied upon to increase over time it meant that revenue surpluses were virtually inevitable in due course. In the course of the fifteen years during which this system operated, housing associations were able to accumulate substantial property portfolios on which they carried low levels of debt, and this put them in a strong position when a later government required them to cover a growing share of development costs from private borrowing (see Chapter 7 later, and Malpass, 2000a).

The introduction of HAG was accompanied by a relaunch of the Housing Corporation, which was given responsibility for registering and regulating housing associations, as well as for the distribution of grant aid. Only registered associations were eligible for grant, and of course this gave the Corporation considerable leverage over associations. It was able to reshape both individual associations as a condition of registration and continued funding, and the sector as a whole by the way grant was distributed. One way of looking at this is to see it as a welcome modernization and re-invigoration of some tired old organizations. Another way is to see it as a step towards the incorporation of a set of voluntary organizations into the apparatus of the welfare state. Associations had a long history of being small, under-funded and therefore insignificant and marginal. The new system brought them towards the centre of housing policy and gave them the resources they had lacked, but at a price in terms of lost independence. This was something that, in all probability, few people worried about at the time. The prospect of being able to make a real impact on some grim inner-city areas was sufficient to compensate for lost autonomy. And for a few years housing association activity thrived, but the growth rates achieved in 1974–77 could not be sustained once the public expenditure cuts following the 1976 financial crisis began to bite, as shown in Table 6.2.

A fuller account of housing associations and their role in housing policy in this period can be found elsewhere (Malpass, 2000b: ch. 8). Here the need is to point to the way in which the growth of housing associations and their migration towards the centre of housing policy represented the thin end of a wedge that threatened the long-established position of local authorities as the main providers of affordable rented housing. It is not being suggested here that the 1974 Act was part of a long term plan to replace councils with housing associations, but there was an openly articulated view that it was necessary to prevent the development of municipal monopolies, especially in inner-city areas subject to redevelopment and publicly funded rehabilitation. As council housing approached a third of the total stock and private renting continued its apparently inexorable decline, there developed a cross-party consensus that it was necessary to

Table 6.2   *New building and renovations by housing associations in Great Britain, 1974–88*

Year	New building	Renovation	Total
1974	9,920	4,132	14,052
1975	14,693	5,078	19,771
1976	15,770	13,544	29,314
1977	25,091	19,630	44,721
1978	22,676	16,079	38,755
1979	17,835	20,097	37,932
1980	21,097	17,715	38,812
1981	19,306	13,770	33,076
1982	13,118	21,795	34,913
1983	16,092	18,036	34,128
1984	16,642	20,701	37,343
1985	13,073	13,419	26,492
1986	12,464	15,035	27,499
1987	12,047	13,267	25,314
1988	11,944	13,636	26,580

Source: *Housing and Construction Statistics* (HMSO).

do something to encourage tenure diversity. The support of the Labour government for housing associations after 1974 stood in contrast to its policies in relation to other areas of the welfare state: in education, for example, it legislated to abolish the direct grant schools and in health it moved towards the abolition of pay-beds in NHS hospitals (although in pensions the introduction of the state earnings related pension scheme, SERPS, included incentives for private occupational schemes).

In retrospect the significance of the Housing Act, 1974, is much clearer than it was at the time. Then new building by local authorities was more than ten times the level achieved by housing associations, and the municipal sector was more than 30 per cent of the total stock compared with less than 2 per cent for housing associations. Neither was it obvious that the local authorities were about to go into permanent decline, first in terms of new building and then as a result of the right to buy. Despite these setbacks local authorities were still building more new houses than the housing associations in 1988. Throughout most of the 1980s housing associations were unable to build as many new houses as they had achieved in the late 1970s. The significance of the 1974 Act, then, lies not in the numbers of houses built but in the way it indicated the willingness of government to depart from the postwar welfare state's emphasis on municipal services. It represented an assimilation of organizations that had been effectively frozen out of the picture in the earlier postwar period. It was not clear to anyone at the time, but the effect of the 1974 Act was to provide housing associations with the opportunity to develop their organizational and financial strength and expertise. The seeds of a way to bypass the local authorities had been sown.

Housing, employment and social security

Earlier sections have discussed welfare state restructuring in terms of the sale of council houses, the residualization of the local authority sector and the development of a potential non-municipal alternative form of social renting. Here the focus shifts to the housing effects of policies in other areas: the abandonment of full employment as a policy objective and attempts to cut or contain the social security budget had serious implications for the housing wellbeing of significant numbers of people. The key point is that to appreciate the full impact on housing of the restructuring of the welfare state we have to look at much more than housing policy. At exactly the time that housing policy was encouraging wider participation in owner occupation the government was pursuing economic policies that were creating a massive increase in the numbers of people for whom mortgaged home ownership was (actually or potentially) more of a liability than a benefit.

In the thirty years after 1945 housing and employment policies worked in mutually supporting ways; after 1975, however, the position was reversed, and from 1980 onwards important changes in social security added to the difficulties of low income households in an increasingly unstable housing market. The central problem was that as housing policy came to place ever greater emphasis on market based solutions to individual housing needs, so employment policy was becoming more tolerant of high levels of unemployment, including much more widespread long term unemployment. Moving from work to benefit inevitably meant a substantial cut in income, and attempts to contain the burgeoning social security budget targeted benefits paid to the unemployed, a significant minority of whom were home owners. Long term unemployment was clearly a threat to the sustainability of home ownership for those directly affected, making it difficult not only to maintain mortgage repayments but also to undertake routine repairs, let alone more expensive refurbishment or improvement.

At the same time, Britain was becoming a much more unequal society, with incomes of lower paid workers tending to fall in real terms, while at the other end of the range real incomes rose strongly (Joseph Rowntree Foundation, 1995: 20). In the 1980s the benefits from cuts in income tax boosted the disposable incomes of the highest paid employees still further, adding to the house price spiral of 1986–88. Policies on employment and on the distribution of income from employment have far reaching implications for housing. Levels of housing wellbeing are closely related to incomes, and were becoming more closely associated in the 1980s. This was a period when policies on employment, income distribution and social security all worked together against the interests of the least well off, while at the same time promoting the interests of the better off, widening inequalities in achieved housing wellbeing. To some extent council housing had helped to break the link between poverty and poor housing, but the policies of the 1980s reversed the trend.

Despite the economic turmoil of the 1970s and the damage done to savings by high inflation, the social security system was developed and improved in significant ways (Timmins, 1996: 344–55). The old family allowance was converted into child benefit (giving more cash directly to mothers), a new state earnings related pension scheme was introduced, there were new benefits for long term sick and disabled people and the decision was made to increase benefits (but not unemployment benefit) each year in line with earnings or prices, whichever was the higher. This approach to benefit up-rating carried with it the implication that claimants might absorb a growing proportion of national income, something that was bound to happen in any case because of growing numbers of pensioners and other demographic changes.

Once the Conservatives came to power in 1979, with their commitment to cuts in public expenditure, they set about cutting back the social security budget and the link to earnings was one of the first casualties. Their task, however, was made more difficult by their own economic policies, which raised the numbers of people out of work and claiming benefits (the bitter irony of the situation was that the Tories fought the 1979 election on the slogan that 'Britain isn't working', and over the next two years the level of unemployment doubled). Social security is inherently a demand-led budget, and so with increasing numbers of claimants the government resorted to cuts in the levels of benefit paid, and restrictions on entitlement. The numbers of people having to rely on the means tested Supplementary Benefit increased by 60 per cent between 1979 and 1983, and unemployed claimants were barred from moving on to the higher rate of benefit paid to other long term claimants. Summing up the cuts in Thatcher's first term MacGregor (1985: 235–6) says:

> Child benefits dropped in mid-term to a thirty year low; earnings related sickness and unemployment benefits were abolished in 1982; support for children in families of the sick, disabled and unemployed on national insurance benefits was cut by up to 23 per cent over these four years; Supplementary Benefit payable to strikers' families was cut by £12.

It is important to locate these changes in the wider context: the British social security system was already less generous than those of neighbouring European countries, and the 1980 budget cut direct taxation by £4.5 billion, none of which would have helped the unemployed (MacGregor, 1985: 234–5).

Between 1979 and 1986 the numbers of people unemployed trebled, reaching 3.1 million according to the official way of counting (Wilcox, 1999: 94). An important aspect of the growth of unemployment at this time was that individuals were likely to find themselves out of work for prolonged periods. Long term unemployment, which, since 1945, had been confined to people who were effectively unemployable, became almost a way of life in the worst affected communities. The marginalized poor were a much larger group in the new welfare state than previously, leading to arguments in some quarters that a new 'underclass' was being created (Murray, 1990). At the same time the number of home owners was also growing, by 2.5 million between 1979 and 1986, raising the sector from 55 per cent to 61.5 per cent of all dwellings in Great Britain. While it is true that unemployed people tended to be concentrated in local authority housing, it is important to remember that 20 per cent of them were home owners, and that the incomes of unemployed people were on average about half what they had previously earned (M. White, 1983: 38–9). (Other sources suggest that one-third of the unemployed in the mid-1980s were home owners, and one-fifth had mortgages: see Department of Health and Social Security, 1984, quoted in Doling and Stafford, 1989: 27.) The unemployed were a sub-set of a growing class of low income home owners, whose numbers were increasing due to the heavy policy emphasis on the virtues of buying rather than renting.

A number of researchers began to investigate and comment on the changing owner occupier sector, drawing attention to its increasing heterogeneity. Karn, Kemeny and Williams (1985), for example, looked at inner-city, predominantly low income, home owners in Birmingham and Liverpool, drawing attention to the extent to which their situation diverged from the positive imagery so often associated with property ownership. Not only were these low income purchasers living in rundown houses and neighbourhoods, where rising values and wealth accumulation could not be taken for granted, but it was sometimes difficult to raise mortgages, and not even certain that investment in necessary repair and modernization work would be matched by increases in value. They pointed to the problems faced by low income purchasers struggling to find the resources to maintain older houses in a decent condition. Their evidence tended to confirm the point previously made by Whitehead (1979: 36), who had argued that the benefits of ownership were contingent upon income and wealth, and that poor home owners might actually be better off as tenants. Encouragement for home ownership needs to be seen in the context of the decline of slum clearance: as local authorities ran down their clearance programmes, so responsibility for maintaining and improving older inner-city housing shifted to individual home owners, many of whom were ill-equipped to shoulder the burden, despite the availability of grants (Thomas, 1986). The English House Condition Survey of 1981 estimated that there were more than half a million houses requiring repairs exceeding £7,000 (to put this figure into context, the average price of houses in 1981 was just over £24,000). A little later the government made it clear that public policy would rest on the belief that, 'The primary responsibility for maintaining and improving private property rests with the owners' (DoE, 1985: para. 9).

The growth of home ownership in the 1980s, coupled with rapid economic restructuring and a widening north–south divide, led commentators to emphasize the differences within the owner occupied sector. Part of this was a focus on the position of marginal owners, people who could only just afford to buy, or who struggled to keep up with mortgage repayments and/or repairs. But as Forrest, Murie and Williams (1990: 103) pointed out, it was also necessary to go beyond marginal groups to marginal localities: home ownership meant different things, and conferred different benefits or costs, in different places. Reviewing the diversity of experience among home owners, Doling and Stafford (1989: 146) pointed out that unemployment in the 1980s had heavily affected groups of workers who had recently provided the recruiting ground for the growth of home ownership, and that as owner occupation had been moving down the income and social class scale, unemployment had been moving up. It is not surprising, then, that the phenomenon of mortgage arrears began to attract attention in this period (Ford, 1984, 1988). Between 1979 and 1985 the number of mortgages increased by 27 per cent, but the number of borrowers in arrears by more than 6 months increased by nearly 500 per cent (Forrest, Murie and Williams, 1990: 29). Mortgage arrears remained a problem for a very small proportion of all mortgaged home owners, but the trend was a sign of the growing diversity of experience. One consequence was a growing number of former home owners becoming homeless and seeking help from local authorities, which, of course, were simultaneously seeing their supply of dwellings going down (Forrest, Murie and Williams, 1990: 103).

Financial deregulation

For many years the financial mainstay of owner occupation had been the ability of the building societies to tap the personal savings market, often acting as a repository for the savings of people who aspired to a mortgage once they had accumulated the necessary deposit. Saving with a building society was a good way to demonstrate one's creditworthiness for a loan from that same society in due course. Once a mortgage was obtained the repayments of interest and capital helped to fund new loans to the next generation of savers, and so on. It was a more or less closed circuit, largely separate from wider financial markets. This separation was reinforced by the way in which the leading societies controlled the market, by regularly agreeing among themselves a recommended set of interest rates to be paid to investors and charged to borrowers. The rates set by this cartel were generally a little below those set by the market. This in turn was advantageous for purchasers, lowering the costs of home ownership, but it tended to lead to shortages and mortgage queues. The low rates paid to investors were tolerated because they were people in the queue, saving their deposits.

The sheltered circuit of mortgage finance came under pressure in the early 1980s, and by the end of the decade the home loans industry had been transformed. The reasons for the change were partly domestic politics and partly international economics. The Thatcher government wanted more competition in financial markets on ideological grounds, but at the same time there were wider international economic forces at work leading towards more openness and competition in financial markets. In 1979 the

Thatcher government removed exchange controls and released commercial banks from the 'corset' which had constrained their operations, thereby making it easier for them to compete with building societies in the mortgage market. At the start of the 1980s banks and insurance companies accounted for only 8 per cent of the mortgage market, but by 1987 they had increased to nearly 50 per cent (Boddy, 1989: 94). This increased competition hastened the demise of the cartel agreement in 1983 and led to legislation in 1986, giving the societies what they wanted to enable them to respond to the new situation, with important implications for both the building societies and the customers. From the point of view of building societies the Building Societies Act, 1986, removed many of the distinctions between them and commercial banks, and the societies became increasingly integrated into the wider market. They were allowed to conduct a wider range of activities, providing financial services other than loans for house purchase. They were also allowed to convert from mutual societies (owned by their members) to public limited company status (owned by shareholders), and by 1988 they could borrow up to 40 per cent of their funds from the wholesale market (as distinct from the retail market of personal savings).

The freeing of the market meant that rates in the home loans sector were brought into line with those operating generally – which meant increases for both borrowers and savers. This obviously increased the cost of a given loan, but it also brought supply and demand into closer relationship, ending mortgage queues. Thus it became easier to borrow for house purchase, but more expensive. The established pattern of saving with one society, from which a loan was later obtained, was largely abandoned, and the whole market became much more open and mobile. From the point of view of consumers, therefore, financial deregulation was a double edged event, helping to fuel the growth of home ownership, but exposing both borrowers and savers to the full effect of market forces from which they had previously been at least partially protected. It has been argued (Stephens, 1993: 308) that deregulation links housing more closely to the macro-economy, exacerbating the effects of boom/bust cycles in the housing market, with serious implications for individuals and institutions. It has also been shown that financial deregulation, by freeing the market, bringing in new institutions and massively increasing the volume of lending, was implicated in triggering the housing market boom of 1986–89 (Hamnett, 1999: 30).

Conclusion

In the period after 1975 the welfare state came under closer scrutiny and attack, and housing was in the forefront, but so was employment policy, and the links between the two deserve closer attention. Housing has been identified as exceptional among welfare state core services in the severity of the attacks on it during the 1980s, but in fact full employment was a much wobblier pillar under the welfare state. Council housing reached a crossroads and, having expanded continually since 1919, it went into both numerical and proportionate decline. At the same time it went from being seen as part of the solution to housing problems to part of the problem to be tackled. The purpose of this chapter has been to develop a perspective on housing and the welfare state that goes beyond existing accounts to show that not only was the public sector cut, residualized and bypassed, but the virtues of the private sector were talked up in the midst of a period when three key developments made it more difficult for more people to satisfy their housing needs in the market: cuts in the scope and value of social security benefits, steeply rising long term unemployment, and market liberalization. These had important, but hard to quantify, implications for the achieved housing welfare of a numerically significant, albeit political marginal, section of the working class.

Accounts of the period have tended to look at the 1980s in terms of privatization and the residualization of local authority housing, but what is needed is a perspective on the restructuring of the welfare state more broadly, and in terms of factors affecting achieved housing wellbeing. The housing studies literature has tended to concentrate on the negative impact of right to buy (RTB) sales on council housing, but has not paid the same sort of attention to the residualization of home ownership. It is simplistic to think in terms of a residual public sector on the one hand and a non-residual, non-problematic private sector on the other. A traditional public services view of the welfare state invites this assumption, or at least neglect of the market. Chapter 1 argued that the state worked through and with the market to ensure or promote housing wellbeing. In the 1980s in particular the state certainly promoted owner occupation and subsidized people to enter; but then it pursued economic and employment policies that left some of them considerably exposed to hardship. Housing was different from health and education in the direct link between employment policy and wellbeing, because of the much larger number of people who relied on their own resources to satisfy their needs. In the early 1980s social and economic policy deliberately created an increase in the numbers of people living in or on the margins of poverty, and housing policy emphasized market based solutions, which were clearly not in the interests of this group. It was no accident that the end of the classic welfare state and the golden age for owner occupation occurred at the same time.

Chapter 7

The New Housing Policy

Since 1988 Britain has experienced two notable transitions, one political and the other economic. The period began with the Conservatives firmly entrenched as the party of government, having just secured their third consecutive election victory. They were returned again in 1992, against expectations, but by then they were deeply divided over the issue of Europe and were subsequently increasingly discredited by accusations of misbehaviour by ministers. The end of the long Tory hegemony was clearly in sight well before the election of 1 May 1997, and, with the Labour Party effectively re-invented as 'New Labour', the only real surprise was the overwhelming scale of the victory (an overall majority of 178). Virtually the same outcome occurred again in 2001, giving the Labour Party its first ever opportunity to govern for two full terms. The economic transition took the form of the dawn of a period of low inflation and low interest rates. From the 1960s governments had treated inflation as a major economic threat, and on several occasions in the 1970s and 1980s inflation exceeded 10 per cent, peaking at around 25 per cent in 1976. Even the Thatcher governments, armed with the theory of monetarism that was supposed to be a cure for inflation, struggled to overcome it: inflation was 18 per cent in 1980 and 9.5 per cent in 1990. However, the 1990s became a decade of low inflation, consistently below 4 per cent from 1992 onwards, and in some years below 2 per cent. In this context interest rates also fell, to nominal rates that had not been seen for more than thirty years. Changes in both inflation and interest rates have had important implications for the housing market.

The housing market in this period has also been much affected by the ups and downs of the economy as a whole. By the spring of 1987 the economy was growing and recovering from the deep recession of the early part of the decade. Unemployment had peaked and was declining. Interest rates were still high, especially by comparison with later years, but in response to a stock market crash in the autumn the chancellor sought to boost activity by lowering rates. This led to mortgage rates falling for a period in 1988 to below 10 per cent, something that had not happened for a decade. And in turn this fuelled demand in a rising housing market. In this febrile situation the chancellor stoked demand still further by announcing in April that he would remove in August the so-called 'double tax relief' enjoyed by unmarried multi-earner mortgaged house buyers.

124

As the economy overheated the chancellor then raised interest rates, resulting in mortgage rates rising from just under 10 per cent in July 1988 to 15.4 per cent by February 1990. This was the highest ever nominal mortgage interest rate. Rates remained high throughout the deep economic recession in 1991–92, which saw unemployment rise to nearly 2.9 million in 1993. The housing market slump of 1989–95 (Hamnett, 1999: 33–43) was the worst in living memory, for, uniquely in the series of booms and slumps since the early 1970s, it coincided with falling inflation and positive interest rates; in other words, house prices actually fell in cash terms and inflation took longer to come to the rescue of owners struggling with mortgage repayments. In the period 1989–93 average house prices in most English regions fell, in some areas by more than a third, and although prices then recovered, in the worst affected regions the average in 1997 was still below the 1989 level (Hamnett, 1999: 35).

During earlier market down-turns inflation had masked falling real values, and during the mid-1970s mortgaged home owners benefited from negative interest rates (where the mortgage rate was less than the rate of inflation). This time, however, between 1.5 and 2 million people found themselves 'in negative equity': that is, their house was worth less than their mortgage (Hamnett, 1999: 5). The worst affected were people who had recently purchased with loans that were the maximum available in relation to both the value of the property and their earnings, and who then found themselves unemployed and unable to maintain repayments. Mortgage arrears rose dramatically (the number of people more than 6 months in arrears rose from 53,000 to 352,000) although remaining a very small proportion of all mortgaged home owners. As a result the numbers of purchasers losing their homes also reached unprecedented levels. In the six years 1990–95 more than 345,000 mortgages were taken into possession by lending institutions (in everyday terms the houses were 'repossessed', and the households evicted: see Ford, Burrows and Nettleton, 2001: 23–4).

Meanwhile, in November 1990 Margaret Thatcher was overthrown by her senior colleagues when it became clear to them that she was no longer an electoral asset. Her successor, John Major, was to remain in office for seven years, but he was opposed not only by a Labour Party intent on re-inventing itself as a electoral force, but also by a significant and vocal section of his own party, the so-called 'Eurosceptics'. Under Thatcher Britain had signed up to important developments in the European Union, in particular the implementation of the Maastricht Treaty, the establishment of a single European market and entry to the European exchange rate mechanism (ERM). The last of these proved to be politically disastrous for the Tories, for after Britain was forced to withdraw from the mechanism in October 1992 the government was never able to recover a lead in the opinion polls. Nevertheless, under Major the Conservatives pressed ahead with further measures to continue the Thatcherite agenda for change in the governance of Britain.

Two key elements, with implications for housing, were privatization and further pressure on public expenditure. It seems reasonable to see privatization as a policy that gained momentum as successive governments after 1979 built on the relatively modest ambitions of the early years. Up to 1986 council house sales had been the largest privatization project, but then the first of the major public utilities, gas, was privatized and, fortified by earlier successes and a new electoral mandate, the government pressed ahead with further measures, including electricity, water, the rump of the coal mining industry and finally the railways. In terms of selling off state owned industries the idea had been pushed about as far as was possible – in the case of the railways many would say beyond what was sustainable. But privatization comes in different forms and during their third term the Conservatives turned their attention to ways of subjecting more public services to 'market testing'. The development of quasi-markets across the field of social policy has been depicted by some writers as a defining feature of government in the 1990s as governments sought to improve efficiency by introducing competition to areas traditionally run on bureaucratic lines (Bartlett, Roberts and Le Grand, 1998).

During the Thatcher years central government developed a deep animosity towards local government in general (albeit with some notable exceptions, such as the Thatcherite London boroughs of Wandsworth and Westminster). This led to some authorities, including the Greater London Council, being abolished altogether, while others saw their budgets cut and their revenue raising powers curtailed. They were also required to market test services hitherto run as in-house operations. This meant inviting private organizations to bid for contracts to run public services on a profit-seeking basis. It was a view of local authorities as 'enablers' rather than service providers; they retained responsibility for making sure that services were provided, but at the extreme all services could be outsourced, potentially reducing the role of local councillors to participation in an annual meeting to review performance and agree new contracts. Compulsory competitive tendering (CCT) was extended to housing management services from 1992.

On the public expenditure front, 'With the exception of the pre-1992 election cycle, public spending on welfare has been remarkably constrained during the period [since the mid-1970s] compared with most of the past century' (Glennerster and Hills, 1998: 308). The ideological stance of the Thatcherite Conservatives demanded cuts in both taxes and spending, but the best they could achieve in practice was to contain the growth of welfare spending, except in housing. Having been singled out for cuts immediately after the 1979 election, housing continued to be the one area of social policy where substantial cuts were implemented. In the period under review this was partly due to switching of expenditure from one heading to another, from housing to social security, and partly due to the way that net investment reflected the impact of capital receipts from council house sales. Nevertheless, the contrast between housing and other programme areas remains striking: since 1990 increases in spending on health and personal social services amounted to 72 per cent, in social security 48 per cent, in education 44 per cent, while in housing there was a reduction of 31 per cent – and this represented a significant recovery from the low point of 1999/2000 (Wilcox, 2003b: 84). Housing expenditure actually increased quite sharply in the early 1990s as the government implemented its new strategy for rented housing (see below), but then, as the housing market recovered, public sector investment fell quickly and was on a downward course at the point when the Labour opposition committed itself to sticking to Tory spending plans for the first two years of its first term. It was only after 2000/01 that housing spending began to rise again.

Finally in this section it is necessary to refer to the impact of Labour in office after eighteen years of Conservative rule. There is already an extensive literature on this subject (Burden *et al.*, 2000; Clarke, Gewirtz and McLaughlin, 2000; Hay, 1999; Powell, 1999, 2002; Savage and Atkinson, 2001). In certain respects Labour has made important changes: for example, handing over control of interest rates to the Bank of England, introducing minimum wage legislation, removing (most) hereditary peers from the House of Lords and devolving some governmental functions to an assembly in Wales and a parliament in Scotland. Labour has also returned to the idea of full employment, although in the context of different economic policies. This stance, however, has not yet been tested in the context of a deep economic recession on the scale of the early 1980s or early 1990s. Labour has put in place measures to tackle child poverty and, in its second term, it demonstrated a willingness to increase public expenditure in order to improve the quality of services. In this sense the contrast with the neglect of investment in key services under the Conservatives is real and important. But the continuities are at least as striking as the changes. Under Tony Blair Labour has shared the Conservatives' enthusiasm for markets, competition and privatization, and an enthusiasm for further reform and modernization of public services that sits quite comfortably with the trajectories set out in earlier years.

An overview of developments in the welfare state since 1988

It was suggested in Chapter 1 that the period of welfare state crisis and retrenchment led to the development of three renegotiated settlements.

These settlements and their application to housing provide the framework for Chapters 8–10, but first this section develops the outline of recent changes in the welfare state in order to contextualize the subsequent more detailed discussion of housing, and to provide a basis for the argument that there has been convergence across programme areas. Without resiling or dissenting from the view that the mid-1970s represented the key turning point in the post-1945 development of the welfare state, there is a case for recognizing the importance of a set of policy changes introduced in or soon after 1988. Although the welfare state as a whole had remained largely intact during Margaret Thatcher's first two terms, the late 1980s saw the introduction of measures that would bring about real and lasting change across the board, leading to a revolution in social policy:

> In the area of social policy, the 1990s will be remembered as the decade in which a major social experiment was implemented in the UK by the Conservative governments. In nearly all areas of welfare provision, new institutional arrangements were introduced designed to extend the principle of markets and competition to the provision of services. At the same time, the principle of free and universal access, fundamental to the concept of the welfare state, was upheld. This combination of free access at the point of delivery, combined with decentralised market-like competition between providers of services, was the key institutional innovation which was referred to as a 'quasi-market'. (Bartlett, Roberts and Le Grand, 1998: 1)

Not to be outdone in this context Labour's 1997 manifesto proclaimed: 'We will be the party of welfare reform' (quoted in Powell and Hewitt, 2002: 61), and so it has proved, but not in ways looked for by its more traditional supporters. Within eighteen months of taking office Labour had introduced a new NHS organization, a welfare to work programme, the basis of a new pensions and social security scheme, a schools policy and a new system for funding higher education (Glennerster, 1999: 29). Labour has belatedly shown a willingness to increase spending on key services to an extent that the Conservatives would not, but its approach to welfare reform has developed very much along lines mapped out by its immediate predecessors: more privatization, marketization and demunicipalization; and more emphasis on competition, consumer choice and state regulation of service providers through complex (and questionable) mechanisms for performance measurement.

According to one leading Conservative policy wonk, David Willetts, 'for us 1988, with the Education Reform Act, the NHS review, the Griffiths report [on social care] and the Housing Act, was the *annus mirabilis* of social policy' (quoted in Timmins, 1996: 433). One of the best sources on this whole episode is the book by Nicholas Timmins (1996) who reveals not only the heated debates carried on within the Thatcher government but also the extent to which ideas (for example, concerning the introduction of student loans) that were subsequently implemented and taken further by a Labour government were then considered too risky. The Education Reform Act, 1988, extended central control via the introduction of a national curriculum for schools and compulsory testing of children at specified key stages (except in Scotland), but it was also decentralizing in the sense that it gave schools the freedom to opt out from local authority control, becoming known as grant maintained schools; where schools did not take this route there was devolution of budgets from local authorities to head teachers and governors. Opting out was justified in terms of choice and diversity, and testing in terms of the imperative of higher standards, all of which are key concepts in the modern welfare state. In pursuit of higher standards in 1992 the government set up a new apparatus for inspecting schools (the Office for Standards in Education, OFSTED), another indicator of the increased emphasis on regulation. Grant maintained status was not widely adopted (only about 5 per cent of all schools took up the option: see Timmins, 1996: 446) and after the 1997 election Labour prevented further opting out, but did not bring grant maintained schools back within local authority control (most converted to foundation status, which gives them continued control over their policies and practices, including selection of pupils: see Brehony and Deem, 2003: 184). Other aspects of the 1988 Act have been modified but largely retained; the Labour government remains committed to choice and diversity in schools and to intervention where schools are seen to be failing, even to the extent of putting in private firms to run them (Brehony and Deem, 2003: 187).

Education was Labour's priority at the 1997 election, at which it promised no return to selection in secondary schools, but it was clear that support for comprehensive education was waning and specialization in schools has become more popular with the leadership. The remaining grammar schools have not been abolished. Labour has continued with the policy of regular testing of children throughout their school careers, and has remained committed to the compilation and publication of school league tables, despite the opposition of many teachers. In the area of higher education Labour has gone further than its predecessors. In 1990 the Conservatives initiated a series of changes affecting higher education, first in terms of the process of replacing student maintenance grants with loans, and then allowing the polytechnics to become universities in 1992. Labour carried this forward, expanding both student numbers and the number of universities. It also went much further, introducing fees payable by students during their courses, and then, amidst great controversy in 2004, insisting on a policy of variable fees, repayable by graduates during the course of their first twenty-five years of employment. This policy change was justified, against critics who argued for a tax funded system, on the grounds that since graduates tended to earn more than non-graduates they should bear some of the cost of their education. In effect the government argued that higher education was both the key to the future success of the economy, and that a degree was a personal consumption good. The insistence that wholly tax funded higher education was unaffordable and that individuals should pay towards the costs of their courses was a good indicator of the drift away from principles formerly seen as lying at the core of the welfare state, and towards the widespread use of direct means-tested charges for services.

Moving on to the NHS, this was the jewel in the crown of the welfare state, the service that Thatcher had had to declare was safe in her hands (even though it was not). By 1987 the funding squeeze had become acute and in January 1988 Thatcher made the surprise announcement of a review of the NHS as a whole. This was to lead to the adoption of the American idea of an internal market in which there would be distinct purchasers (the health authorities and fund holding general practitioners) and providers (the hospitals), while retaining a fully tax funded service that was free at the point of use. This, of course, did not of itself solve the funding crisis, but it did offer the theoretical prospect of greater efficiency, choice and diversity. At the same time the government introduced trust status for hospitals opting for self-government; unlike grant maintained status for schools, this model was widely adopted and continued by Labour, which proposed to develop the concept further in the form of foundation hospitals. The Labour government proclaimed itself to be abolishing the Tories' internal market, but it did not revert to the old regime and retained the purchaser/provider split. Carrying forward its own modernization plans Labour has embarked on a major hospital building programme, and has claimed to have introduced the most fundamental reforms since 1948 (Department of Health, 2000).

Alongside the perennial issue of the cost of hospital services in the mid-1980s there developed a new concern about the rapidly increasing cost to the Exchequer of private nursing and residential care homes (which was itself largely due to policy changes in the early part of the decade). The dilemma was that a way of reducing the cost of hospitals was to move people into the community, especially elderly people and those in long stay learning disability hospitals, but this would only work financially if the costs of community care could be contained. In 1986 Sir Roy Griffiths (who had earlier reported on the management of the health service) was asked to produce a further report on community care. His report, submitted in 1988, eventually led to the NHS and Community Care Act, 1990, and to substantial reforms implemented from 1993. The story has been told elsewhere (Means and Smith, 1994; Timmins, 1996) and here it is sufficient to note that the thrust of the reforms was to emphasize the role of local social services departments as enablers rather than providers of community care services. Local authorities were to be responsible for community care plans, which were expected to show how to make maximum use of providers in the independent sector – this was a term used to embrace voluntary, not-for-profit organizations as well as private profit-seeking businesses. Again, choice and diversity were key concepts.

The largest spending programme of all, social security, was not significantly affected by the burst of late 1980s reforms, largely because there had just been major changes in the Social Security Act, 1986, which, among other things, introduced the Social Fund, to provide loans instead of grants to poor people to meet the cost of items that could not be paid for out of normal weekly benefits. Later, the Child Support Agency was set up in 1990 to pursue absent fathers who reneged on maintenance payments in the knowledge that the state would have to provide. Somewhat later, however, some important changes were made. In 1993, for example, unemployment benefit was replaced by 'job seekers' allowance'; more than just a name change, this made payment conditional on claimants signing a jobseeking agreement, and entitlement to benefit was reduced from 12 to 6 months. The cost of invalidity benefit was also tackled by the introduction of more stringent medical tests. Finally the Conservatives made changes to the state earnings related pension scheme, with the intention of cutting its long term cost to the Exchequer (Timmins, 1996: 515).

Labour has continued with the same broad approach, making state benefits more conditional and encouraging people to make their own private provision, especially in the area of pensions. Labour's New Deal for the unemployed, for example, insisted that young people would receive benefit only if they agreed to one of four choices involving work, training or education – doing nothing meant no benefit. On pensions, Labour has introduced a minimum income guarantee for the least well off pensioners, a state second pension to replace SERPS for low paid workers, and the option of a private stakeholder pension. The issue of pensions is an area of policy where the government is very clearly of the view that people should be making more provision for themselves rather than relying on the state. Private, personal pensions introduced by the Tories continue to be supported by Labour, despite the very poor value for money offered by many money purchase products. The shift from collective to individual provision is particularly clear in this area, strengthening the link between what you save and what you get in the long run. This means that income inequalities generated in the labour market will be continued and possibly enhanced in old age.

Despite Labour's rather belated enthusiasm for increased spending on welfare and its attempts to define its position as representing a 'third way' (Giddens, 1998b), there are important continuities with the policies of the previous government. Support for markets, privatization and public–private partnerships is strong, as is commitment to individual responsibility and direct payment for services. Devolved management and demunicipalization is coupled with strong central control through new technologies of performance measurement. Finally, before we return to housing:

> third way thinking broadly dictates that savings should be made by reducing spending in areas either where state support masks costs that individuals should be meeting themselves, or where private and voluntary agencies can provide services more cheaply ... prime candidates in the first category are retirement pensions and higher education. In both cases the Blair governments have been keen to reduce these expensive commitments by encouraging private sector take-up where possible – occupational and stakeholder pensions for those deemed able to make their own provision for retirement, and loans in place of grants for those students from better-off families entering higher education. In the second category, housing has come to be regarded as an area which should be left primarily to the private sector, with private ownership and private renting, supported by some social housing, being the major form of provision. (Ellison and Pierson, 2003: 8–9)

Taken together the thrust of policy in a number of key areas is to load the cost of services onto individuals and families: students are to enter their working lives with substantial debts, they are then to take out more debt in order to buy a house, while all the time being urged to save for their retirement. Each one of these policies looked at in isolation has a certain plausibility about it, but seen together they begin to look like an unsustainable strategy for the longer term.

The emergence of the new housing policy

There is widespread agreement among analysts and commentators that housing has slipped down the order of political priorities in recent years. In contrast to earlier periods discussed in previous chapters, housing has ceased to be the sort of issue that wins elections. Housing continued to work well for the Conservatives at the three elections between 1979 and 1987, in a period when the Party had something positive to offer significant groups of voters, whether they were existing or aspiring home owners. However, by 1992 the housing market was in deep recession, and no-one wanted to talk about it. It was also virtually ignored by all political parties in 1997 and 2001. Academic commentators began to wonder whether there was a future for housing policy. Kleinman (1996) talked about the collapse of housing policy as it had been formulated in the postwar period, while Bramley (1997) and Hills (1998) suggested that British housing policy had become fragmented and subsumed within other programmes, including social security, planning and economic and community regeneration. However, although housing policy is undoubtedly different from the days when governments sought to impress the voters with the sheer scale of their building programmes, it is nonetheless still important. Housing is too important for the economy as well as for the wealth and wellbeing of the people for governments not to have policies on the subject. The long established mantra of 'a decent home...within reach of every family' (DoE, 1995: 3; see also DETR, 2000: 7) continues to be the basic goal of policy to which all political parties give assent. The way in which that goal is approached varies over time, according to the dynamics of the underlying problem and prevailing views about how to proceed. Housing policy has not disappeared but it has been refashioned for contemporary social, economic and political circumstances. Kleinman (1996) is quite right to say that housing policy as we knew it in the first thirty years after 1945 has collapsed, but a new orthodoxy, in terms of the way the problem is formulated and what to do about it, has been developed.

Throughout their first two terms in office after 1979 Conservative housing policy had been built around one big idea: the expansion of owner occupation, chiefly through the sale of council houses. It has been claimed by one former Conservative housing minister (Young, 1991: 8) that in 1986/87 a 'fundamental and much needed review' of policy was undertaken, and during the election campaign in the spring of 1987 a number of radical ideas were brought forward, amounting to a new strategy for rental housing. This was designed to sit alongside the continuing commitment to owner occupation as the main form of housing consumption. These ideas were subsequently elaborated in a White Paper (DoE, 1987) and carried forward through the Housing Act, 1988, and the Local Government and Housing Act, 1989. The new strategy was driven by recognition of the need to expand overall supply, while continuing to reduce the amount of local authority housing. It therefore needs to be understood in terms of the three main parts of the rental sector.

First, in relation to local authorities, the government planned to step up its attack on their role as providers and to move them towards a more strategic enabling role. This represented a step change, moving beyond the right to buy towards a much more aggressive, in principle challenge to the role that local authorities had developed over a period of seventy years. For the first time ministers were questioning the need for local authorities to be involved in the direct provision and management of rented housing. For example, William Waldegrave, housing minister in 1987–88, suggested that, 'The next great push after the right to buy should be to get rid of the state as a big landlord and bring housing back to the community' (Waldegrave, 1987). The meaning of the phrase 'back to the community' was not spelled out, but its use was interesting in the context of proposals that were about transferring the ownership of parts of the council sector to private landlords, not a group of citizens usually associated with having the interests of the community at heart. The idea of community ownership resurfaced some years later, from a somewhat different direction, but also in the context of removing local authorities from the landlord role (Institute for Public Policy Research, 2000).

Specific proposals brought forward at the time of the 1987 general election included the ring fencing of local authority housing revenue accounts (to prevent councils using their local tax income to subsidize rents), housing action trusts (to remove the most challenging estates from local authority control for improvement and sale by newly created bodies) and tenants' choice (a scheme to allow council tenants to choose a new, non-municipal landlord). Each of these can be understood as an attempt to reduce the scale of local authority housing. Ring fencing would tend to cause rents to rise, thereby encouraging more people to consider exercising their right to buy, while the other two schemes were explicitly about hiving off parts of the stock to new owners, in a way that had never been proposed before. Hitherto no government had even considered forcing local authorities to sell houses except to individual tenants. In the event, although legislated for in the Housing Act, 1988, neither housing action trusts nor tenants' choice made much direct impact, largely because of unanticipated opposition from tenants, but ring fencing became part of a wider restructuring of local authority housing finance, which did have an immediate impact on rents and resources available to local authorities to maintain and improve their dwellings (Malpass and Means, 1993; Malpass *et al.*, 1993).

On the new strategic role of local authorities the White Paper of 1987 had little say beyond the following:

> there will no longer be the same presumption that the local authority itself should take direct action to meet new or increasing demands. The future role of local authorities will essentially be a strategic one identifying housing needs and demands, encouraging innovative methods of provision by other bodies to meet such needs, maximising the use of private finance, and encouraging the new interest in the revival of the independent rented sector. In order to fulfil this strategic role they will have to work closely with housing associations; private landlords;

developers; and building societies and other providers of finance. Local authorities are being encouraged to adopt this new approach in preparing their housing investment programmes for 1988/89, and in reviewing and improving the quality of their housing strategies. (DoE, 1987: 14)

However, the system evolved over the next several years and local authorities were subjected to a stream of guidance on how to present their strategies (Cole and Goodchild, 1995; Lambert and Malpass, 1998). The system has continued to change since 1997 but there has been no retreat from the idea that local authority involvement in housing should be primarily strategic rather than operational, and where they continue to provide housing authorities are now required to separate the two roles. One of the favoured ways for achieving this split is for local authorities to transfer ownership of all their houses to new landlords. The story of the emergence of large scale voluntary transfer (LSVT) after 1987 is a fascinating example of how a local initiative in opposition to government policy (specifically, tenants' choice) grew into a mainstream policy (Malpass and Mullins, 2002). Local authorities began to come forward with proposals to transfer their houses to newly established housing associations in 1988 but the idea was not taken up as government policy until 1992, and by 1995 the White Paper was urging all authorities to at least consider transfer.

The further decline of local authorities as housing landlords represented an intensification of an existing trend, but for housing associations the new strategy developed in the late 1980s marked a turning point after the uncertainties of the early Thatcher years during which they had suffered by being bracketed with the local authorities. Now, however, housing associations had been singled out for support in the context of the government's recognition that there was a considerable unmet need for additional affordable rented housing. The Thatcher governments were so viscerally opposed to local authorities that they turned to housing associations, which were rapidly redefined as part of a newly designated independent rented sector, bracketed with commercial private landlords. In the event the links between the associations and the public sector were too close, and the differences between them and profit seeking private landlords too great, so that this label never became established. Instead the term 'social housing' became more widely used to embrace both local authorities and housing associations. The key to the growth of housing associations in the first half of the 1990s was a set of changes enabling them to borrow large amounts of private finance to supplement Exchequer grants. At the same time, the aggregate level of the Approved Development Programme (ADP) was at record levels. The grant rate as a proportion of the cost of each new dwelling went down as private finance increased, thereby permitting greater overall output, but at the price of substantially higher rents (for a fuller explanation and discussion see Malpass, 2000b: ch. 10).

At the same time as housing associations were being groomed to take over as the main suppliers of new subsidized housing, investment in private renting was being encouraged by rent deregulation. From early 1989 landlords were free to establish new tenancies on the basis of rents freely negotiated with tenants and on terms known as assured or assured shorthold, tenancies that gave tenants less security than the old regulated tenancies. The incentive for landlords to invest was thus the possibility of a higher return on capital and easier access to vacant possession (Kemp, 1993). It was not so clear what would attract more tenants into the private sector, apart from lack of alternatives.

Integral to the new rental housing strategy was tolerance of higher rents, and the higher Exchequer costs implicit in this due to the impact on housing benefit. Ministers referred to housing benefit 'taking the strain' of higher rents across the board. In the local authority sector the government wanted higher rents partly to encourage more tenants to reconsider other tenure options, and partly to generate overall savings in public expenditure (in this sector higher rents created surpluses that could be used to offset the increased burden of housing benefit). In the housing association sector higher rents were needed to meet the higher costs of borrowing from private finance institutions, but overall the government pursued a strategy of shifting from general subsidy (sometimes called bricks and mortar subsidy) to means-tested assistance with housing costs. However, the outcome was not quite as anticipated, and the housing benefit bill increased by a factor of four, from £2.5 billion to over £10 billion, between 1989/90 and 1994/95 (Wilcox, 1999). The sheer scale of the bill for housing benefit was only one of the problems highlighted by deregulation of private renting and the changes in the housing associations' financial regime. Unsurprisingly, by the mid-1990s the government had rediscovered the virtues of general subsidy for people on permanently low incomes (DoE, 1995: 4), and the strong upward pressure on rents was eased; indeed the government began to look for ways to prevent social landlords increasing rents beyond centrally approved rates, and in the private sector it began to introduce ways of limiting the rents on which benefit would be paid. These were essentially cosmetic temporary measures, pending the sort of fundamental reform that had long been recognized to be necessary (Kemp, 2000).

A significant proportion of the increased cost of housing benefit was covered by cuts in mortgage interest tax relief (MITR). This was a reform that had been advocated for years by a wide spectrum of informed opinion (e.g., NFHA, 1985) but stoutly rejected by Margaret Thatcher. Almost as soon as Thatcher was deposed the process of phasing out MITR was put in train. This needs to be seen in the context of a wider sea change in the pattern of housing finance in Britain. First, by the 1990s subsidy, which had been such a dominant feature of the system for over seventy years, was being squeezed across all tenures. The cuts in grant rates for new housing association schemes has been mentioned above, and at the same time general subsidy was being rapidly withdrawn from local authorities. By 1994/95 the aggregate housing revenue account for all English local authorities moved from deficit into surplus (although some individual local authorities continued to receive subsidy); this had never happened before. Second, the 1990s saw not only a shift in public expenditure from general subsidy into housing benefit but also a shift from public borrowing to private finance for social housing investment (much of the cost of which was borne by the public purse via housing benefit).

New Labour and the new housing policy

When Labour took office after eighteen years in opposition they inherited a housing policy, and a housing policy context, that were both quite different from the late 1970s. Policy had moved on from the sorts of concerns about shortage and house building targets that had dominated debates for much of the post-Second World War period, and it had moved on from the idea that the state should boost supply by various forms of subsidy. The new housing policy can be summed up in four points:

1   It was characterized much less by subsidy, and more by taxation (including the removal of surpluses from local authority housing revenue accounts) and targeted assistance delivered through the social security system.
2   After decades during which policy had facilitated the transformation and modernization of the housing market, it was the restructuring of social rented housing that was now the focus of attention.
3   This was linked in part to contemporary ideas about the role of democratic local government, and in part to methods of financing measures to tackle the problems (now including variable levels of demand) associated with the growing residualization of social rented housing.
4   After a period when policy was dominated by the issue of tenure, problems of supply and demand had begun to re-emerge, but whereas hitherto policy had been framed in terms of rather simplistic assumptions about the desirability of expanding owner occupation, it was becoming clear that in future it would be necessary to recognize the co-existence of high demand in some areas and low demand in others.

The government's position on housing policy for the new millennium was set out in a Green Paper in April 2000 (DETR, 2000: 10–14):

- a stronger role for local authorities to reflect variations in circumstances around the country
- support for sustainable home ownership
- new approaches to improve the quality of social rented housing and housing management, including a commitment to bring all social housing up to a decent standard within ten years
- improvements in the delivery of affordable housing
- reforms to lettings policies to give tenants in social housing real choice over the homes they live in
- strengthening of protection available to homeless families
- review of tenure arrangements for social housing
- social sector rents to be maintained at affordable, sub-market levels
- restructuring of social sector rents to put them on a fairer, affordable basis
- development of housing benefit to improve customer service, tackle fraud and error and improve incentives to work.

Owner occupation (which had grown from 55 per cent in 1979 to 67 per cent in 1997) was deeply entrenched as the centrepiece of housing policy, and this was not a position that the new government wished to challenge in any way, but it carried on with the policy of phasing out MITR, which was finally removed in 2000. Labour also inherited and embraced the new strategy for rental housing, with its well established trajectories in relation to each sub-sector: more council houses were sold to new owners in large scale voluntary transfers in Labour's first three years than in the previous nine years under the Conservatives, and further increases were planned (DETR, 2000: 61; Malpass and Mullins, 2002); the number of new council houses built fell below the previous record lows achieved under the Tories, as Table 7.1 indicates, while housing associations continued to be the main providers of new affordable housing; and on private renting, Labour positively endorsed the policy of encouraging further growth (DETR, 2000: 44–52).

The figures in Table 7.1 refer only to new houses, and it is possible to argue that this is a rather restricted measure of provision (for an alternative angle on the supply of dwellings by housing associations see Malpass, 2000b: 226). Nevertheless, the table indicates that local authorities have been effectively eliminated as builders of new houses, while housing associations have not been able to sustain their role as an alternative supplier of affordable houses. For several years after 1988 aggregate output by local authorities and housing associations remained around 30,000 and

Table 7.1 *Houses completed in Great Britain, 1988–2002*

Year	Local authorities	Housing associations	Private builders	Total
1988	18,997	12,781	199,876	231,654
1989	16,452	13,934	179,593	209,979
1990	15,686	17,469	160,635	193,790
1991	9,651	20,022	153,969	183,642
1992	4,141	25,470	140,977	170,588
1993	2,076	35,286	140,966	178,328
1994	1,869	36,612	147,819	186,300
1995	1,445	38,284	150,859	190,588
1996	862	32,148	147,370	180,380
1997	468	27,502	152,548	180,518
1998	428	23,325	146,486	170,239
1999	165	23,315	149,151	172,631
2000	302	22,910	144,250	167,462
2001	480	21,242	140,490	162,212
2002	331	19,554	151,097	170,982

Source: Data from Wilcox (2003b; original source *Housing Statistics*).

then rose to a peak of almost 40,000 by 1995, but once the cuts in the Housing Corporation's ADP kicked in there was a downward trend, continuing up to 2002, by which time the production of affordable rented housing had fallen to the lowest peacetime level since 1924. By 2002 housing associations were producing at only half the rate achieved seven years earlier (and this was despite substantial growth in the sector due to stock transfer). The level of production by housing associations needs to be seen in the context of a series of studies estimating the requirement for new social housing to exceed 60,000 dwellings per annum (Bramley, 1990; Environment Committee, 1995; Holmans, 1995a; Holmans, Morrison and Whitehead, 1998; Whitehead and Kleinman, 1992). Private builders, for their part, were never able to recover the levels of output achieved in the late 1980s, despite the return of boom conditions in the housing market in recent years. The failure of supply to respond to rising prices in this period is particularly striking and sufficiently puzzling for the Chancellor to commission a report as to the reasons (Barker, 2003).

Table 7.2 shows that the downward trend in public investment in social housing continued for three years under Labour. Real, inflation adjusted, investment remained below half the 1989/90 level for six years under Labour after 1997. There are grounds for saying that 1989/90 is not a fair

Table 7.2   *Gross social housing investment in Great Britain, 1987/88–2003/4*
(excluding private finance)

Year	£million cash	£million 2001/02 prices
1987/88	5,206	8,803
1988/89	5,634	8,932
1989/90	7,248	10,988
1990/91	5,743	7,881
1991/92	5,944	7,688
1992/93	6,533	8,185
1993/94	6,422	7,852
1994/95	5,864	7,076
1995/96	5,264	6,176
1996/97	4,806	5,465
1997/98	4,061	4,480
1998/99	4,133	4,437
1999/2000	4,029	4,223
2000/01	4,474	4,586
2001/02	4,975	4,975
2002/03	5,382	5,210
2003/04 (estimate)	6,058	5,725

Source: Data from Wilcox (2003b; original source *Public Expenditure Plans*).

benchmark, for the level of spending in that year was artificially boosted by local authorities anticipating the impact of the transition to a new financial regime (Malpass *et al.*, 1993). Nevertheless, embedded within these figures are some important trends in different components: for example, taking 1988/89 as a better comparator, inflation adjusted spending by English local authorities on renovating their own houses remained below that level throughout the period up to 2000/01, and although spending by the Housing Corporation in England rose by nearly 150 per cent in real terms in 1988/89 to 1992/93, it then fell back even more, by more than 75 per cent by 1988/99. It is only since 2001 that the Corporation's ADP has shown signs of significant growth (Wilcox, 2003b: 152–4).

Academic commentaries on Labour's housing policy have tended to see it as broadly a continuation of trajectories established before 1997 (Cowan and Marsh, 2001; Ford, 2003; Kemp, 1999), but it is necessary to acknowledge that a certain distinctiveness has emerged. In early moves the new government increased local authority capital spending, abandoned compulsory competitive tendering for local authority housing management and removed contentious parts of the Conservatives' homelessness policy. CCT had failed to attract much interest among private organizations and the majority of contracts were won by in-house bids. In place of CCT Labour introduced its own approach to improving efficiency and effectiveness, Best Value (which is discussed in more detail in a later chapter). Here it is enough to note that social housing providers have come under increasing pressure through the application of best value and other measures of performance, including inspection. It is arguable that they are more closely monitored and controlled now than before 1997.

Two further indicators of continuity concern the reform of housing benefit, where Labour has followed the Conservatives' strategy of putting off the sort of fundamental reform that is known to be necessary, and the problem of meeting unmet demand for housing in the more economically buoyant parts of the country. Here again Labour has followed the Conservatives' line of relying on private enterprise to produce a high proportion of new output. This needs to be contrasted with the approach of fifty years ago, when a Conservative government aiming for 300,000 dwellings a year also relied on private builders for the majority, but was prepared to use the local authorities to make good any shortfall (Merrett, 1979). Now, however, social housing organizations are not only not used in that way but they are themselves reliant on private builders to deliver a significant proportion of their new dwellings.

Conclusion

This chapter has sought to make two main points. First it has aimed to show that trends in mainstream welfare state services since 1988 (marketization, privatization, choice, individual as opposed to collective provision, etc.) have both reflected trajectories already established in housing, and marched in step with more recent developments in housing. Second, it has argued that contemporary housing policy is built on a new orthodoxy, much of which was established after 1988 and before the general election of 1997. In the present period it is no longer the marginality of housing in relation to the welfare state that is so striking but its centrality to current developments. The next three chapters deal with key aspects of contemporary housing policy that relate directly to current and emergent issues in the welfare state as a whole. Housing provides a rich context in which to explore the implications for wellbeing of wider reliance on markets, residualization and demunicipalization.

Chapter 8

Housing, Wellbeing and the Market

The starting point for this chapter is the idea of a new political/economic settlement, based on a smaller role for the state in both managing the economy and delivering welfare services. Housing provides a good context within which to examine what happens when the state withdraws from labour market regulation, positively encouraging the notion of flexibility/insecurity, and at the same time promotes market based mechanisms for the distribution of a basic determinant of wellbeing. The stated aim of housing policy in the early twenty-first century is 'to offer everyone the opportunity of a decent home and so promote social cohesion, well-being and self-dependence' (DETR, 2000: 16), and there are important questions to be asked about the extent to which the market can be relied upon to achieve this goal.

At the present time almost 80 per cent of households rely on the private market for their housing, the vast majority being, or planning to be, in the owner occupier sector. Private renting continues to play a role (accommodating about 10 per cent of households) and the Blair governments have expressed support for a healthy and expanding private rental sector, partly because it is believed to aid labour flexibility and mobility (DETR, 2000: 44–5). However, most people who rent privately do so as a temporary stage in housing careers that will take them into owner occupation. Accordingly, therefore, this chapter concentrates on owner occupation as the dominant, and preferred, form of the housing market in the present period.

Government support for owner occupation is nearly as old as the welfare state itself, and throughout the period since the 1953 housing White Paper it has been promoted as a 'good thing' from the points of view of both individual households and society as a whole. It is undoubtedly true that the growth of home ownership has been highly advantageous to large numbers of people, not only purchasers but also all those trades and professions that have prospered from the business generated by the processes of buying and selling, maintaining and improving, furnishing and personalizing houses. Owner occupation has broadened the distribution of wealth in Britain, and houses have come to represent the main form of wealth held by individuals (apart from the richest and poorest households: Hamnett, 1999: 106–7).

Owning, as distinct from renting, has also been seen by some writers as fostering a sense of psychological wellbeing or ontological security (Saunders, 1990), although the contingent nature of this and other advantages of owner occupation has been asserted by others (Forrest, Murie and Williams, 1990). Owner occupation, as an individualized, market based form of provision, allows consumers to reap the full effects of the advantages of ownership, but it also heaps on them the costs of any disadvantages. For much of the period after 1945 owner occupation was discussed largely in terms of its benefits, but the housing market slump of the early 1990s severely challenged simplistic assumptions about security, affordability and wealth accumulation (Bramley, Munro and Pawson, 2004; Forrest and Murie, 1994; Hamnett, 1999). In the aftermath of the worst shock to the housing system since the Second World War, even former cheerleaders for owner occupation such as Mark Boleat (1997: 60) were forced to admit that 'housing is now a risky investment', and as Murie (1998: 94) has pointed out the debate has become focused around the question of sustainable home ownership.

The housing Green Paper of 2000 continued the emphasis on sustainable home ownership, defined as 'where owners can afford it in the long term' (DETR, 2000: 30). However, it is arguable that from an analytical point of view the focus should be rather wider than the single question of whether owners can hang on to their homes in the long term. In evaluating owner occupation it is important to look at risks that do not necessarily threaten security of tenure but may nevertheless have an impact on wealth and wellbeing. These would include a wide variety of contingencies, from lower returns than could have been obtained from non-housing investment, or from buying a different house, possibly at a different time, to implications for health arising from external developments such as road schemes, or for the quality of education of children because of changing school catchment areas. But, going beyond risk, owner occupation is increasingly characterized by inequality:

> The home ownership market in Britain has functioned as a massive, though far from random, lottery, distributing differential gains and losses to millions of owners across the country and over time. It is far from random because there is a broadly consistent pattern of gains and losses depending on type of property bought, where and when, and who bought it. (Hamnett, 1999: 10–11)

Increased risk and inequality are not concepts normally associated with the welfare state, at least historically. On the contrary, defenders of the postwar welfare state, such as Richard Titmuss, framed their arguments in terms of the responsibility of the state for *reducing* the risks and inequalities generated in a competitive capitalist economy. Now, in the modernized and restructured welfare state, risk and inequality are part of the everyday experience of the housing mainstream, and the growth of owner occupation reflects a wider tendency to transfer responsibility for welfare provision from the state to the individual and from the public to the private sector. Accordingly, risk and inequality are the two main themes explored in this chapter. First, in relation to risk, the argument is that changes in the housing and labour markets and in aspects of government policy have combined to increase the levels of risk to which home owners are exposed:

> If the golden age of home ownership was one in which the sector was expanding most rapidly because of demographic and demand factors, and properties were appreciating in value (again because of these factors and rising affluence), it is also important to recognise that underpinning the golden age were generous tax relief, financial privileges and a safety net, both in terms of the social security system and the availability of good quality council housing. These factors meant that the home ownership sector and home owners themselves were not fully exposed to risk. After the golden age the safety nets were withdrawn. The alternative tenures are much less attractive, the financial privileges are less and the economic context leaves people much more exposed to risk. (Murie, 1998: 96)

This is close to the point made by Ford, Burrows and Nettleton (2001: vi) who refer to 'a radical realignment that has occurred between the spheres of work, welfare and housing over the last two decades; a realignment that has made home ownership a far riskier undertaking than was hitherto the case'. While some writers have depicted the housing market as being in crisis in the early 1990s, Ford, Burrows and Nettleton (2001: 44) are at pains to point out that that episode masked more profound and long term transformations in the labour market and the social security system, leading to permanently higher levels of risk for home owners.

Second, in relation to inequality, owner occupation needs to be understood as an engine of social and economic inequality, amplifying differences generated elsewhere, principally in the labour market. This is about recognizing that although all markets are essentially mechanisms for distributing goods and services according to the spending power and preferences of consumers, the housing market is different in at least two crucial respects: it has an investment dimension and a spatial dimension. Irrespective of any expectation of a real increase in value over time, the sheer durability of houses means that home owners acquire an asset which will ultimately be re-sold. What you buy, when and where, and how long you hang on to it, will be reflected in its value at the point of resale. Location is well known to be an important factor in determining the value of houses, and one reason for this is that where a house is located determines the owner's access to a variety of scarce resources, such as shops, leisure facilities, transport links and schools. This effectively means that the people with the most money secure the best houses in the most sought after neighbourhoods, where prices are highest. People buying houses are also buying access to the facilities and benefits of the neighbourhood, tangible and intangible, which may have a critical influence on their wider life chances (Forrest, Murie and Williams, 1990: 128). In other words, the housing market is a way of sorting the population into socially distinct locations reflecting purchasing power, which is largely a reflection of earned income. It then bestows on those different groups different rates of capital appreciation and differential access to valued resources, thereby amplifying the differences in their starting points.

Owner occupation in contemporary Britain

One of the enduring features of home ownership is its popularity; surveys of household tenure preferences consistently report large majorities identifying owner occupation as their favoured tenure, even in the wake of the market crisis of the early 1990s (Council of Mortgage Lenders, 2004: 41; J. Smith, 2002). This needs to be seen in the context of a highly dynamic and diverse sector of the British housing system. Dynamism and diversity are key concepts for understanding the owner occupied sector today. Dynamism can be analysed in terms of growth, maturation and change. The present size of the owner occupied sector, 69 per cent of the total, is the product of growth from a position of about 10 per cent in 1914. This has been achieved by a combination of new building and transfers of existing dwellings from other tenures. In the period between 1919 and 1939, for example, nearly 2 million newly built houses were added to the owner occupied sector in England and Wales, and more than 1 million were transferred from private renting (DoE, 1977b: 39). Then, in the thirty years after 1945 a further 3.9 million were built and 2.6 million transferred. Since the Second World War, private sector new building has been virtually monopolized by the market for owner occupation, with negligible investment in private renting. And since 1980 transfers from the local authority sector have become the major source of supply complementing new building, adding just over 2 million dwellings by 2003.

As it has grown in size so owner occupation has also matured in the sense that home owners have achieved a more balanced age profile. In the early growth phases the majority of purchasers were relatively young people, and elderly people were under-represented, but over the years the numbers of elderly home owners have increased substantially. Owner occupation has also broadened to include a much wider cross section of the population in terms of class and income position. Again, the early expansion took in mainly middle-class salaried people (but see the discussion in Chapter 3 earlier), although a characteristic of growth since the 1960s has been the increasing proportions of working-class people buying their own homes. This is discussed below as an aspect of diversity.

Owner occupation has changed in terms of its political and economic significance, and the role that it plays in the housing system, as it has grown from being small and insignificant to large and dominant. In the first half of the twentieth century governments were largely indifferent to it and housing policy was framed more in terms of the assumed need to revive investment in private renting. But as owner occupation became more popular and as governments came to realize that private renting was not going to revive, policy swung ever more firmly behind the idea that buying a house was to be encouraged as a 'basic and natural desire' (DoE, 1977a: 50). In the 1980s the rate of growth of home ownership replaced the number of new houses built as the key performance indicator for housing ministers, and great political importance was attached to the putative electoral implications of the rise of working-class home ownership. In economic terms, owner occupation has come to play an important role in relation to both growth and management of the economy. The building, maintenance and improvement of owner occupied houses accounts for a significant proportion of the work of the construction industry, while the business of buying and selling also generates large numbers of jobs. House prices, and people's expectations about whether they are going to rise or fall, influence consumer spending and therefore the rate of growth in the economy. When house prices are rising strongly consumers feel better off and are ready to increase debt fuelled spending, underpinned by the appreciating asset represented by their houses. In short, the state of the housing market and the wider economy are intimately bound together (Maclennan, 1994; Maclennan *et al.*, 1997).

The owner occupier sector has also changed in the sense that the arrangements for mortgage lending have become much more open and integrated with commercial banking. In the early years of the twentieth century private mortgages (where individual investors lent money directly to house purchasers in deals brokered by solicitors) were not unusual, but then for several decades the building societies dominated the scene. Eventually, in the 1980s, their privileged position was eroded by the wider deregulation of the finance industry, and a number of the larger societies converted into banks. In recent years banks have taken over from building societies as the main suppliers of mortgage finance. As mentioned in Chapter 7, deregulation had an impact on the housing market by making access to mortgages much quicker and easier, albeit at market rates of interest rather than the slightly lower rates that had previously prevailed. Mortgage lending has become much more openly competitive; in the past lenders would advertise for investors, never for borrowers, but now there is an active market in short-term discounted mortgage deals as lenders seek to attract new business. This has had the effect of breaking the long term relationship between lender and borrower, and encouraged borrowers to shop around for the best terms on a regular basis. And this in turn can be seen to be implicated in high rates of equity withdrawal as re-mortgaging owners are tempted to increase their debt to fund non-housing expenditure. By 2001, re-mortgaging (i.e., by non-moving owners) amounted to nearly a third of all new lending, and half of all re-mortgaging borrowers used the opportunity to withdraw equity (J. Smith, 2002). As recently as the 1980s equity withdrawal was much more difficult, because interest on mortgage debt attracted tax relief which was not available on other forms of borrowing, and therefore there was a requirement that debts secured against a property were used exclusively for purchasing or improving that property.

Turning to the idea of diversity, in a situation where more than 16 million households own or are buying their own homes there is inevitably tremendous variation in terms of the type, size, quality, location and value of dwellings in this part of the housing system; this is not a 'one size fits all' sector. Owner occupation is markedly more diverse than the other main tenure categories, embracing most of the oldest houses in the country, as well as the majority of those built since 1919; in contrast to social renting, virtually all of which was built or converted for low income households, the range of dwellings within owner occupation runs from the very smallest and humblest to the largest and grandest. Local authority housing, on the other hand, is much more uniform, almost all of it having been purpose built in the period 1919–79 (the majority after 1945), and 40 per cent of housing association dwellings have been built since 1980 (although this sector includes a significant proportion of acquired older properties, and its composition is changing because of the transfer of former council houses: ODPM, 2001: 19). Owner occupation is also socially diverse, including not only very high proportions of the better off sections of the population but also significant numbers of lower income groups – by the late 1990s a majority of households in the lowest income decile (the poorest 10 per cent) were home owners (Ford, Burrows and Nettleton, 2001: 44) and in 2001 some 61 per cent of workers whose jobs were classified as semi-routine or routine were home owners (Council of Mortgage Lenders, 2004: 43; P. Williams, 2003: 32). This social diversity is reflected in house values, with the most expensive houses changing hands at more than a thousand times the prices of the cheapest. These sorts of price differences are influenced by both the size and quality of dwellings and their location, with large houses in sought-after parts of central London commanding a substantial premium.

House prices, and affordability, vary considerably across the country, reflecting differences in economic activity. London prices have always been the highest in the country, and, as a rule, the further from London the lower the average price: in 2002 the Greater London average was more than two and a half times the average in the north of England and in Scotland (Wilcox, 2003b: 133). These averages are important indicators but it must be remembered that behind them lies wide variation within regions, and the figures can be misleading because of the different mixes of houses in the samples used to compile the averages. One attempt to look at affordability using comparable samples of dwellings has suggested that in the latter part of 2002 half of all households in England in the age range 20–39 could not afford to buy a house, even one at the lowest quartile price (Wilcox, 2003a). Fortunately, many of these households had already bought, thereby highlighting the need for care in relation to conclusions drawn from evidence for a particular point in time. Wilcox based his calculations on specific assumptions: he looked at the proportions of working households in the age range 20–39 who could not afford to buy a 4/5 room house at the lower quartile price with a 95 per cent mortgage and a loan to income ratio of 3 to 1. But of course, affordability is a subjective judgement, and some people will, under certain circumstances, happily borrow more than three times their income, while others would feel stretched at that level of debt. It often depends on what other demands the household income has to bear, how long a given level of debt charge will have to be borne and perceptions of value for money.

One result of the popularity of owner occupation among both consumers and governments has been the introduction of various schemes to facilitate access to the sector among people whose incomes prevent them from paying the full market price. These low cost home ownership schemes include the secure tenants' right to buy, shared ownership (where the occupier pays a mortgage on part of the house and rent on the rest) and equity loans schemes that allow purchasers to limit their mortgage costs to 75 per cent of the purchase price (Bennett, 2002). In volume terms low cost home ownership schemes have made very little impact, but in political terms they create an impression of policy action while imposing little cost on government funds (Boleat, 1997: 58).

The growing risks of owner occupation

For much of the period since 1945 owner occupation was, and was seen as, a secure and virtually risk-free investment: 'Since the early 1940s, the trend in house prices has been steadily upward, with two exceptions – the first half of the 1950s and the beginning of the 1990s. Adjusted for general inflation, house prices rose fourfold between 1943 and 1994, at an average annual rate of 2.7%' (Cutler, 1995). Owning a house was associated with security of tenure, wealth accumulation and freedom of choice in relation to key decisions about buying and selling and investment in repairs and improvements. More recent experience, especially in the housing market slump of the early 1990s, has shown that these benefits are contingent rather than intrinsic. In certain circumstances all of these alleged benefits can flip over to become problems. Security is dependent on having continued ability to meet mortgage costs; freedom to move is dependent upon finding a buyer willing to pay an acceptable price and finding an affordable place to move to. Freedom to improve the property can become a burden of responsibility for unaffordable repairs, and wealth accumulation can melt away in a falling market. These are the main risks of owner occupation, which need to be set alongside the notion of choice. Every time a choice is exercised in a market there is an accompanying risk.

This section considers four main causes of increased risk in the owner occupied sector in Britain: instability in the housing market, the dismantling of the various forms of financial support previously available to home owners, changes in the labour market and the arrival of an era of low inflation and rising levels of personal debt. These indicators are considered in turn, but their full impact is enhanced by the ways in which they act together.

Market instability

Whereas the previous section discussed dynamism in the owner occupied sector in terms of changes over a long period, it is now necessary to point to shorter term fluctuations in market activity. Over the period since the early 1970s the British housing market has experienced three boom–slump cycles (Bramley, Munro and Pawson, 2004; Hamnett, 1999), and it appears that instability has become a permanent feature of the market. Housing market booms seem to start with escalating prices in London, spreading out across the country over a year or two (this was the case in the 1980s boom, and appears to be true of the price spiral of the early 2000s). In the boom phase of the market cycle house prices tend to rise faster than earnings and prices generally, which has the peculiar dual effect of making owner occupation less affordable while simultaneously increasing demand. Aspiring purchasers feel they must buy now before prices move beyond their reach, and the more people who think this way the more demand rises and prices are further inflated. In these circumstances the housing market becomes a newsworthy topic, with prominent media coverage of the gains being made by existing owners and stories of outrageous prices being both demanded and paid (Hamnett, 1999: chs 1 and 2), and of course, the more the media cover stories of this kind the more frenzied is the public response.

Price spirals of this kind squeeze out some potential purchasers, but others are drawn into the market earlier than they might have been by the promise of financial gains and the knowledge that to delay is to risk prolonged exclusion from the advantages of ownership. There is evidence to show that during booms mortgage lenders are inclined to lend higher multiples of income. This can be defended as a response to competitive market pressures but its effect is to stoke up the rate of price increases. The long run ratio of average house prices to average earnings is about 3.5:1, but during boom periods it increases to 5:1 or more. Once prices move to an unsustainable relationship with earnings then the market is in danger of tipping over into slump, a phase during which the reasons that drove the boom operate in reverse: falling prices become self-propelling as purchasers hold off in expectation of better deals in future.

How does instability increase risk? Boom–slump cycles do not affect everyone in the same way or to the same degree. The numbers of people affected and the extent to which they are damaged (financially and psychologically) are empirical questions, which need to be related to particular historical events. Boom–slump cycles vary in severity and their impact is influenced by what is happening at the same time. The cycle of boom and slump in the late 1980s and early 1990s was the most severe in living memory and remains the benchmark for current debate, but the impact of that cycle would not have been as great had it not been for the effect of financial deregulation on the upswing, and of the economic recession on the downswing. In principle, though, the scale and intensity of risk need to be distinguished from the actuality – not everyone who is at risk of losing their home does so, although this is not to diminish the real stress experienced by people who are aware of their insecurity.

During the upswing the people at risk are would-be purchasers, especially first time buyers, who face risks whether they decide to buy or to delay. In a rising market the primary problem is access; existing owners simply ride the wave, their ability to buy at inflated prices underpinned by the rising prices of their own houses. In these circumstances, first time buyers may feel that they must jump on board the fast moving housing market or risk being left behind. They see the contrast between their position, where savings cannot keep up with house prices, and that of existing owners, for whom rising prices are a boon, not a threat. First time buyers who decide to take the chance may be tempted or pressurized into borrowing more than they can comfortably afford, leading to repayments that are unsustainable in the long term. The temptation is increased where buyers perceive that by borrowing just that little bit more they can secure a house with locational advantages that will reduce the risk of future losses. When prices are rising strongly there is also the risk of buyers being gazumped, when an offer to buy has been accepted and then, after costs have been incurred, another buyer makes a higher offer, which the seller is tempted to accept. This can be very frustrating and expensive for purchasers who lose the houses they thought they were buying. For a report of empirical research on consumer behaviour during both boom and slump phases see Munro (2000).

It is during the downswing phase that most risk is concentrated, the crucial factors determining exposure to risk being the debt–equity ratio and the need to sell. Existing owners with low debt–equity ratios are effectively immune from the risk of losing their home or of finding that the size of their mortgage exceeds the value of their house. The higher the proportion of debt to equity then the greater the risk that falling prices will lead to negative equity (i.e., where the home is worth less than the mortgage), but not all of those in this situation will be at risk of losing their home. Owners with negative equity who do not need to sell during a downswing may not be seriously affected. It is recent buyers, especially those who bought with high percentage loans at the very peak of the market and who then need to sell at an early date, who are more likely to be at risk of negative equity. This is a very particular group of people, a sub-set of the much larger group experiencing negative equity – in the early 1990s slump the total number was said to exceed 1.5 million (Dorling and Cornford, 1995; Hamnett, 1999: 5).

For the majority negative equity was gradually eliminated as prices recovered. But the evidence from the early 1990s graphically demonstrates the damage inflicted by the combination of house prices falling in cash as well as real terms at a time of high and rising unemployment. Whereas in previous housing market slumps inflation had prevented prices from falling in cash terms, the crisis of negative equity in the 1990s was made worse by falling inflation. The volume of transactions at high prices in the late 1980s meant that there were large numbers of people with very high debt–equity ratios, and these were the people who lost their homes in record numbers as unemployment robbed them of the ability to sustain mortgage repayments and the falling market made it virtually impossible to sell their homes. Mortgage arrears and possessions (i.e., where the lender takes possession of the dwelling) had been rising during the previous couple of decades, but broadly in line with the growing number of mortgaged home owners. Suddenly possessions rose from under 16,000 in 1989 to nearly 44,000 in 1990 before reaching a peak at 75,500 in 1991; arrears peaked in 1992, when more than 350,000 borrowers were more than six payments behind (this should be compared with the figure of 53,000 in 1988: Ford, Burrows and Nettleton, 2001: 23).

Policy changes

However, dramatic as they were, the events of the early 1990s should not obscure the underlying trend towards greater insecurity in the housing market. As mentioned above, policy support for owner occupation is almost as old as the welfare state, but one of the most remarkable aspects of policy towards it over the last thirty years or so is the way in which successive British governments have maintained a stream of rhetorical encouragement while pursuing policies that have made buying a house a much riskier undertaking. They have gradually stripped away a series of supports, the first of which to be abandoned, in 1975, was the long established policy of full employment. Full employment was immensely important to the growth of owner occupation and its abandonment at the very time that increasing numbers of working-class households – the ones most at risk of unemployment – were taking out mortgages was a blow to their aspirations and security. Next came financial deregulation in the mid-1980s, which, as mentioned above, made it easier to borrow but at the price of higher interest rates. Deregulation also opened up the market for low cost endowment mortgages, whereby borrowers paid interest on the full amount of their mortgage for the whole of the loan period, in the expectation that with-profits life assurance policies maturing at that point would cover the full repayment of the loan. These mortgages became hugely popular, accounting for 84 per cent of new loans in 1988, but doubts about their ability to deliver anticipated returns have seriously eroded the market, which was down to 13 per cent by 2000 (J. Smith, 2001). However, they have turned out to be a risky gamble, and in 2004 it was estimated that 80 per cent of the remaining 8.5 million endowment mortgages would not meet their target of repaying the full loan (Treasury Select Committee, 2004).

Cuts in entitlement to income support for unemployed mortgaged home owners weakened the social security safety net and shifted the burden of responsibility onto individuals. From 1986 unemployed mortgagors were restricted to help with only half of their interest payments (repayments of principal had never been covered), and the ceiling on eligible mortgages was reduced. Income support for mortgage interest (ISMI) was later, in 1995, removed altogether for existing borrowers during the first eight weeks of unemployment, and restricted to half for the next eighteen weeks. At the same time the rules were tightened for new borrowers, denying them assistance for the first thirty-nine weeks of any claim (Ford, Burrows and Nettleton, 2001: 84). The cost of ISMI was on an ascending curve when the first restrictions were introduced, having risen by a factor of five since 1980. The restrictions failed to quell further substantial increases in the housing market crisis of the early 1990s, and by 1993 more than half a million households were relying on Income Support to cover their mortgage interest charges (Holmans, 1997: 180), when the cost peaked at over £1,200 million (Wilcox, 2003b: 201). However, the cost to the Treasury was actually falling, because of market recovery, before the 1995 restrictions.

These changes in the social security safety net for mortgaged home owners were accompanied by government exhortation to borrowers to protect themselves through private insurance. This was a classic example of the privatization of risk, shifting responsibility and financial costs from the state to individuals. But it is in the nature of private insurance that the very people most likely to need to make a claim are the least likely to be in a position to afford to meet the cost of the premiums. Take-up of private insurance to cover mortgage costs remains low, at only 31 per cent in 2001 (J. Smith, 2002), and as Ford, Burrows and Nettleton (2001: 106) have pointed out, 'the available evidence indicates that neither public nor private safety net provision is satisfactory'.

The phasing out of mortgage interest tax relief (MITR) is simpler to explain but rather more complicated to assess. Before 1974 relief was available on the full amount of mortgage interest at the tax-payer's marginal rate, but from then until 1983 MITR was restricted to the interest payable on the first £25,000 of eligible debt; the ceiling was then raised to £30,000. Higher rate tax-payers were given relief at that rate until 1991/92. Throughout this period, however, the £30,000 ceiling was maintained, with the result that the value of relief to individual purchasers fell steeply; when it was introduced the ceiling was more than twice the average mortgage for first time buyers, but rising house prices meant that by 1992 it was significantly less than the average amount borrowed by first time buyers. Over the next eight years MITR was gradually phased out, and was finally removed in April 2000.

Assessing the effects of MITR and its withdrawal is complex, because although in volume terms at its peak in 1990/91 it was costing the Treasury up to £7.7 billion (Wilcox, 2003b: 195), the distribution of the benefit of all this money is less clear cut. In a market where prices are freely determined between sellers and buyers it was arguable that the effect of tax relief was merely to allow prices to rise to a higher level than they would have reached in the absence of the relief. This is based on the view that in the long run prices reflect wage levels and that what is important to purchasers is how much a house at a given price is going to cost them in terms of weekly or monthly outgoings. To the extent that purchasers calculate the price they are prepared to pay for a house by reference to what it will cost them each week or month then tax relief simply enabled them to service a higher level of debt, and therefore pay higher prices, for a given level of regular expenditure. On this view tax relief was capitalized in the form of higher house prices and the beneficiaries, therefore, were not house buyers but sellers. One estimate suggests that MITR might have inflated house prices by 5 per cent (Council of Mortgage Leaders, 2004: 28).

However, there were occasions when tax relief was of considerable help to purchasers. In the late 1970s when interest rates rose to unprecedented levels tax relief really did provide relief from the full effect of the increased cost, absorbing 30 per cent of the increase, but later, in 1990, when interest rates again rose to even higher levels the restrictions on tax relief then in place meant that it provided much less protection (Holmans, 1997: 182). It should also be recognized that until 1990 MITR was available at the tax-payer's marginal rate, which meant that it was of much greater help to higher earners, and in this sense the cuts in the highest levels of income tax under the Conservative governments of the 1980s helped to make the system fairer.

In the context of diminishing financial support for owner occupiers, it is perhaps not surprising that governments have not introduced effective measures to help low income owners with housing costs. Nevertheless, the need for such measures has increased as the numbers of owners living on pensions and other forms of low income have risen. Burrows (2003: 1–2) has made the telling point that half of all poor people in Britain are home owners, but they receive only 8 per cent of the financial assistance distributed to low income households to assist with housing costs.

Changing labour markets

Labour market conditions, especially levels of remuneration and security of employment, have profound implications for the demand for, and sustainability of, owner occupied housing, which absorbs significant proportions of household income over prolonged periods (Allen and Hamnett, 1991). The importance of full employment for the growth of owner occupation in the postwar decades has been stressed above, and it is now necessary to recognize the implications of contemporary labour market trends. Britain has moved into a phase in which discussion of the labour market is dominated by notions of flexibility and insecurity, which, on the face of it, would be expected to have negative consequences for owner occupation:

> with respect to the last quarter of the [twentieth] century, a number of commentators have pointed to [a] major change in the structure of employment: the decline of the traditional full-time employment contract and its replacement by a variety of non-standard contracts. This development has often been seen as linked to a growing divergence

between a core workforce of relatively privileged full-time employees and a secondary workforce of those with sub-standard terms of employment. Those on non-standard contracts are thought to constitute a 'flexible workforce', which could be easily disposed of to help employers cope with the increased volatility of product market conditions in an increasingly competitive and global economic environment. (Gallie, 2000: 295–6)

The key features of the contemporary labour market include the growth of part-time employment, self-employment and temporary work. Although a majority of women now have paid employment, growth in the period 1971–97 was mainly due to part-time jobs. In relation to self-employment and temporary employment the importance of the changes should not be over-emphasized: by 1998 only 12.1 per cent of people were self-employed and only 7.1 per cent were temporary employees (Gallie, 2000: 296–300). However, in an analysis examining the links between changing labour markets and housing Ford *et al.* (2001: ch. 3) make the point that the trends are upwards and that self-employment and temporary employment are seen as less secure. They refer to the tendency for re-employment after a spell of unemployment to be at lower pay and also note the growth in the numbers of low paid jobs. Their interpretation of the evidence suggests an increasingly insecure labour market in which people are required to move jobs more often and to cope with periods of unemployment. They also point to the increased risks, especially for mortgaged home owners, in this context. These include the risk of not only falling into arrears with mortgage repayments but also finding that home ownership is not sustainable in the longer run. In addition it is arguable that insecurity and flexibility will exclude and deter some people from entering owner occupation in the first place.

There are two caveats to be entered in relation to the position taken by Ford *et al.* First, although their work is consistent with a widespread view about the changing nature of employment in contemporary globalized capitalism, this is contested territory (Doogan, 2001; Elliott and Atkinson, 1998; Heery and Salmon, 2000). Terms such as insecurity are used differently by different people. Nevertheless, there is evidence that more people report *feeling* insecure at work (OECD, 1997, quoted in Heery and Salmon, 2000: 39). Whether the underlying evidence supports this perception is debated, but the reasons why people might feel insecure are clear enough. During the 1980s, not only was unemployment very high for some years but also there were structural changes in the economy which had knock-on effects on the labour market. Large numbers of men lost their jobs in manufacturing industries and coal mining, and some never worked again. This was associated with a fall in male participation rates in the labour force in the latter years of the twentieth century, and a marked rise in the numbers claiming long term sick and disability benefits (Lindsay, 2003). Also in the 1980s a succession of legislative measures sought to weaken the position of the trade unions, to deregulate the labour market and to reduce the protection formerly available to workers. Then the early 1990s economic recession was perceived to have affected a wider range of workers, including those in jobs and industries (such as financial services) not previously regarded as being at high risk of unemployment. At the same time there has been more public debate about the notion of globalization, with, on the one hand, some high profile examples of employers relocating their activities to countries with lower labour costs, while, on the other hand, ministers have talked up the need for workers to be flexible and to recognize that there are no longer any 'jobs for life'. As Taylor-Gooby (2000: 6–7) has pointed out there seems to be an explosion of concern about risk, and fear of unemployment exceeds the real risk. Perception is the basis of decision making, and so it might be expected that people would adjust their housing market behaviour to reflect their understanding of the risks. This might lead to later entry to owner occupation and more cautious borrowing.

The second caveat concerns the housing market itself and the timing of research. Ford *et al.* based much of their analysis on evidence from the first half of the 1990s, when the economy and the housing market were in poor shape. An analysis based on housing and labour market conditions in the early 2000s would lead to less pessimistic conclusions. The insecurity thesis and the apparently widespread public perception of insecurity are not reflected in the continuing popularity of home ownership and levels of housing market activity, or in the doubling of house prices over the period 1997–2003 (Vass, 2003).

The impact of low inflation

From the point of view of home owners, the arrival of an era of low inflation has removed an important cushion, because although nominal interest rates are much lower than in the high inflationary years, low inflation means that the burden of debt repayment remains heavy for longer. Add to this the requirement to repay debts arising from higher education, and the need to save for old age, and young people contemplating buying a house face some difficult calculations. It can be shown that, on the assumption of a real interest rate of 3 per cent, inflation at 10 per cent implies a heavier mortgage costs burden on household income in the early years than would arise if inflation was only 2.5 per cent, but after year ten of a 25-year loan, mortgage costs absorb a higher proportion of income in the low inflation environment (Cutler, 2002). Moreover, low inflation also means that the debt to value ratio erodes more slowly, and therefore owners accumulate equity more slowly. Boleat (1997: 59–60) has admitted that:

> It was inflation that largely took the risk out of house purchase ... In retrospect, there is little denying that for much of the 1970s and 1980s, the real security on which mortgage lenders lent, on which insurers relied, and on which valuers also relied, was inflation rather than any implicit value of bricks and mortar as an investment.

In the present period not only is there low inflation but also a higher proportion of home owners are exposed to the risks of debt. First, in relation to debt secured against property, one estimate (quoted by Hamnett, 1999: 56) suggests that in 1947 only 15 per cent of home owners had mortgages; over the years the proportion has risen to 57 per cent by 2001 (Holmans, 1997: 178; Wilcox, 2003b: 44) suggests that the proportion was just over 60 per cent in England and Wales in 1994). As mentioned above, the active and competitive mortgage market in recent years has encouraged borrowers to shop around, to remortgage on a regular basis and to increase their debt and to release some of their equity (J. Smith, 2001, 2003). As a result the total amount of debt secured against dwellings increased by about a quarter in the five years up to 2003 (Hamilton, 2003). Low inflation and low interest rates are said to make owner occupation more affordable than in the past, and this is true in the sense that existing owners have seen debt charges fall substantially since the early 1990s, and new borrowers pay less for a given level of debt than they would have had to pay in the past. However, it is necessary to compare the very different positions of existing and new purchasers. In practice low interest rates tend to fuel the rise in house prices, to the considerable benefit of existing owners, but leaving purchasers no better off, and more exposed to the risk of rising interest rates (Vass, 2003). When mortgages can be obtained for 4 per cent, a rise of 2 percentage points would increase mortgage costs by 50 per cent for borrowers in the early years of a repayment mortgage. This needs to be seen in the context of increasing numbers of people who are already heavily committed: there has been a doubling in two years in the numbers of people spending more than a quarter of their income on mortgage costs (Vass, 2003).

Second, in relation to unsecured debt, the evidence suggests that debt to income ratios rose significantly between 1995 and 2000 at all points on the income distribution, and by most for households with the highest ratios (generally those with the lowest incomes). Among the lowest income households unsecured debt to income ratios more than doubled in this period, although the proportions of households reporting their unsecured debts as a 'heavy burden' or 'somewhat of a burden' were broadly stable at around 11 per cent and 30 per cent respectively (Cox, Whitely and Brierley, 2002). In general, for home owners household debt is underpinned by property values, and the growth in indebtedness can be seen as fuelled by perceptions of rapidly rising house prices. Heavily indebted households could be vulnerable in the event of a major correction in the housing market and/or rising unemployment.

Finally in this section, it is necessary to draw a distinction between the degree of risk in the system and the numbers of people likely to be at risk. This is a reference to the idea that not only has owner occupation become riskier for the reasons just discussed, but there are now more low income home owners than ever before. The maturation of the sector means that there are more elderly home owners, and, as previously mentioned, the expansion of the market has drawn in increasing numbers of people in jobs that are vulnerable to rising unemployment and industrial restructuring. In 1993 29 per cent of home owners had no earned income (Holmans, 1997: 180), and, as noted above, in the early 2000s half of all poor households are home owners. And this points to the observation that the risks, and benefits, of home ownership are unevenly distributed.

Owner occupation and inequality

Although owner occupation is associated with a wider spread of wealth, it should also be seen as an engine of inequality, not only reflecting but amplifying inequalities generated in the labour market and elsewhere. There can be no doubt that, by redistributing the ownership of domestic property from the few to the many, the growth of owner occupation has enabled a large proportion of the population to acquire valuable capital assets and to accumulate wealth on a scale not previously contemplated. However, within the owner occupier market there is very wide variation in the amounts of wealth accumulated by owners in different circumstances. And in an era when owner occupation is not only the main source of wealth accumulation for the majority of people but also a key factor in determining access to credit and locational advantage (in relation to spatially distributed scarce urban resources), to be excluded from that market is more disadvantaging today than at any time in the past.

Owner occupation is a system for rewarding people who are generally better off in the first place. For a large majority of people, access to owner occupation is income related (very few can buy their first house outright, and therefore buying is dependent on ability to raise a mortgage and to sustain regular repayments). This means that many low income households are excluded from the benefits (and risks) of owning, although, as already mentioned, it does not mean that there are no poor home owners – people can become poor after buying their home, and outright owners have average incomes well below those of mortgaged owners, reflecting the generally lower incomes of elderly people. On average, purchasing owners (as distinct from outright owners) have incomes more than three times the average of council tenants (Wilcox, 2003b: 121). While wealth accumulation cannot be guaranteed to home owners, there is a high probability of gains over time, but for non-owners there is the certainty that they will not benefit from increasing property prices. In fact not only do tenants not benefit from higher valuations, they tend to face increases in rents as a consequence. Thus their different relationship to changes in property prices tends to widen the differences between owners and tenants, accentuating pre-existing income differences. This could be addressed through the tax system, but the exclusion of the principal home from liability for capital gains tax and the high (and regularly raised) threshold for inheritance tax signal that equity, fairness and tenure neutrality are less important to governments than encouragement of owner occupation.

To the extent that access to owner occupation is dependent upon income then it is interesting to speculate on the implications of the increased numbers of women in the labour force. In the early years of the twentieth century women constituted 29 per cent of the total work force, and the demands of child care tended to mean that it was difficult for married women to remain in paid work, but by 2000 around 53 per cent of women over the age of 16 were in employment, and women made up 46 per cent of all workers (Lindsay, 2003). There are two aspects to consider: first, the continued tendency for women's incomes to be lower than men's suggests that the housing market would reflect this form of inequality in the sense that households dependent on women's earnings would, on the whole, be disadvantaged compared to households with male earnings; second, however, the rising curve of female employment implies a growth of two-earner households, which in turn suggests that these would have an advantage over one-earner households, whether male or female. In principle it would seem plausible to argue that two-earner households, with enhanced purchasing power, would tend to lift house prices, and that this would produce a situation in which two incomes became necessary. Thus one-income households would become a relatively disadvantaged group; clearly this cannot be any more than a tendency because there are single-earner households with incomes above those achieved in others where there are two earners. However, it does suggest that the possession of two incomes is likely to be more important for the sustainability of owner occupation among low income households, and that, as a direct consequence, family break-up is more likely to have an adverse impact on women in such households (Early and Mulholland, 1995). The general point here, though, is that to the extent that the market adjusts to the increased spending power of two-earner households then single earners are disadvantaged, and single earners who are women are, on the whole, more likely to be disadvantaged to a greater degree.

One of the alleged benefits of the market is that it gives consumers choice but, as the previous paragraph has indicated, choice is not evenly distributed; the main constraint is purchasing power (in the case of housing this is usually a combination of down payment and access to credit). As in any market, those with the greatest purchasing power have the widest choice, and effectively monopolize the most desirable houses commanding the highest prices. The majority of first time buyers seek loans covering a high proportion of purchase price, which means that income is the key determinant of the level at which they enter the market. In some circumstances down payments can be crucial, as will be discussed below. During the 1990s average advances to first time buyers ran at 84.3 per cent of the purchase price (Wilcox, 2003b: 127), and it is interesting to note that as the housing market recovered and prices rose after 1996 the average percentage advance fell, implying that additional down payments were necessary to make housing affordable, and/or that rising prices squeezed some people – those on lower incomes who required high percentage loans – out of the market altogether. There is evidence to suggest that both of these effects have been at work in London in recent years; median deposits placed by first time buyers increased threefold, to £17,000, between 1997 and 2001, and median earnings of first time buyers increased by more than two-thirds in the same period, much more than earnings generally (Office of the Deputy Prime Minister, or ODPM, 2002).

The main point to be made here is that inequalities in incomes tend to be mapped onto the housing market, with the better off in the highest priced houses in the most desirable locations, and low income marginal purchasers having to make do with the meanest and least well located dwellings (hence the popular notion of climbing the 'housing ladder' as income rises and wealth accumulates). Widening income inequalities since the late 1970s, fuelled by tax cuts for the rich in the 1980s, promoted greater price variation, with implications for mobility and wealth accumulation. The definition and measurement of the gains made by owner occupiers has been energetically debated in the housing literature (Duncan, 1990; Forrest, Murie and Williams, 1990; Hamnett, 1999; Saunders, 1990; Saunders and Harris, 1988), and there is no need to do more here than acknowledge that there are different ways of approaching the problem. While there can be no certainties in this area, it is nevertheless clear that the experience of home owners in the British housing market since 1945 has been that house prices have tended to rise, and although it is possible to identify periods when prices were falling in real terms, in the longer run houses have proved to be a very good form of investment. In general it can be said that people buying high priced houses are likely to make larger capital gains in absolute terms. However, the picture is complicated by time, geography and social class. A study of home owners in the south east of England in 1993 by Hamnett (1999: ch. 4) reports evidence to support the idea that higher socio-economic groups buy more expensive houses and make higher absolute gains, but that this is partly due to greater mobility – gains reflect the number of moves and the tendency to trade up each time. Hamnett (1999: 100) concludes that:

> Measured over their entire housing career ... professional and managerial owners gained almost twice as much in absolute terms as manual groups, which reflects the more expensive property they are able to buy ... In the long run, professionals and managers gain more than other groups in both absolute and percentage terms ... Class and income strongly influence gains for comparable cohorts of buyers, but over the long term date of purchase is the most important determinant of absolute gains. An unskilled worker who bought in the 1960s or 1970s will, almost inevitably, have a larger gain than a professional or managerial owner who bought in the last few years but, when length of time in the housing market is held constant, social class reasserts its importance.

Hamnett's evidence related to the south east, and it is important to acknowledge the wide variations in prices around the country (Bramley, Munro and Pawson, 2004: ch. 3). In 2002 the average house price in the UK was £128,634, but in Greater London it was £206,839, and in Yorkshire and Humberside only £88,041. Thus the Yorkshire and Humberside average was only 42.5 per cent of the London average, and the gap has grown wider over the years. In 1969 the Yorkshire and Humberside average was 55 per cent of the London average. A person who bought a house in Bradford or Leeds in 1969 at the regional average price of £3,436 would have accumulated £84,605 by 2002, whereas a similar buyer in London would have gained just over £200,000 in the same time (Building Societies Association, 1979; Wilcox, 2003b). Some consolation can be drawn from the fact that house prices vary more than incomes on a regional basis, making owner occupation more affordable in the north.

In addition to regional price differences there is also evidence of variation in relative price levels over time in local housing markets. A factor that seems to be of increasing significance in this context is the relationship between house prices and school catchment areas, although research evidence is thin. Butler and Robson (2003: 5) report that estate agents in London are increasingly marketing houses on the basis of their school catchment area, arguing that this is a reflection of the introduction of parental choice and the publication of school league tables. Being in the right catchment area can add tens of thousands of pounds to the value of a house. Education is just one of the geographically distributed resources influencing prices in the housing market, and, of course, it is safe to assume that the better off use their superior purchasing power to maximize access to these benefits and privileges.

Another form of inter-generational assistance is, of course, inheritance, although there is little reliable evidence on the extent of inherited housing wealth or its impact on housing market activity (Hamnett, 1991; Hamnett and Seavers, 1996). It has been suggested that the avalanche of inherited housing wealth that was being forecast in the 1980s has not arrived, possibly because of equity withdrawal before death and increased demands arising from the costs of nursing and residential care in old age (Bramley, Munro and Pawson, 2004). Nevertheless, it is clear that only the descendants of owner occupiers stand to benefit from inherited housing wealth, and that houses represent such a significant proportion of personal wealth, even though individual dwellings vary widely in value, that at some level owner occupation must have an impact on inequality through inheritance. Taxation could be used as a way of tackling this aspect of the amplification of inequality, but with the threshold for inheritance tax at about twice the average house value, most estates escape the tax net altogether.

Conclusion

As Munro (2000: 150) has pointed out, it would be difficult to argue that the modern privatized, market based, housing system has been forced upon a reluctant population. Despite the shock of recession, falling house prices and mass eviction in the early 1990s owner occupation is still the tenure of choice for the majority. It remains popular, especially in comparison with other tenure options. However, as this chapter has shown, owner occupation in the modern era is associated with risk and inequality. These are complex, having geographical, temporal, generational, class and gender dimensions, but they tend to work in ways that imply least risk and most gain for people already benefiting from advantageous labour market positions (either their own or those of earlier generations of their families). So although most people most of the time probably feel that they are benefiting from the housing market, it is clear that as a method of distribution and redistribution the market is the antithesis of the egalitarianism and collectivism of the postwar welfare state. As such the owner occupier market and its popularity with governments and voters indicates the distance travelled since those days more than half a century ago.

Chapter 9

Social Change, Social Exclusion and Social Housing

It was argued in Chapter 1 that a distinctive feature of local authority housing in Britain for much of the twentieth century was that it was neither universal nor wholly residual. However, the flip side of a large and expanding owner occupier market is a smaller and different social rented sector, and over the last thirty years a process of chronic residualization has set in as two protracted restructuring processes, affecting both the housing market and the welfare state, have worked together to turn social housing into a tenure increasingly occupied by the least well off. Underlying this chapter is the idea that whereas after 1945 the welfare state was largely oriented towards nuclear families consisting of one (usually male) wage earner and dependent women and children, a new social settlement acknowledges a far wider range of households and different patterns of dependency. This is reflected in changes in the housing system, which, to a greater extent than some other, more solidly established core areas of the welfare state, exhibits the implications of confining public services to certain low income sections of the population. The employed working class, previously constituting the majority of tenants in social renting, have to a large extent transferred into owner occupation. At the same time, a range of households that were virtually invisible to the postwar welfare state (unemployed, single people, lone parents, elderly people, people with disabilities and members of minority ethnic communities) have become much more numerous in social renting as a whole. As a result, social housing now plays a quite different role in the overall housing system: from being associated with affluence and privilege it has become a tenure linked to poverty and social exclusion. To put it another way, social housing has moved from working class to non-working class (Forrest and Murie, 1988: 67).

The reason that this is important is because of the policy responses that are evoked by different distributions of population by tenure. It has been argued in earlier chapters that housing policy throughout the twentieth century gave greater priority to meeting the needs and demands of the employed population, in particular the skilled working class rather than the poor and unemployed. The emphasis shifted over time from public to private (owner occupied) provision but at all times the needs of the better off were the main consideration. The less well off remained for decades in the declining private rented sector, only gradually moving into public housing as private renting became more scarce and as the better off moved out into owner occupation. Now, for the first time people outside the active labour force, on very low incomes, form the majority in social renting, a development that raises interesting policy questions about how governments respond to situations where the people directly affected generally have little political or economic power.

Poverty and social exclusion

Earlier chapters have made repeated reference to residualization, and to warnings from academic commentators in particular that social rented housing in Britain was moving in this direction. Since the 1990s, however, debate about social housing has become increasingly enmeshed with a new discourse, around the notion of social exclusion. It is, therefore, necessary to be clear about the meaning of social exclusion and how it relates to the idea of residualization. Distinguishing between the two is important, not least in relation to understanding current policy: to tackle one is not necessarily to tackle the other, as will be discussed in a later section.

The residualization of social housing is a process of change in terms of who lives in the sector and what it does in the wider housing system. Social exclusion, however, is a broader concept which is crucial to understanding the modern welfare state, and in particular the residualized role of social renting. It is a difficult, slippery and contested concept, which is, according to Atkinson (2000: 1,039), subject to as many theories as there are theorists – and there is now a considerable literature to choose from (Anderson and Sim, 2000; Byrne, 1999; Griffiths and Stewart, 1998; *Housing Studies*, November 1998; Jordan, 1996; Levitas, 1998; Madanipour, Cars and Allen, 1998; Room, 1990, 1991, 1995). It is generally understood to have come to prominence in Britain only in the 1990s, having originated within mainland Europe, specifically in France in the 1970s (Atkinson, 2000: 1,039). Although social exclusion has been defined in a variety of ways, there is general agreement that it means more than poverty, referring not just to spending power but also to the quality of relationships between citizens and the societies in which they live. It also implies a process, something that is done to people, rather than a static condition; as such it is to be preferred to the idea of the underclass (McNicol, 1987; Murray, 1990). In a widely read and appreciated account Ruth Levitas (1998) takes the underclass as one of three discourses through which to explore social exclusion, the others being redistributionist and social integrationist approaches.

Byrne (1999: 2) takes a different line, emphasizing the multi-dimensional nature of exclusion, and the significance of spatial separation in urban areas. The idea of divided cities was discussed 160 years ago by Engels (1844) but retains considerable currency among contemporary scholars (Buck *et al.*, 2002; Fainstein, Gordon and Harloe, 1992; Hamnett, 2003; Pacione, 1997), and no account of housing in Britain can afford to ignore the implications of spatial differences.

A key question invited by the very notion of social exclusion is, 'exclusion from what?' (although it has been argued – Castel, 1995, quoted in Marsh and Mullins, 1998: 754 – that it is not necessary to provide an answer). Somerville (1998: 761–2) suggests that the question is commonly answered in terms of exclusion from the labour market and denial of citizenship rights. However, Byrne (1999: 2) endorses the definition put forward by Madanipour, Cars and Allen (1998), which is couched in terms of exclusion from participation in decision making and political processes, access to employment and material resources and integration into common cultural practices. This comes close to the idea that social exclusion is about being 'cut off from the mainstream' (Lee, 1998: 57). Unfortunately, there are problems with defining exclusion in relation to the labour market, citizenship and the mainstream. A focus on labour markets can be seen as too narrow and simplistic, inviting a binary (in or out) view of a much more complicated phenomenon – some workers are in secure, well paid employment, while others are insecure, low paid and often in and out of work. And how do we account for unpaid domestic and caring work, much of it done by women? Citizenship is itself a contested concept, which needs to be understood in relation to particular geographical and temporal contexts. And the notion of the mainstream, while useful and appealing, demands specification: if social exclusion is about more than poverty then the mainstream must be defined in terms other than spending power (if not then it is scarcely different from the notion of relative poverty developed by Townsend, 1979; Mack and Lansley, 1985; and Gordon and Pantazis 1995). The idea of a mainstream connects to the argument that there is a new social settlement that is more broadly based and no longer exclusively white and heterosexual. The social mainstream needs to be defined in inclusive terms, accommodating difference, and not implying sameness. But there remains room for argument about whether members of some groups (for example, Hell's Angels or fox hunters) are mainstream.

The conventional starting point for discussion of citizenship, in Britain at least, is the work of T. H. Marshall (1950). This is also a useful starting point in the context of an interest in the welfare state, because Marshall saw the development of social rights, embodied in the postwar welfare state, as complementing the civil and political rights won in earlier periods, and thereby rounding out of the notion of citizenship. Advocates of the welfare state, such as Richard Titmuss, made much of the importance of the claim that the postwar welfare state extended to all citizens the right to use a range of key public services with 'no sense of inferiority, pauperism, shame or stigma ... no attribution that one was becoming a public burden'. In this way the welfare state was seen as a socially integrating device, and this idea has persisted into discussions of citizenship and social exclusion in the present period:

> We define social exclusion in relation first of all to social rights. We investigate what social rights a citizen has to employment, housing, health care, etc., how effectively national policies enable citizens to secure these rights and what other barriers [exist] which exclude people from these rights. (Room, 1991: 5)

Similarly, Berghman (1995) and A. Walker and C. Walker (1997) accept the idea that the social rights associated with the welfare state promote social integration, but there are grounds for questioning this assumption, not least because, as was argued in Chapter 1, generalizations about the welfare state are risky. It is simplistic to assume that the welfare state as a whole and in every branch has always and unproblematically promoted social solidarity and inclusion. It is necessary, first, to look at claims about the inclusiveness of the welfare state in the past, and second, to consider the dynamic nature of the concept of citizenship. Although social exclusion is discussed as a contemporary phenomenon, it can be identified in the postwar welfare state, a point that is implicit in the observation that the welfare state was constructed around white working families and that some groups of people were virtually invisible – either denied access altogether or subject to forms of provision that continued to be stigmatizing: this idea was captured in the titles of two books about the poverty of services for people with learning disabilities and elderly people in the 1960s: *Put Away* (P. Morris, 1969) and *Sans Everything* (Robb, 1967). It has been argued that the universalism of the postwar welfare state was deeply circumscribed and highly conditional (Langan and Clarke, 1993: 28). Some services were more circumscribed than others, and while family allowances, the NHS and education up to the school leaving age were open to all, other services, especially public housing and means-tested welfare benefits, were not. It can be argued that in the postwar period council housing played an integrative role, in relation to important fractions of the social and economic mainstream, providing good quality modern homes for the employed working class. But it is much more difficult to make the same case today. Social rented housing is no longer a mainstream tenure, and access to it is, in practice, confined to members of groups who were formerly largely excluded from it, as subsequent sections of this chapter will explore.

Meanwhile, those groups of skilled workers who were the majority of new tenants in the 1940s and 1950s have moved on to home ownership, and are, in effect, now excluded from social renting. While the growth of owner occupation is routinely referred to in terms of consumer preferences, it is also partly explicable in terms of the retreat of the state in this area of social provision, implying an obligation on those who can to house themselves, leaving the state to support those who cannot. Housing provides an example of the general point made by Dean (2004: 1), who observes that, 'policy makers of the so-called "third way" have been insisting, on the one hand, that we can have no rights without responsibilities, while implying, on the other, that we cannot be properly responsible if we allow ourselves to be dependent – and dependent on the state, especially'. This illustrates the idea of a new social settlement and draws attention to the dynamic nature of the concept of citizenship. The new social settlement recognizes a wider range of households and social groups, but it is not a straightforward matter of these groups being absorbed into the full range of services on equal terms with everyone else (the mainstream). Formerly excluded groups (including those described above as virtually invisible to the postwar welfare state) are now accommodated in social housing, but this does not signal social inclusion; on the contrary, it is a case of social exclusion continuing to be practised, but in a different way. Far from access to, and participation in, social housing being a measure of inclusion, as stated by Room, it is a reflection and reinforcement of pre-existing exclusion. This is implicit in the social reconstruction of social renting as a residual sector; the very term residual is reminiscent of the deliberately stigmatizing nineteenth-century Poor Law. As the better off, higher status groups have abandoned council housing, so it has been reconstituted as a site of social exclusion. In the new social settlement those formerly included through their status as council tenants have moved on, and demonstrate their citizenship in the new way, taking responsibility for meeting their accommodation needs through house purchase.

In the period since the 1980s there has been a drift towards seeing citizens as consumers, people with choices (Lee and Murie, 1997: 4), and this links to the New Labour emphasis on the virtues of work as the generator of the resources that empower people to make choices. Consumers are people with money in their pockets, and employment is the chief source of spending power; indeed, 'making work pay' has become a mantra of New Labour (the similarity of this slogan to the New Poor Law (of 1834) notion of less eligibility is chilling). For New Labour it seems that labour market activity, not access to public services, is the key badge of citizenship. The corollary is that non-involvement in the labour force is a cause of social exclusion. Although the government has defined social exclusion as, 'a shorthand term for what can happen when people or areas suffer from a combination of linked problems such as unemployment, poor skills, low income, unfair discrimination, poor housing, high crime, bad health and family breakdown' (Social Exclusion Unit, 2004: 4), the chief remedy is seen as moving people from benefit into work. The list of ills that comprise social exclusion is remarkably similar to the famous five giants identified by William Beveridge in 1942, but the prescription is decidedly different, focusing on the importance of the excluded changing their ways and joining the mainstream, and the most important route into the mainstream is by obtaining employment, although there are other behavioural pressures.

Levitas (1998) has chronicled New Labour's increasing commitment, in the period before the 1997 general election, to paid work as the salvation of the excluded. She quotes, for example, Tony Blair arguing that the new workless class must be brought back into society and into useful work; and Gordon Brown saying that 'the core value is work ... work and employment will be our first priority' (Levitas, 1998: 138–9). This approach has continued, with ministers still talking about the need to tackle the 'culture of worklessness' and arguing that the problem is not the lack of jobs but the 'poverty of aspiration' among the excluded (Browne, 2004). The focus seems to have shifted from the rights of citizens to the obligations on them, chiefly in the form of the obligation to work and then to consume. Bauman (1998: 90) goes so far as to define the poor in contemporary consumer society as 'flawed consumers':

> First and foremost, the poor of today are 'non-consumers', not 'unemployed'; they are defined in the first place through being flawed consumers, since the most crucial of social duties which they do not fulfil is that of being active and effective buyers of the goods and services the market offers.

In modern Britain shopping has become a civic duty; after all, it makes the money go round and creates opportunities for others to demonstrate their citizenship by working too. And in this context, buying a house is the biggest item of expenditure that anyone can make, and it is therefore the clearest demonstration of citizenship. This contrasts with the observation that, 'To many, social renting has become a symbol of failure in a consumer society – a tenure of last resort' (Taylor, 1998: 820). To the government's slogan of 'work for those who can, support for those who cannot' (Social Exclusion Unit, 2004: 9) can now be added another strapline for the times: home ownership for those who can, renting for those who cannot.

This discussion suggests that, in the case of housing at least, it is insufficient and unhelpful to define social exclusion as denial of social rights measured in terms of access to public services. Where the social mainstream has abandoned a service, and access to it is effectively confined to the least well off, workless and benefit dependent groups in society, then that service itself becomes a sign of social exclusion. The social exclusion debate takes us beyond poverty and beyond the observation that social housing has become a part of the housing system predominantly accommodating the least well off. It highlights the way in which the institutions of the welfare state can contribute to social exclusion, but it is important to note here that social housing is not the only, or the primary, cause of exclusion. Social exclusion is generated elsewhere, especially in the education system and the labour market, and people bring it with them when they become tenants of social landlords (routes into social housing tend to prioritize people who are already socially excluded by virtue of being outside the labour force, dependent on state benefits, long term sick, disabled or elderly).

This highlights both the multi-dimensional nature of the problem and the way in which social housing can reinforce social exclusion. First, as already mentioned, social housing has become identified with exclusion and is itself stigmatizing, a tangible sign of spoilt identity or less than full citizenship. Second, social housing acts as a means of congregating the excluded in what then become 'excluded places' (Skifter Anderson, 2002, 2003), thereby influencing their access to other spatially distributed resources. Such areas are often characterized by poorly performing public services (especially schools), lack of spending power (and therefore limited choice and competition in local shops) and poor public transport links to the local labour market. As Byrne (1999: 110) has argued, 'With income the rich are separate from the rest of us. With space it is the poor who are separated off. Indeed spatial exclusion is the most visible and evident form of exclusion.' Third, social rented housing not only denies tenants access to the wealth accumulation that is such a valued (if not guaranteed) quality of owner occupation, it also denies access to credit secured against the home, thereby further restricting consumption activity.

A final point to be made here concerns the need to avoid the impression that social exclusion is exclusive to social housing. Clearly it is not. One measure would be that in the 10 per cent most deprived wards in England, the majority (57 per cent) of people live in the private sector (ODPM, 2003: 57). There is a large and contested literature about the best ways to measure area deprivation, and about the effectiveness of area based initiatives in reaching people experiencing deprivation and exclusion. But one thing is clear: while a high proportion of the tenants of social rented housing experience social exclusion (to a greater or lesser extent), tenure based measures fail to reach a significant proportion of the excluded population (Lee and Murie, 1997: 53).

Social change and social housing

This section looks at the evidence underpinning some of the more general propositions discussed above. It is concerned to demonstrate two distinct processes, one social and demographic and the other housing. The changing social composition of the British population has been mapped onto the housing system in a particular way, with important implications for the role and character of, and prospects for, the social rented sector. Early discussions of the residualization of public housing (Forrest and Murie, 1988; Malpass, 1990) tended to concentrate on the housing process, looking at the way in which council housing was becoming a tenure for the least well off. Here, however, the objective is to link this to the wider process of social change, making the connection between what is happening in housing and the notion of a new social settlement.

Building on the discussion of social change in Chapter 2, there are several key dimensions to develop. The general theme is one of increasing diversity, moving away from the assumed model of the white nuclear family with one income and a number of dependent children. First, although the total population has increased over the last forty years, the number of separate households has increased at a faster rate (and is expected to continue to do so – projections suggest an increase of nearly a fifth between 1996 and 2021: DETR, 1999). This is largely due to 'an enormous growth in single person households at both ends of the age range – young people leaving home, and elderly people' (Coleman, 2000: 78). In 1961 some 42 per cent of households in England and Wales contained one or two people; by 1991 the figure had risen to 62 per cent. Over the same period there was a 50 per cent fall in the proportion of households with five or more people. By the mid-1990s households with dependent children were in a minority, constituting just under a third of all households. Second, however, there has been a considerable growth in the numbers of lone parent households with dependent children, up from 2 per cent in 1961 to 7 per cent of all households by 1996, at which time they amounted to no less than a quarter of all households with dependent children (Coleman, 2000: 79). This growth has been partly due to increased rates of divorce, but by 1992 more than a third of lone parents were never-married women.

Third, there has been a growth in the proportion of the population counted as economically inactive (which means that they are neither in paid employment nor seeking it). This category includes elderly and retired people, who account for a substantial proportion of its growth, and younger people not seeking employment because of caring responsibilities or because they are sick or disabled. In 1962 just under 17 per cent of households in England had no-one in employment, but by 1993 the proportion had more than doubled, to 39 per cent (Holmans, 1995b: 111). Admittedly this was a year of economic recession, and the figure for 1990 was significantly lower at 34 per cent, but even this was still twice the 1962 level. More recently the government has claimed that the rate of worklessness among working-age people has been on a falling trend since 1999 (ONS, 2004). Holmans (1995b) has shown that the increase in the proportion of non-working households is partly a demographic effect of the rising numbers of elderly people, and partly due to more elderly people living alone in retirement. Holmans (1995b: 112) also argues that the growth in the numbers of economically inactive households below retirement age is mainly due to the declining participation rates among men over 45 years of age rather than the rising numbers of lone parents. The falling level of employment among men in this age group is probably best explained in terms of the impact of recession and economic restructuring, especially in the early 1980s, when many manufacturing jobs were lost.

The final dimension to be considered concerns the growth in the numbers of households belonging to minority ethnic communities. This is difficult territory, about which it is dangerous to generalize and where there is plenty of room to contest definitions and to question the reliability of statistics. In their discussion of changes in immigration and ethnicity across the twentieth century Peach *et al.* (2000) distinguish between the earlier episodes of immigration by Irish, Jewish and Polish people from the later, post-1945, immigration from the Caribbean, the Indian sub-continent and Africa. These later arrivals, including people born in Britain to immigrant parents, amounted to around 3 million by 1991. The largest sub-group was people originally from India (over 800,000), followed by people from the Caribbean (half a million). Peach *et al.* make the point that immigration from the Caribbean and south Asia after 1945 was stimulated by the demand for labour in certain sectors of the British economy, specifically in relation to low paid jobs, and that migrant communities tended to congregate in inner urban neighbourhoods for the same reasons – lack of demand from white people. Over time the different minority communities developed in characteristic ways, in terms of factors including employment and housing tenure. For example, in the early 1990s black-Caribbean male unemployment was more than twice the rate experienced by white men, whereas Peach *et al.* (2000: 153) acknowledge the economic divergence within the Asian population but conclude that 'Indians have made one of the most successful adaptations to British economic life.'

These four factors – more small households (many of them consisting exclusively of elderly people or young people who have recently left the parental home), more single parents, more households with no income from employment and more people belonging to minority ethnic communities – have contributed to a dramatic re-shaping of British society, and to the emergence of new patterns of dependency to be addressed, in part at least, by public services. Of course, this is not to imply that everyone in these (overlapping) groups is in the same situation. Obviously, not all elderly people, single parents and members of minority communities are poor or socially excluded; but to be a member of one or more of these categories is to be at higher risk of poverty and exclusion.

Turning now to the way the population is mapped onto the housing system in the present period, the residualization of social housing can be understood as the outcome of three processes: the shrinkage of the total supply, together with the (linked) departure of the better off and higher socio-economic groups, and the tendency for those left behind and new entrants to be less well off and in lower socio-economic groups. In addition, there are the policies that have helped to promote these processes. In some respects the policies of the last twenty-five years have been perverse: the number of social rented sector dwellings available for rent by people on low incomes has fallen while the numbers of economically inactive people have increased. The contrast with fifty years ago is stark: then local authorities were the main suppliers of new houses and new entrants were overwhelmingly people with relatively good earnings; now the sector as a whole has shrunk by 30 per cent since 1981 and is still in decline, and most new tenants have no earned income.

The great expansion of council housing after the Second World War overwhelmingly benefited white families with at least one earned income. This was partly because of the social composition of the population at that time, and partly because of policy factors, which emphasized the building of family-sized houses (as distinct from small dwellings aimed at elderly people and other small households), and managerial practices which tended to favour white families with long periods of local residence over newly arrived families (Henderson and Karn, 1987; S. Smith, 1989). The institutionalized bias against single people of working age, elderly people, low income households and members of minority ethnic communities in those days can be seen as a form of social exclusion. The transformation of social housing, and council housing in particular, is striking, and now the link between social housing and the socially excluded is strong. In 1962 only 11 per cent of households renting from local councils in England had no earned income, and 55 per cent had two or more earners. By 1993, however, 66 per cent of council tenants had no earned income, and only 14 per cent had two or more earners (Holmans, 1995b: 111).

Forty years ago non-earners were under-represented in council housing, but now they are heavily over-represented. To put it another way, forty years ago council tenants were more likely to be in work than were owner occupiers, but now they are more than twice as likely to be not working.

Other indicators include the fact that social rented sector tenants tend to be older than owner occupiers as a group (although not outright owners), and elderly people are over-represented in this sector. There are also more lone parents in social renting (18 per cent in England in 2001/02 compared with 7 per cent overall: ODPM, 2003: 41). People who are permanently sick or disabled are three times as common in social renting as elsewhere (12 per cent as against 4 per cent overall). And, not surprisingly, social rented sector tenants have average incomes that are only 40 per cent of the overall average. A corollary of low income and exclusion from the labour force is benefit dependency, of which one key indicator is that more than 60 per cent of social rented sector tenants were claiming housing benefit in 2002, and a majority of that group also claimed income support (Wilcox, 2003b: 206–9).

Having established who lives in social rented housing in the early 2000s it is necessary to consider mobility into and out of social renting. The two groups are markedly different, and for obvious economic and life cycle reasons. According to the Survey of English Housing, the effect of the right to buy between 1980 and 1993 was to remove from council housing some 800,000 households headed by someone in full-time employment at the time of purchase, and to this total must be added a not insignificant number of other tenants moving into the owner occupied sector by buying on the open market (Holmans, 2000: 113). The majority of these purchasers have been shown to be people sufficiently advanced in their working lives to be able to qualify for large right to buy discounts and/or to be able to afford the costs of mortgage repayments; in the three years to 2001/02 the average weekly income of people moving out of social renting was twice that of tenants in the sector as a whole (ODPM, 2003: 42). Among new entrants, on the other hand, more than three-quarters of those who were newly formed households in this period were under 35, while almost a third of new tenants who came from owner occupation were over 65. This pattern of movements into and out of social housing has contributed to a characteristic bi-polar age distribution in social housing, with large numbers of tenants under 35 and over 65 (Burrows, 1997, 1999; DETR, 2000: 54).

The stock of dwellings remaining in the social rented sector is significantly different now compared with the period before the introduction of the right to buy twenty-five years ago. The effect of so many tenants buying houses on the more attractive estates has left behind a stock that contains a much higher proportion of flats than is found in the owner occupier sector. Another indicator of difference is that council tenants are much more likely to live in houses valued in the lowest council tax band (60 per cent as compared with 13 per cent for owner occupiers: ODPM, 2003: 16), and it has been claimed that 'Nationally, council housing continues to dominate in the majority of poor neighbourhoods' (Social Exclusion Unit, 1998: para. 1.16). The stripping out of much of the best quality and most desirable social rented housing has left remaining and prospective tenants with less choice and fewer options to acquire equivalent accommodation. While the sector has been shrinking in size it has also been starved of resources for repairs and improvements, to the extent that it was admitted in 2000 that there was a £19 billion backlog of repairs to be carried out (DETR, 2000: 5), and more recently the government has referred to more than 1.5 million social rented sector tenants living in dwellings that fail the 'decent homes standard' (ODPM, 2003: 13).

In this situation, where social renting is perceived to accommodate the least well off, in dwellings needing repair, on estates that are labelled as places of crime and anti-social behaviour, it is not surprising that survey evidence consistently shows very low proportions – around 10–15 per cent – of people stating a preference for social renting over other tenures (DETR, 2000: 30; J. Smith, 2001: 15). This is, of course, a lower proportion than actually live in social renting, reinforcing the notion that it is a tenure of last resort. There are two important points to add here. First, the departure and exclusion of the better off is as significant for understanding social renting in the early twenty-first century as the increasing proportions of tenants on low incomes and with no earned incomes. This sorting of the population by income, employment status and tenure is the antithesis of the solidaristic, integrationist model of the postwar welfare state. Second, social renting is in a sense a less than adequate residual service, for it provides for only some of those who need assistance with housing costs (a fifth of housing benefit recipients in 1999 were people in the private rented sector: Wilcox, 2003b: 210), and there is no evidence of government intention to alter this situation.

The residualization of social renting can, then, be understood in terms of a number of dimensions:

1   The stock remaining today is what has been left behind after twenty-five years of selective transfer of the best and most attractive houses through the right to buy.
2   The people living in social renting are to a large and increasing extent the economically residualized, marginalized poor and socially excluded.
3   The sector has been transformed into one that is popularly and officially perceived as playing a residual role, a safety net accommodating those whose low incomes mean that they cannot afford open market rents or prices.

Residualization, social exclusion and policy

Having established the importance of the social exclusion debate for understanding social housing, and the extent to which social renting has become residualized, the next question concerns the policy implications: what, if anything, needs to be done about the situation? On the one hand there is a body of opinion which holds that accommodating the poor and socially excluded is precisely the right role for social housing, and that it has taken far too long to redress the mistakes and misallocation of the past. On the other hand the argument is that a residualized social rented sector is undesirable because of the belief that services confined to the poor will be poor services, and because of the way in which other indicators of social and economic disadvantage become geographically concentrated and therefore mutually reinforcing. This section does not seek to resolve the issue, but to look at the policies adopted by governments, particularly in the period since 1997. In doing so it concentrates on the important distinction between residualization and social exclusion. These are different problems and imply different interventions. It is a mistake to see the language of social exclusion as simply a New Labour way of talking about its policy for tackling residualization. The process of residualization is about the concentration of the socially excluded in social housing, and therefore it is closely linked to the social exclusion debate. The two ideas are also linked to the extent that a residualized social rented sector reinforces the exclusion of those housed within it. The argument to be developed here, however, is that to tackle one is not necessarily to tackle the other, that residualization is not the target of policy in the present period, and that the strategy for tackling social exclusion has little to do with housing.

The historical narrative of previous chapters has shown that the residualization of social rented housing has been under way for a long time, and that the difficulties currently faced by tenants, social housing providers and governments were not unforeseen. For at least fifteen years before 1997 governments and local authorities had been concerned about the problems posed by increasingly unpopular and rundown estates. But policy under the Conservatives had been contradictory and overall the effect was to intensify the physical decline of the sector in terms of both quantitative and qualitative measures. Policy in that period was quite openly about turning social housing into a more residual sector. The Conservatives under Margaret Thatcher defined council housing as part of the problem to be tackled, reversing sixty years during which local authorities had been seen as part of the solution. The more they talked up the problematic status of council housing, the more it became a self-fulfilling prophecy, deflecting demand from people who had some choice about their housing and lowering the morale of staff and tenants alike. The Thatcherites' remedy was to starve the sector of investment resources, reinforcing the process of decline, and to sell off as much public housing as possible, initially to individual sitting tenants, then through the disposal of whole estates to private developers and later via Housing Action Trusts, or HATs (which were intended to take the most rundown estates and prepare them for privatization). This whole approach was shot through with irony: for example, affluent council tenants who in the past had been vilified by Tory rhetoric as feather-bedded recipients of unwarranted subsidy were now encouraged to buy with the aid of substantial discounts; and the success of the right to buy depended on tenants seeing their own homes as desirable and worth buying. In the case of HATs the irony took a different form, and all six in the first wave proposed by the government were rejected by tenants who preferred to stay with the council (Karn, 1993).

The right to buy was presented as a policy designed to promote owner occupation but, as argued in Chapter 6, its effect was also to residualize the local authority sector, by removing both the better off working tenants and the most desirable houses. In the long run and for those left behind or trying to get into the sector the right to buy has been a disaster, reducing choice, intensifying social exclusion and exacerbating a problem that is very difficult to tackle effectively. As if the carrot of discounted prices was not sufficient to drive the right to buy the government adopted a new approach to setting rents and subsidies in 1980 (Malpass, 1990). This forced steep increases in rent as a result of withdrawal of subsidy, a policy which made sense in terms of consciously deterrent prices, but which operated in such a way that increases in rental income were not reflected in resources available for repairs and improvements. The strategy was reinvigorated in 1989, with a further hike in rents and a steep fall in the level of investment in essential works (Malpass *et al.*, 1993). It became clear that rent and subsidy policy was more concerned with promoting the right to buy than with addressing the increasingly obvious problems of the housing stock. In this sense, then, central government policy was the agent of disrepair, although the local authorities, as the owners of the houses, were blamed for lack of repairs and investment. Another aspect of policy in this period, therefore, was a programme of centrally orchestrated investment (Estate Action) targeted on specific areas (Pinto, 1993), designed to demonstrate that while the local authorities could not be trusted to invest appropriately the government could.

Looking at housing policy under the Labour governments since 1997, it soon becomes clear that tackling residualization is not a priority. That is to say, reversing residualization is not on the agenda, although coping with it is. To try to stem the residualization process and begin to reverse the decline of social housing would imply measures designed to broaden its social base. It would mean trying to change the role of social housing within the wider housing system, by returning the sector to a position where it became a tenure of choice rather than necessity. A strategy to alter the tenure preference gradient would require action across the housing system as a whole, with the aim of producing a more tenure-neutral pattern of housing options. In practice, however, such a radical approach is barely conceivable, largely because residualization is not only the inescapable consequence of half a century of housing policy but also an integral part of the social settlement of the new welfare state. Indeed, the residual role for social renting is unquestioningly and absolutely accepted, because it is implicit in the commitment to the market, especially owner occupation, as the mainstream way of providing for the social mainstream. It is enshrined in the New Labour view of the world, and specifically in the Green Paper, which listed as one of Labour's key principles for housing policy: 'Giving responsibility to individuals to provide their own homes where they can, providing support for those who cannot' (DETR, 2000: 16). So much for choice.

The government's attitude to social housing is revealed in two reports commissioned in 2003. The first was the report of the Home Ownership Task Force, which had been asked to look at ways to help social sector tenants and others into home ownership (Housing Corporation, 2003a). The other was the report of a review of problems of housing supply. In the present period Britain faces a pressing need to increase the supply of new houses, and in 2003 concern about the 'issues underlying the lack of supply' and poor response to rising demand led the chancellor to commission a report (Barker, 2003, 2004). This confirmed that there was growing evidence of a persistent inadequate supply, and concluded that Britain needed a more flexible housing market, in which supply responded more strongly to changes in price. The Barker report also recommended an increased supply of social housing, of between 17,000 and 26,000 dwellings per year, but although this would represent a doubling of current rates it would only restore output to the level achieved in the year before Labour came into office (and even returning to mid-1990s levels of social housing production would leave new supply well below other estimates of need: see Bacon, 2000: 10).

Elsewhere, official publications refer to the plan to provide 200,000 homes in certain designated parts of the south east of England in the period up to 2016, but they have become remarkably coy about quantitative output estimates or targets for the social rented sector (on the basis that these decisions have been devolved to Scotland and Wales and the new regional housing bodies in England: ODPM, 2003, 2004a). However, in March 2004 it was announced that nearly £3.5 billion would be invested in the production of 67,000 affordable homes in England over the next two years (ODPM, 2004c). Although this represents a significant increase over recent years, it remains clear that the market is to be relied upon for providing by far the largest proportion of new dwellings. This is consistent with the known preference of the Blair government for private solutions wherever possible, and represents a continuation of the approach pursued by governments of all political complexions since the late 1960s, but it is interesting that in circumstances where there are clearly acknowledged problems about supply from private enterprise the government has decided not to deploy a means of building houses that had proved very effective in the past. Volume building by local authorities, which was the key to high levels of output in the period 1945–68, is now out of the question. It is a measure of how far the Labour Party has travelled that since 1997 output by social housing providers has continued to fall in both absolute terms and as a proportion of all new building.

Council house building had been reduced to derisory levels by the outgoing Conservatives but has fallen further under Labour. Overall output by local authorities and housing associations has just crept above 20 per cent of the total in three years since 1992, and since Labour came into office it has not exceeded 15.5 per cent. These very low levels of new building have contributed to a continuing overall decline in the stock of social renting, which fell by half a million dwellings between 1992 and 2002 (Wilcox, 2003b: 90). It is interesting that the language of the Green Paper is positive about both owner occupation and private renting, 'encouraging' growth and 'promoting' expansion, but in relation to social renting the language is much more equivocal, referring to improving the quality rather than the quantity of the stock. A shortfall in the supply of social rented housing can be seen as a way of persuading people to opt for private sector solutions.

An interesting indicator of the stance of the government in this area is the changing interpretations of the term 'affordable housing', especially in the context of the increasing policy emphasis on the use of the planning system to deliver it. As local authorities scaled down their building activities in the 1980s they were encouraged to provide sites in their ownership for housing associations, but in due course municipal land banks became depleted, and government turned increasingly to the planning system to deliver affordable housing from private sector developments, as a condition of planning permission and as a way of capturing for the good of the community some of the gains from development. Over time the definition of affordable housing in this context has changed and broadened; initially it was taken to refer to new social rented dwellings, to be owned and managed by a housing association, but by the time of the Green Paper it was being defined as 'housing that is either let at sub-market rents or sold at prices at the lower end of prevailing market levels' (DETR, 2000: 70). This is yet another step away from social renting as a form of provision encouraged and supported by government, for developers generally prefer to provide dwellings for open market sale, rather than for social renting. It is also a step away from helping those households whose low income leaves them unable to afford open market prices, albeit ones at the lower end of the scale.

Another, related, indicator of the government's stance on social housing is the so-called key worker scheme, which helped 9,000 people to buy homes between September 2001 and March 2004. This was launched as the starter home initiative in the Green Paper of 2000 (DETR, 2000: 37–8), and was based on giving assistance to low income workers in certain designated areas and occupations to buy homes that they could not otherwise afford. The scheme, which was relaunched as 'Key worker living' in March 2004 (ODPM, 2004b), continues to be run through housing associations (although the ODPM's promotional leaflet is coy about this fact), and it continues to cover workers in the health service, teachers, police, probation and prison staff and fire fighters in London, the south east and the east of England. The emphasis is on providing equity loans of up to £50,000 to help such people buy houses at open market prices, or shared ownership (where the occupier buys at least 25 per cent of the equity and pays rent on the remainder). There is also the possibility of 'intermediate renting', which is defined as 75–80 per cent of the local market rent. The scheme is open to criticism on a number of grounds, including the inequitable targeting of specific groups of public sector workers, but not others playing (arguably) equally important roles in contemporary society. It is also economically illiterate, because of the way that it amplifies demand in an already unbalanced market, and because it ignores the obvious remedy for struggling public sector workers: higher wages. The key worker scheme has been given a high profile by the ODPM, but in fact it is expected to have only a very small quantitative impact, in a restricted area, albeit at enormous expense. It is said to involve the expenditure of £1 billion in the three years to 2006, but is only expected to accommodate 12,000 workers in this period – surely one of the worst value for money housing projects ever invented by a British government (ODPM, 2004a: 24).

However, leaving these criticisms aside, the most relevant point in the present context concerns what the key worker scheme is not, rather than what it is. It is not social renting. In the past local authorities ran key worker schemes, which provided council houses for workers needed by local employers, especially workers recruited from outside the locality. In the present period, however, where some public sector employers have problems recruiting and retaining staff at the given rates of pay, the response is not to deem a social renting solution as suitable for workers for whom house purchase is clearly unaffordable, but to give them subsidized

access to owner occupation. A government interested in reversing the residualization process might have seized on this as an opportunity to broaden
the social mix within social renting. The fact that it has not done so suggests that it has either given up on social renting, seeing it as irredeemably
residual, or that it accepts that residualization is the right way to go.

So far, this review of contemporary housing policy has looked at supply
and the marginal role accorded to social housing. Turning to policies
specific to social housing, the first point to make concerns the right to buy,
which was emblematic of 1980s Conservatism and the Thatcherite assault
on social housing – and which the New Labour government has left
in place. However, there have been some adjustments to the scheme,
principally in terms of lower discounts (Murie and Ferrari, 2003: 10–11),
but retention of the right to buy is a powerful indicator of the Labour
government's current view of social renting:

> We want to establish a [social housing] sector in which tenants have
> real choice over their housing, where they can take responsibility for
> their homes in the same way that owner occupiers can; where tenants
> are empowered in the decision making processes that affect their
> homes; where tenants choose their homes rather than being pushed into
> them; and where there is a wider range of housing providers competing
> for tenants' custom and offering high quality, good value services.
> (DETR, 2000: 56)

This is a vision of a marketized social rented sector, with all the emphasis
on choice, empowerment and competition. The Green Paper devoted a
whole chapter to the subject of choice in the letting of social housing, and so
it is appropriate to look at what was proposed (DETR, 2000: 78–92). The
debate about the letting of social housing had been given a particular turn by
an influential report (Page, 1993), which argued that as housing associations
took over from local authorities as the main providers of new social rented
dwellings they were at risk of repeating the mistakes of the past, including
the suggestion that by allocating according to housing need, together with an
imperative to give half of all new schemes to people who were statutorily
homeless, they were creating ghettos of low income and socially excluded
households. In the wake of this report allocation according to housing need
came to be implicated in the residualization of social housing, and the Green
Paper combined discussion of choice with proposals for a retreat from points
based allocations systems. The government's position was confused and
ambivalent. On the one hand it said that it did 'not believe that social housing should only be allocated to the poorest and most vulnerable members of
the community', but on the other hand, it did believe that, 'priority ... should
generally continue to be given to people in the greatest housing need and for

whom suitable private sector housing is not an affordable option' (DETR, 2000: 80). Later in the same chapter it suggested low priority in lettings arrangements for people 'who do not need social housing because they are capable of finding suitable housing in the private sector. They would not normally get social housing if someone with greater priority wanted it' (DETR, 2000: 82–3). This is as clear an endorsement of the residual status of social housing as can be found in the contemporary official literature on the subject. It also highlights the reason that housing need became associated with residualization: need had been redefined in terms of income and affordability. To the question, 'Does this household need a home?' had been added the question, 'and can they afford to get one using their own resources?'

On the specific proposal to introduce a greater element of choice into the letting of social rented housing, there is just one simple point to be made. So long as the people who are given the choice remain those who are defined to be in housing need in the way just discussed, then there will be no impact on the social make-up of the sector. This is not to argue against choice, but to point out that the proposals for choice based lettings are not designed to reverse the residualization process. The key issue remains that those people who have choice (as a result of their spending power) do not generally choose social housing, and the quotes from the Green Paper in the previous paragraph indicate that nothing is to be done to encourage them to change their minds.

Choice in the lettings process is about empowering tenants and prospective tenants as individuals. In addition the government has introduced compulsory 'tenants' compacts', under which every local authority must set up a mechanism for consulting its tenants. The 'best value' approach to service provision also requires local authorities to involve tenants in the regular service reviews that are an integral part of the process. These may be effective ways of improving the responsiveness and the overall quality of services, but they are very unlikely to have any impact on the wider and rising tide of residualization. That is not surprising, and neither is it a criticism, for these measures are not designed to tackle residualization.

Although Labour has allowed the social rented sector to continue to shrink, it has, nevertheless, placed considerable emphasis on improving the quality of the remaining stock. One of the new government's first acts was to redeem its election promise to release local authorities' accumulated capital receipts from the sale of assets. This amounted to several billion pounds made available for investment, nearly all of which went into renovation rather than new building. Subsequently the government has maintained pressure on local authorities to tackle the backlog of repairs and to move towards ensuring that all their dwellings meet the 'decent homes standard' by 2010. This is linked to the importance attached to tackling disadvantage through neighbourhood renewal and community regeneration. At the outset the new government seemed to equate social exclusion with social housing, for the brief given to the newly established Social Exclusion Unit was to 'develop integrated and sustainable approaches to the problems of the worst housing estates, including crime, drugs, unemployment, community breakdown and bad schools etc' (Social Exclusion Unit, 1998). However, this was soon modified in the light of the growing realization that although council housing might dominate the majority of poor neighbourhoods, the problems were much wider. In fact the focus shifted away from housing in the National Strategy for Neighbourhood Renewal:

> Some neighbourhoods would have no future if their housing were not improved. But there has consistently been more emphasis on regenerating the physical environment than on changing the prospects of the people who live there. This means tackling poor schools, inadequate adult skills, lack of job opportunities and childcare, improving health, and providing attractive and affordable local leisure activities for children and teenagers. (Social Exclusion Unit, 1998: para. 2.14)

There has been a lot of hand wringing introspection about the amounts of money spent on physical regeneration of estates in the past and the apparent failure of this investment to deliver sustainable improvement; but it is possible to argue that such investment was always likely to disappoint in the absence of a wider understanding. One wider perspective would be to say that improving the physical environment of social housing estates needed to be set alongside other measures designed to broaden the appeal and accessibility of this sector as a whole. This would be a strategy to tackle (i.e., reverse) residualization. Another perspective, the social exclusion perspective, places the emphasis on changing the people: for example, by helping them to obtain the educational qualifications and other skills that they need in order to gain paid employment. Tackling social exclusion is an approach that is not concerned with changing the role that social rented housing plays in the wider housing system; it is about changing a number of other factors that affect life and life chances for people living in social renting.

The same report (Social Exclusion Unit, 1998) identified five strategic themes:

- getting the people to work
- getting the place to work
- building a future for young people
- access to services
- making government work better.

The second of these referred to housing management and unpopular housing, but in general the analysis and prescriptions of the Social Exclusion Unit have tended to concentrate on matters other than housing. A key emphasis is on the importance of work; for example, a review published in 2004 said that, 'measures to tackle the economic causes of social exclusion have delivered significant results in terms of employment rates, but persistent levels of worklessness and concentrations of high unemployment in particular areas suggest the need for greater emphasis on employment in regeneration programmes for deprived neighbourhoods' (Social Exclusion Unit, 2004: 2). The review had very little to say about housing, which is revealing in itself, for it seems to confirm the interpretation developed above concerning the acceptance of the residual status of social housing. However, to the extent that social rented housing remains the tenure of last resort it will continue to be a factor in perpetuating social exclusion. To try to tackle social exclusion without simultaneously seeking to do something about social housing is an incomplete strategy.

Conclusion

Historically social rented housing was neither universal nor residual, and as such it did not fit comfortably into the welfare state. Now it has become clearly and increasingly residual, and as such it fits more neatly into the modern welfare state. In terms of their housing conditions the poor have always had the worst of it: they were failed by the market and by housing policy which developed in ways that favoured, and continue to favour, the better off. As the least well off have moved into social renting they have found that it is no longer the high quality service and badge of inclusion that it once was. Having been excluded from social renting they are now excluded by it.

This chapter has made the point that it is necessary to understand social exclusion operating in different ways at different times. As the concept of citizenship has changed, with increasing emphasis on work and consumption, so social rented housing has become more associated with poverty and social exclusion. Residualization happens when the poor and socially excluded move into social renting, but tackling exclusion will not deal with residualization, which is about the role that social renting plays in the wider housing system. It has been shown above that residualization was positively promoted by government policies over a prolonged period, especially from 1979 to 1997, and that reversing the process has not become an objective of policy action since the change of government in 1997. On the contrary, all the evidence points to acceptance of a residual status for social housing. However, to the extent that a residualized social housing sector is a factor in reinforcing and perpetuating social exclusion it cannot be ignored if exclusion is to be tackled successfully. Indeed, a policy of promoting social inclusion through measures designed to get more people into employment might actually intensify problems of residualization, to the extent that the newly included took the opportunity of higher (earned) income to move away into owner occupied housing, as they are currently encouraged to do by both popular prejudice and government policy. Unless the reputation of social housing is addressed, this is exactly what they are likely to do. The conclusion is that a fully rounded policy to address social exclusion needs to include measures to reverse the process of residualization, and that requires housing policy measures designed to modify the current steep preference gradient which leads people who can afford it to abandon social housing as soon as they can.

Chapter 10

The New Organization of Social Housing

Having looked at the changing social composition of social rented housing and its role in contemporary society, this chapter turns to the question of the transformation of the mechanisms and organizations responsible for the delivery of social housing. The transition from municipal to non-municipal dominance of social renting represents a profound change from patterns established during the twentieth century and apparently still deeply entrenched as recently as the late 1980s. But this is merely the head-line event, behind which lies a further set of changes in terms of the financing, management and accountability of social housing providers as a whole. And this in turn needs to be seen in the context of the construction of a new organizational settlement for the welfare state, implicit in New Labour references to the modernization of public services, and in academic debates around the transition from local government to local governance.

Local authorities played a leading role in the implementation of public policy and the delivery of key welfare state services in the postwar period (although it has been argued (Loughlin, Gelfand and Young, 1985) that they were already in decline before 1939). It was more or less taken for granted that general purpose, multi-functional local authorities were, and should be, responsible for the delivery of a range of public services. This organizational model had two defining features: first, it provided a formal mechanism of accountability, for not only were the staff answerable to the councillors but also the latter were answerable to the public at regular elec-tions. Second, public services were delivered by large functional departments characterized by strong vertical integration and weak horizontal links, giving rise to the notion of administrative 'silos'. Within departments there were two chief modes of co-ordination, bureaucracy and professionalism (Clarke and Newman, 1997: 4). Bureaucracy, in particular, has become the butt of much criticism, but historically it was seen as an improvement on previ-ous arrangements, since it provided a more rational, open and impartial approach (Clarke and Newman, 1997: 5). Professionalism is often con-trasted with bureaucracy but the two co-existed in local government, and a number of local government occupations (including housing management) self-consciously pursued professionalizing projects, partly as a means of improving the quality of service offered to the public and partly as a way of establishing a basis of authority in decision making. Professional expertise provided senior staff with a counter-balancing basis of authority in discussions with elected members around policy and operational decisions.

The crisis of the welfare state in the mid-1970s sharpened criticism of municipal services, which were attacked for being inefficient and remote from the public – the very word bureaucratic became a term of abuse. And professionalism also came in for criticism on the grounds that it was a self-serving project, a set of restrictive practices contributing to the impression that public services were oriented towards the needs and interests of providers rather than users, and that the claim to expertise was bogus – apparently demonstrated, for example, by the seemingly unstoppable series of child abuse cases where social workers were repeatedly shown to have failed to take appropriate action. The established organizational model came under attack from politicians from left and right, and from academics including the public choice theorists and others who argued that public services were too much influenced by producer interests. For these critics the remedy was to redress the balance through a more market oriented approach in which competition would empower consumers. Influential writers such as Osborne and Gaebler (1992), claiming to perceive a global paradigm shift in attitudes to government, called for nothing less than the 'reinvention of government'. Or, as Minogue, Polidano and Hulme (1998: 18) have put it, the new public management has been driving out the devalued currency of the old public administration. This also had long term implications for local democracy, and it is important to see the modernization process as embracing the democratic side of local government as well as administration and management.

The notion of new public management means different things to different people (Ferlie *et al.*, 1996), but it has been defined by Dunleavy and Hood (1994) as 'a handy shorthand, a summary description of a way of reorganising public sector bodies to bring their management, reporting and accounting approaches closer to a particular perception of business methods'. This has involved attempts to reduce the overall size of the public administrative bureaucracy by privatization, outsourcing through external contracts, competition (including the use of internal and quasi markets) and increased use of performance monitoring. Under the Conservatives in the 1980s emphasis was placed on privatization and competition, and on the extensive use of performance management techniques based on target setting and output measurement. Local authorities were required to put key services (such as refuse collection, and later, in the 1990s, housing management) out to tender, encouraging private firms to compete for contracts to undertake work previously carried out in-house. In this context the idea of the enabling local authority emerged; local authorities were encouraged to see themselves as playing a strategic role, ensuring that services were efficiently and effectively provided in their areas, but not necessarily by them (Bramley, 1993; Goodlad, 1993). Another aspect of developments at this time was the purchaser–provider split within local authority departments, a distinction that was implicit in competitive tendering.

Some aspects of new public management, such as compulsory competitive tendering, worked better in some services than others, and the stance of government has changed over time. Other aspects have endured as the process of modernization has been relentlessly driven forward under the New Labour government since 1997 (Office of Public Service Reform, 2002). New Labour has sought to present itself as not as openly hostile to local government as were the Thatcher and Major governments, and compulsory competitive tendering has given way to the so-called 'best value' approach, which involves the setting of objectives, establishing a programme of performance reviews, publishing a performance plan, undergoing independent inspection and audit, and ultimately being subject to intervention by the Secretary of State if services fail (DETR, 1998; Woods, 2000: 141). It has been claimed that it is possible to discern a shift from new public management to 'modern management', which is concerned with long term effectiveness as well as short term efficiency, less focused on institutional reform and presented more as a set of tools to achieve policy outcomes, and more concerned with collaboration, partnership and joined-up government (Newman, 2000: 47).

Other writers have put it somewhat differently. Rhodes (2000: xiii–xiv), for example, has argued that one of the unintended outcomes of attempts to introduce new public management (NPM) in Britain has been the creation of new policy ideas, and that 'The delicious irony is that the new ideas were not those of NPM but of local governance'. According to this analysis, the drive for a market based method of policy co-ordination was unsuccessful, but the attempt to move in this direction itself stimulated a response that has led to a new style of service delivery based on complex partnerships, coalitions and networks spanning the public, private and voluntary sectors. Rhodes (1999: xviii) has also claimed that governance has become the defining narrative of British government in the present period. In dictionary terms the words government and governance are synonyms, but different uses of the term governance give rise to confusion and it is necessary to provide some clarification. Governance gained currency in the 1990s, first in relation to the concept of corporate governance, or how organizations manage their internal and external accountability; this refers chiefly to the role of directors as the people responsible for the proper running of organizations on behalf of shareholders and/or other stakeholders. The issue of corporate governance attracted attention partly as a result of a number of high profile scandals in private enterprise, and partly because of questions arising as to the accountability of the increasing numbers of private and voluntary organizations used to deliver services that had previously been within the public sector.

A second usage of the word governance arose as a way of capturing the idea that there had been a decisive shift away from the old local government model towards a more fragmented pattern of service provision, relying on a range of non-municipal organizations:

> [Governance] can be broadly defined as a concern with governing, achieving collective action in the realm of public affairs, in conditions where it is not possible to rest on recourse to the authority of the state. Governance involves working across boundaries within the public sector or between the public sector and private or voluntary sectors. It focuses attention on a set of actors that are drawn from but also beyond the formal institutions of government. A key concern is processes of networking and partnership. Governance recognises the capacity to get things done which does not rest on the power of government to command or use its authority. Governing becomes an interactive process because no single actor has knowledge and resource capacity to tackle problems unilaterally. (Stoker, 2000: 3)

The need to find a term to capture the importance of the fragmentation of service delivery is understandable, but the adoption of governance is potentially confusing, to the extent that governance was already a generic label within a body of literature that defined three distinct modes of co-ordination: markets (based on competition and the price mechanism), hierarchies (based on commands from above) and networks (based on trust, reciprocity and diplomacy: see Thompson *et al.*, 1991; Williamson, 1975). Research on changes in British local government in the 1990s began to identify local governance with network co-ordination, standing between the public sector bureaucracy and the market. Thus Rhodes (1997: 15) referred to 'self-organising inter-organisational networks characterised by inter-dependence, resource exchange, rules of the game and significant autonomy from the state' (see also Rhodes, 1999: xvii). The appeal of networks is understandable – after all, the demunicipalization of local service delivery is a move away from the hierarchical, bureaucratic style of traditional town hall department-based administration, and there has been a rowing back from the outright privatization, marketization and faith in competition that characterized the Thatcherite approach to new public management.

Network co-ordination appears to be the only analytical category available, but in practice it is more complicated and less clear-cut. There are grounds for scepticism about the extent to which network co-ordination adequately captured the complexity of the modernized public service delivery system. While some writers have speculated about the idea of the new governance as 'governing without government' (Rhodes, 1996), others, for example Hoggett (1996), have acknowledged that governments do not willingly give up power and control, and therefore the perpetuation of hierarchical relations, albeit in new forms, is to be expected. The rapid growth of regulatory structures and processes is one potent indicator of this tendency, and a key theme in the remainder of this chapter is that greater managerial freedom in terms of operational decisions has been accompanied by a growth of central regulation and performance monitoring.

However one theorizes it there is no denying the scale and importance of the transformation of the organization and delivery of public services in the last twenty years or so. There has been a hollowing out of local government, demonstrated by the transfer of service delivery to non-municipal organizations and the marginalization of local councillors. The trend established under the Conservatives has been taken forward by New Labour since 1997, and Tony Blair himself has insisted that the modernization of local government must mean the abandonment of the all-purpose local authority delivering a wide range of services (Blair, 1998, 2002). The commitment and the direction of change is nowhere clearer than in housing. The story told in earlier chapters was one of municipal dominance of social housing provision, and of minimal central government involvement in local decision making. In matters of investment, rent setting, allocations and the organization of housing management local authorities enjoyed considerable, but never unfettered, autonomy (Malpass and Murie, 1999). From the early 1970s, when central government first attempted to remove local councillors' freedom to set rents, the trend has been consistently towards less public housing, less municipal control over social housing as a whole, and greater central government prescription, direction and regulation.

Towards a new pattern of ownership

As recently as 1987 local authorities owned over 90 per cent of all social housing in Britain, but by 2003 that figure had fallen to less than two-thirds (Pawson and Fancy, 2003; Wilcox, 2003b: 90), and it is generally expected that the trend will continue. Indeed, in the housing Green Paper of 2000 the government speculated that the local authority share might fall to half by 2004, and implied the possibility of the transfer of 2 million council houses over a ten-year period (DETR, 2000: 61). So far the pace of transfers has fallen well short of that vision, but it is clear that the brakes have come off the transfer programme (Murie and Nevin, 2001: 37).

In terms of numbers, by the end of 2003 nearly 1,000,000 dwellings had been transferred; 42 authorities had transferred part of their stock and 115 had ceased to own any houses. This means that nearly 30 per cent of all housing authorities had no houses, so for these councils the enabling role was all that was left to them.

The seismic importance of the transformation of social housing through stock transfer should not be under-estimated. After decades in which local authorities had robustly defended themselves against the pretensions of the voluntary sector, within a generation the previously marginalized housing association sector may, indeed probably will, come to replace municipal landlords altogether. In this process, the housing association sector is itself being transformed by the creation of a plethora of new organizations, differing in important ways from traditional associations. This raises some interesting questions about why the shift away from council housing is happening, and why now. What is driving the process, and what are the implications in terms of both the services offered to tenants and the governance and accountability systems? In considering these issues it is also necessary to remember that stock transfer is having an impact not only on council housing but also on the structure and dynamics of the whole of the registered social landlord (RSL) sector into which the dwellings are being moved.

Even if the pace of change is not as fast as expected (Cole and Furbey, 1994: 1), the eclipse of council housing is now apparently politically irreversible – a development that was, if not inconceivable twenty years ago, certainly not predicted. The small scale antecedents of whole-stock transfer had not led insiders to foresee the way that policy followed practice from 1988 onwards. In the early 1980s there were one-off experiments in transferring the ownership of rundown estates, such as the Cantril Farm/ Stockbridge Village on Merseyside and Thamesmead in south east London. Later there were local authority-led sales of estates to private developers for refurbishment and open market sale (Usher, 1987), but the idea of transferring the whole of a local authority's housing stock to a newly established housing association was not part of the then Conservative government's view of the way forward. To reinforce this point it is worth noting that large scale stock transfer was not legislated for in the Housing Act, 1988, and when local authorities developed the idea they did so under pre-existing powers contained in the Housing Act, 1985, amended by the Housing and Planning Act, 1986, which had been introduced with estate disposal rather than whole stock transfer in mind (Mullen, 2001: 500). The focus of policy up to that time was on transferring problematic rundown estates to Housing Action Trusts, for subsequent improvement and disposal, and the so-called tenants' choice initiative, which again implied partial stock transfers (DoE, 1987).

Underpinning the government's stance at that time was the idea that substantial numbers of tenants were frustrated by the performance of their local authorities and keen to seek new landlords. It was also assumed that there was a set of landlord organizations waiting to take over parts of the council stock. In practice this analysis proved to be unfounded, and HATs and tenants' choice were essentially failed initiatives, but their effect was to jolt a number of local authorities into radical action to combat a perceived threat to the integrity of affordable rented housing at a local level. Stock transfer was developed by local authorities themselves: 'Rather than dissatisfied tenants driving a transfer process it was disabled landlords who sought to resolve their dilemmas through transfer' (Murie and Nevin, 2001: 31).

The lack of tenant enthusiasm for transfer is striking (a quarter of transfer ballots have resulted in rejection by tenants: Pawson, 2004), and this has continued to influence the dynamics of the transfer process, which invariably requires a package of incentives and guarantees for existing tenants in order to generate sufficient support for a successful ballot. There is scope for debate about the relative importance of senior officers and councillors in moves to initiate transfer in the early years. It seems likely that different motivations dominated in different places; it has been suggested (S. Lowe, 2004: 49) that the initiative was taken by chief housing officers, a view supported by more recent research (Pawson and Fancy, 2003: 10). It was also sometimes the case that local politicians saw advantages in transfer, although whether this was primarily in terms of protecting and enhancing the provision of social housing, or off-loading a problematic service while at the same time generating a substantial capital receipt, is open to interpretation.

Stock transfer provides a fascinating example of the development of housing policy, illustrating how an idea that emerged as a tactical response in opposition to central government was subsequently taken over by the centre and turned into a mainstream policy (Malpass and Mullins, 2002). It is in this context that it is appropriate to refer to policy following practice. In the early years, between 1988 and 1992, central government responded in an ad hoc way to local transfer proposals as they came forward. Local authorities showed that transfer was a viable approach, in the sense that tenants could be persuaded to vote for it, and banks would lend the money. Once this had been demonstrated, the centre adopted transfer as its own policy, and laid down guidelines and established an annual programme, on which prospective transferring authorities were required secure a place (DoE, 1992). One of the guidelines was that no more than 5,000 dwellings should be transferred to a single new landlord, implying that the larger local authorities would need to devise ways of breaking up their housing stocks among two or more housing associations. At the same time, there was the somewhat contradictory expectation that existing associations would become involved in transfers; the contradictoriness of this was that in practice only the larger associations would be in a position to bid to take over council housing estates. By 1995 the centre was making it clear that it would like to see all authorities at least considering the merits of stock transfer (DoE, 1995: 29).

The change of government in 1997 led some people to think that stock transfer had run its course, but in fact New Labour proved even more enthusiastic, although it retained a cumbersome decision making framework, with built-in delays, distortions and increased costs. A curious feature of the development of stock transfer policy is that all governments since 1987 have made it abundantly clear that they want to see an end to local authorities as housing landlords, but they have left local authorities themselves to trigger the process. Local authorities then have to secure both a place in the annual national programme and a positive vote from tenants. Empowering tenants in this way has both distorted and increased the cost of each local transfer, giving existing tenants the opportunity to demand concessions and guarantees, about things such as the right to buy and rent levels, that will be denied to new tenants. Moreover, where tenants vote against transfer the government has made it known that they can expect no additional investment funds from traditional sources. This can leave councils that favour transfer in the unenviable position of having responsibility for improving the quality of their housing, but no means of doing so.

Despite these peculiarities, transfer fitted neatly with the New Labour leadership's modernization agenda. After its early period of extreme fiscal rectitude, sticking to the previous Conservative government's spending plans, Labour increased the flow of resources into public services, but the money for modernization and improvement came with strings attached: it was contingent on further 'reform' and organizational change, including increased involvement of the private sector in the delivery of essential public services. In the case of housing this needs to be explored in terms of at least two dimensions. First, transfer was presented as the government's favoured way of raising the money for the physical modernization of public housing. It was committed to increased expenditure on public services, but health and education were the priorities, not housing. If resources were to be found to invest in new social housing, and to tackle the huge backlog of repairs (estimated to be £19 billion in social housing as a whole: DETR, 2000: 5) it was clear that they would have to be funded in ways that did not count as public expenditure (DETR, 2000: 59). Stock transfer has remained the clear favourite with government, but two other options have been offered to local authorities: arm's length management organizations (ALMOs), which have attracted the interest of high performing councils keen to retain ownership of their housing, and the private finance initiative (PFI), which has not made much impact so far.

Attempts to persuade the Treasury to alter the public spending conventions failed (Hawksworth and Wilcox, 1995), partly, it may be surmised, because finance was not the only issue: the government supported the transfer of council housing for other reasons, to do with its wider modernization agenda. At one level stock transfer can be understood as a massive re-mortgaging exercise, although if the object was merely to release resources for investment there were clearly cheaper ways of doing so than re-mortgaging the entire stock. The organization acquiring the stock has to arrange a loan both to buy the houses and to fund the promised investment. In the majority of transfers before 2000 this left the selling authority with a capital receipt after repayment of outstanding housing debt (sometimes the receipt also permitted the council to pay off its debts entirely). The total amount raised for stock transfer in England between 1988/89 and 2002/03 was £11.18 billion, of which £5.5 billion was for purchase, with the balance for repairs and improvements and other costs (Wilcox, 2003b: 157). In the early years of transfer, activity was concentrated in rural and suburban areas, where there were high positive valuations that made transfer a financially viable and attractive proposition. In the mid-1990s the government introduced the Estates Renewal Challenge Fund (ERCF) as a device for facilitating transfer in urban areas where valuations were low or negative. This was a time-limited fund, but the government subsequently provided substantial Treasury support to facilitate transfer in authorities where the authority was left with 'overhanging debt' after disposal of its low value stock (for details see Gibb, 2003: 94; Wilcox, 2003b: 158). The government's commitment to transfer was tested by the volume of Treasury support – £900 million – required to support the highly contested transfer of the 81,000 dwellings owned by Glasgow City Council (Gibb, 2003: 102).

Finance has often been presented as the key driver of stock transfer, because the finance for repairs and improvements is dependent upon transfer out of the public sector. But finance is, in a sense, a red herring, because there was no necessary link between investment and transfer. If raising the money for investment had been the only issue then ways could have been found (and were suggested, e.g., by Hawksworth and Wilcox, 1995) to achieve this without sacrificing local authority ownership and control of a valuable public asset. But, of course, the reality was that the loss of the local authority role was not a sacrifice from the point of view of the government – it was the point of the exercise, and finance for investment was merely a device for driving this through. Thus modernization of the stock was only part of the story, serving to support the other dimension of New Labour's view of modernization, namely the separation of the management of public services from the bureaucratic and politicized confines of the town hall. From this point of view, transfer to a new, or at least different, landlord organization provides not only investment that does not count as public expenditure but also the opportunity for managers to manage in new, flexible, more business-like ways, and to make decisions that are informed by what is right for the business without having to worry about political pressure from elected members.

This raises the question of whether stock transfer represents a form of privatization. Some critics of the process, notably the campaigning organization, Defend Council Housing, depict transfer as privatization because of the reliance on private finance, the status of RSLs as private bodies and the rhetoric around business plans and management principles. Others (Pawson, 2004) have countered that stock transfer should not be seen as privatization, chiefly because the new landlord organizations are non-profit distributing and their operations are heavily influenced by the public policy framework and the ethos of social businesses (the idea that organizations can be run in business-like ways while retaining a commitment to social purposes). Although they rely on loans from private institutions this is not a relevant criterion, for local authorities have also always borrowed in similar ways. However, private finance has had an effect on business management, raising the profile of finance and treasury functions within organizations. RSLs routinely strive to make surpluses in order to demonstrate their financial rectitude and thereby preserve their future borrowing power, but surpluses are distinct from profits in the sense that they are not distributed to shareholders in the form of dividends; in other words, the returns to investors in RSLs are not proportional to the performance of the organization. All surpluses are retained and can only be spent on developing the service.

It is more fruitful to see stock transfer as part of the wider development of the managerialist welfare state (Clarke, Gewirtz and McLaughlin, 2000), which needs to be looked at in terms of both management and accountability. Tony Blair (1998: 11–12) has made clear his view that the idea of the local authority providing services is a 'flawed model', and that 'the council was – and often still is – an unresponsive and incompetent landlord'. In this he was echoing criticisms made by the Audit Commission, which concluded that:

> the professional independence and standing of chief housing officers needs to be strengthened, to enable them to withstand undue local political pressures...
>
> Management must be free to manage, within overall policy directions established by members. In the Commission's view, attempts by elected members to do officers' jobs for them will lead – and have led – to poorer services. (Audit Commission, 1986: 30–1)

The notion of 'undue' local political pressure is interesting, and invites the response that it is undue central political pressure that is preventing local authorities from continuing to provide a service that local voters and rate-payers have supported and developed over many decades. The marginalization of democratically elected local councillors is clearly one of the main drivers of stock transfer and the whole 'modernization' process. Although councillors have been criticized for becoming too involved in operational decisions it does not necessarily follow that taking housing out of the town hall system will result in better quality services, for it is by no means established that housing associations are better landlords than local authorities. Research since the 1980s has failed to demonstrate a consistent pattern:

> Most of the research commentaries in this area and many of the political ones have arrived at a view that tenure is not the key factor determining the quality of service. RSLs do not uniformly deliver a better service than local authorities. There are good performers in each category of 'social landlord'. Stock transfer does not necessarily provide a guarantee of continuing good quality future service. (Murie and Nevin, 2001: 42)

It appears that stock transfer is not a case of 'evidence based policy', built on 'what works', two key ideas said to underpin the New Labour approach (Davies, Nulty and Smith, 2000). As Murie and Nevin (2001) have pointed out, the Green Paper discussion of transfer was strikingly uncritical, reflecting a settled position based on conviction rather than evidence. It would not be surprising if the organizations taking over from local authorities performed well, at least at first, because after all they have something to prove to the tenants that were persuaded to vote for transfer, and the finances have been stacked in their favour.

When local authority housing departments convert themselves into housing associations and move out to their new offices they leave behind the possibility of 'undue local political pressure', which is something that staff at all levels appreciate about their new status. However, there are major questions about the accountability structures in the RSL sector and their efficiency. Tony Blair may regard the local authority as a flawed model, but RSLs also attract criticism for the weakness of boards of directors and the undemocratic nature of their recruitment processes. For many years local authorities in general remained suspicious of housing associations because of their apparent lack of accountability and their tendency to recruit new board members informally from within their own social circles. Historically housing associations had little commitment to tenant involvement or representation on boards, and although there are shareholders (each entitled to just one share) with the formal power to elect board members, it is the board itself that decides how many shares to issue and to whom. An important feature of the development of stock transfer has been the tendency to set up new organizations, rather than to transfer to existing RSLs. This may be explained partly in terms of the benefits accruing to senior staff, but it is also arguable that it reflects a critique of established RSLs. Stock transfer organizations have adopted an approach to governance and accountability that is much more open and democratic, with reserved places on the board for tenants and local councillors. Initially it was not possible for councillors to constitute more than 20 per cent of the board, but since the Housing Act, 1996, councillors and tenants may each make up as much as 49 per cent; typically this results in tenants, councillors and 'independents' each occupying a third of the seats. It is also interesting that the post-1996 pattern is often referred to as the 'local housing company' model, perhaps as a further sign of distance from the governance arrangements associated with traditional housing associations.

The creation of a new body at the point of transfer provides an opportunity for new organizational structures and management systems to be introduced. Research by Pawson and Fancy (2003: 12) reported that newly created transfer associations typically differ significantly from their municipal antecedents. The same research also drew attention to the dynamic nature of post-transfer organizations, in the sense that half of the organizations surveyed had entered into group structures of one kind or another (Pawson and Fancy, 2003: 16). Although central government initially expressed a clear preference for relatively small transfer organizations it has proved unable to hold the line, or to prevent subsequent growth, strategic alliances or mergers. The limit of 12,000 dwellings in any single transfer has been breached and relaxed, most obviously in the case of Glasgow, where all 81,000 dwellings were transferred to a single organization (albeit with a plan to pass the stock on to 60 small local organizations: Gibb, 2003), but also in Bradford, Knowsley and Walsall. There is a tendency on business grounds (economies of scale, ability to borrow at lower rates) for active RSLs to merge or form alliances in group structures. There is therefore a tension between the argument that transfer would lead to smaller and more locally responsive organizations and the way in which these independent organizations respond to the business pressures on them.

After more than fifteen years of transfer activity, the organizational pattern is increasingly diverse. Some early transfers resulted in well resourced and ambitious organizations that were able to take full advantage of the conditions in the early 1990s which enabled them to grow and to expand their geographical scope. Others, especially the partial transfers by urban authorities, have led to organizations with a quite different approach, happy to work within existing boundaries. Not only do organizations reflect the circumstances prevailing at the time of their creation but they display distinct patterns of change subsequently. This raises the wider question of the impact of stock transfer organizations on the RSL sector as a whole, and vice versa.

The changing not-for-profit sector

Stock transfer should be understood as a process driven mainly by concerns about local authorities as major housing suppliers, and as such it is about transforming council housing and modernizing local government, but at the same time it is also transforming the not-for-profit sector into which the dwellings and their management are moved. Transfer does not necessarily reflect particular enthusiasm for housing associations; rather it is a reflection that they were already in existence, providing a model that could be adopted, adapted and modified. As mentioned above, local authorities had historically not shown much support for or commitment to housing associations, and in transferring their stocks of housing they have overwhelmingly chosen to set up new organizations that resemble (but are distinct from) traditional associations. In 1992 the housing association sector in Great Britain consisted of 733,000 dwellings; it was growing quickly as a result of heavy investment in new building and stock transfer, and by 2002 it had more than doubled in size, reaching nearly 1.7 million (Wilcox, 2003b: 90). Throughout the period, taken as a whole, stock transfer has been the main source of growth. The creation of around 200 new RSLs has not only added to the stock but also significantly added to the number of large housing associations; the majority of newly created stock transfer associations came into existence with more than 2,500 dwellings (some with very many more), and this immediately made them much larger than 90 per cent of existing associations. In 1989 there were 45 associations with more than 2,500 dwellings, owning 54 per cent of the total housing association stock in England; by 1997 there were 116 associations in this category, owning 74 per cent of the total (Malpass, 2000b: 237–8). The effect of stock transfer, then, has been to accentuate the tendency for housing association dwellings to be concentrated in a relatively small number of large organizations.

Stock transfer organizations are now the majority of the largest associations in England, and it is interesting to speculate on their impact on the sector as a whole. Are they likely to swamp the traditions of the existing organizations? And would this be regarded as a good thing? Or are they likely to conform to the established customs and mores? Is the shared regulatory framework likely to bring about greater organizational similarity in both structure (isomorphism) and behaviour? In the long run the influence is likely to run both ways, but already key institutions such as the

Housing Corporation and the National Housing Federation (NHF) have responded to the presence of stock transfer organizations by changing the ways in which they operate and the ways in which they view the sector. For the Housing Corporation the task of regulation has been affected by the need to manage the risks associated with very large new players, initially with higher levels of borrowing than is normal among traditional associations (in the long term transfer organizations have the potential to become financially strong and cash rich as debts are paid off – this would generate a different set of problems for the government and the Corporation). For the NHF the problem of incorporating these new organizations in a way that preserves some semblance of a unified not-for-profit housing sector has involved substantial shifts of power between member organizations, and the need to address specific stock transfer issues in its role as the trade body in negotiations with government (for example, in relation to the impact of government policy on rent restructuring).

However, while it is inevitable that stock transfer has had, and will continue to have, a significant impact on the RSL sector in a variety of ways, it is only one factor influencing change. It has been argued elsewhere (Malpass, 2000b: 265) that the modern housing association sector is effectively the creation of successive governments since the early 1960s, and policy action has continued to affect the form and direction of change. The re-introduction of private finance as a significant source of investment capital since 1989 has had a major impact, a key factor in what R. Walker (1998) has described as a shift from comfort to competition. As mentioned above, in relation to stock transfer, private finance has been both a way of generating capital outside the confines of the public expenditure conventions and an integral part of the modernization process in the sense that it sharpens the business pressures on organizations to perform efficiently and effectively. The fact that private finance became an important influence on established associations at the same time that stock transfer emerged meant that the sector as a whole was already entering an important period of change, and this in turn meant that assessing the impact of transfer organizations was more difficult.

Historically housing associations had relied to a large extent on private investors for their development finance (and their difficulties in the area were the main cause of their low levels of output throughout most of the twentieth century). From 1974 to 1989, however, they were boosted by a public finance regime that included generous capital grants, amounting to around 80 per cent of development costs, and loans for the balance. This had the great short term advantage of promoting growth, while in the longer term allowing associations to build up substantial property assets that were largely unencumbered by debt. In a sense the period 1974–89 can be seen as a pump priming exercise, boosting associations to the point where they were able to operate effectively in the capital markets; it was, with the benefit of hindsight, a necessary investment of public funds that lifted housing associations to a level where they could take over from local authorities as the main providers of new social rented housing.

The shift to a system that required associations to raise more than half their capital from private investors can be understood in different ways. First, like stock transfer it was a bottom-up initiative in response to the implications of government policy. It was housing associations themselves that started exploring the possibilities of raising capital on their own account, as a way of maintaining their building programmes in the face of the falling levels of funding from the Exchequer. Once the Treasury agreed to define private borrowing by housing associations as not public expenditure then the way was opened for this to become a mainstream way of funding development (Malpass, 2000c: 178–9). Second, private finance was a way of making the associations' assets 'work', in the sense that loans for new building were secured against the value of existing houses. Third, the move to private finance can be seen as the adoption of direct borrowing, in much the same way that the shift from private renting to owner occupation represented the rise of direct borrowing by consumers. In both cases groups that had historically been unable to raise sufficient credit on their own account had relied on intermediaries (private landlords or the Exchequer), but in due course they had achieved a position where they could undertake direct borrowing. In the same way that owner occupation represents the modernized form of the housing market (Harloe, 1985: xxiii), independent, privately financed, housing associations can be seen as the modernized form of social housing provider.

There is a debate to be had as to how far housing associations and other forms of not-for-profit housing providers are independent of government, but it is clear that they are heavily regulated and managed by or on behalf of government. As a result they are highly suggestible; for example, the geographical expansion of housing associations that had previously operated within long established territories can be seen as a direct response to government enthusiasm for competition in the early 1990s, which led it, through the Housing Corporation, to urge associations to widen their horizons and to compete with each other in new areas. This episode was mercifully short lived but RSLs continue to be shaped and reshaped by government policy. As the chosen instruments of policy for the delivery of affordable housing RSLs are constantly exposed to attempts to get them to follow the twists and turns of government by initiative, whether it be rent restructuring, choice based lettings, key worker housing or new methods of building procurement. Each of these is a central government policy shaping RSL behaviour in the first decade of the twenty-first century.

One longstanding issue has been the large number of registered associations in England (as long ago as 1971 it was being argued that there were too many: Cohen Committee, 1971: 75) and from the outset of the new regime in 1975 the Corporation tended to channel development funds to a relatively small group of associations – the ones it could rely on to deliver. More recently there have been suggestions that the Corporation was establishing a 'super league' of large developing associations (Malpass, 2000b: 7, 237), and this seems to be confirmed by the announcement that in 2004–06 some 80 per cent of the development programme in England would be carried out by just 70 RSLs (this represents an extension of existing practice, for although in recent years 3–400 associations have received development grant, in 2003 approximately 56 per cent went to just 42 associations: Housing Corporation, 2003b, 2004).

All this implies that over the next few years the shape of the not-for-profit sector will continue to change, in the direction of increasing dominance of stock transfer organizations and a small number of actively expanding associations, which are mostly already in the group of the top associations by size. At the same time we can expect further refinement of the 'technologies of control' (Foucault, 1977) through which central government seeks to monitor and influence the performance of apparently independent organizations.

Managerialism and social housing

The discussion so far has concentrated on the transformation of social housing from a municipal to an increasingly non-municipal service; in this context reference has been made to the marginalization of local democratic processes and accountability, and to the increased employment of private finance, partly as a way of generating resources for the physical modernization of the stock but also as a way of achieving organizational modernization by inculcating a more business-like approach. This section moves on to consider further aspects of the new organizational settlement of the welfare state. It is helpful to think in terms of managerialism and a managerialist transformation, as a challenge to the bureaucratic and professional styles that characterized the postwar welfare state. Clarke, Gewirtz and McLaughlin (2000: 8–10) suggest that:

> Managerialisation refers to...social and organisational processes linked to the establishment of a claim about who possesses the right to direct, co-ordinate or run organisations...[A] central issue in the managerialisation of public services has been the concerted effort to displace or subordinate the claims of professionalism. It can no longer

be assumed that 'professionals know best'; rather we are invited to accept that managers 'do the right thing'...[M]anagerialism has tended to subordinate other principles of judgement to the managerial calculus of economy and efficiency. National debates about 'the future of welfare' have been framed by questions of cost and the managerial agenda of 'driving down costs', concentrating on the 'core business' and providing 'value for money'.

An integral part of the managerialist approach is an emphasis on consumerism, relating to service users as customers with choices, rather than as clients to be advised or instructed. The notion of empowerment is much debated and needs to be considered here. At the same time, however, the fragmentation of the welfare state and the rise of managerialism have been accompanied by the development of a set of mechanisms and processes that enable central government and its agents to influence and steer the activities of service delivery organizations. The marginalization of democratic accountability at the local level has been followed by the rise of accountability directly upwards to government through inspection and performance monitoring, and downwards to service users as customers rather than voters. In the case of housing the managerialist turn is well entrenched: professionalism (never strongly embedded) is threatened, choice and consumerism are established mantras and a sophisticated monitoring, regulation and inspection regime is in place.

Taking these in turn, the emergence of housing management as a professional occupation is usually traced back to Octavia Hill and her followers in the first half of the twentieth century. However, while it is true that the women working in the Octavia Hill method and tradition were, on the whole, much better trained and much more likely to be university graduates than their male contemporaries, and had a credible claim to professional expertise, there were major barriers to a successful professionalization project. First, the fact that they were all women was a factor, as was their commitment to working with the poor (as a generalization it can be said that occupations that are exclusively or predominantly female tend to struggle to achieve high status, as do occupations that work with low status clients). Second, the majority of posts in the rapidly expanding local authority sector were occupied by men, and housing management was effectively redefined as a technical/administrative task. The professionals remained mainly outside the emergent municipal mainstream, confined to the tiny voluntary sector. It is interesting that after the Second World War, when local authorities were the overwhelmingly dominant providers of new houses for more than a decade, there was no attempt to professionalize housing management. (The contrast with the experience of town and country planning is striking – here the introduction of major planning legislation in 1947 led to official encouragement for the establishment of university courses to develop a cadre of trained professionals: Cullingworth, 1975. Similar housing courses did not emerge until the 1970s.) It was as late as 1965 that a unified professional body was established and a more effective professional project was developed in the context of a rapidly growing municipal housing sector. However, there remained the difficulty of defining exactly what the occupation was, and wherein lay its claim to special knowledge and expertise, a task that was made more difficult by the wide variety of ways in which different local authorities chose to organize their housing services (Kemp and Williams, 1991; Malpass and Murie, 1999: ch. 11).

Attempts were made to develop professional status for housing management, arguably as a strategy to counter the increasing assertiveness of councillors in the larger and more politicized local authorities from 1965 in London and the mid-1970s elsewhere (Barron, Crawley and Wood, 1991; Gyford, Leach and Game, 1989; Stoker, 1991), and as a means of staking a claim to parity of power and esteem alongside the other more established professions in local government. But, as Furbey, Reid and Cole (2001) have argued, housing never had more than a weak and fragile claim to professional standing, and they also acknowledge that the 'claims to professional status in housing have become less sustainable than ever'. The intrinsic weakness of the case has been further undermined by the rise of managerialism and the progressive removal of housing from the municipal environment in which it was grounded and where it was nurtured by particular circumstances. In the not-for-profit world of single purpose organizations, with generally compliant boards of directors, there is not the same pressure to assert a distinctive professional claim.

Turning to the customer orientation, this is itself a threat to the claims of professionalism, to the extent that it involves a rebalancing of the relationship between consumer and provider. Empowering service users was an essential part of the strategy to improve quality and efficiency in the public sector where it was held that dominant producer interests were a barrier to change. Tenant participation in housing has a long, if not very distinguished, history, enjoying a period of growth and popularity in the 1970s (Cooper and Hawtin, 1997). The Thatcherite Conservatives were more intent on encouraging individual tenants to use their right to buy as a way of exiting council housing, and support for collective action was based on seeing it as a way of attacking local authorities. However, more recently it has become established as a key part of government policy, at least in rhetorical terms which present it as something of a panacea for the problems of social housing (Carr, Sefton-Green and Tissier, 2001: 157). It is also implicit in the emphasis placed by New Labour on public service users as customers with rights and choices. The government introduced compulsory Tenants' Participation Compacts, which all local authorities were required to have in place from April 2000. These Compacts are statements of how tenants can become involved in local decisions, what councils and tenants have jointly decided to do, and how implementation is to be monitored. It has been pointed out that the use of term 'compact' in this context is interesting: unlike the word contract it implies no conferring of legally enforceable rights. 'This is an example of the government being more concerned with establishing appropriate machinery to achieve their policy goals than with legal rights' (Carr, Sefton-Green and Tissier, 2001: 161).

The whole area of tenant participation is problematic, beset with difficulties in actually stimulating active involvement by more than a tiny proportion of tenants, which fuels debates about how representative such activists are. The central irony of the present situation is that government seems to be keener on tenant participation than are tenants themselves, revealing that what should be bottom-up is actually top-down. This impression is reinforced by remembering that tenant empowerment does not extend to the freedom to vote for their local authority to be allowed to invest in its own stock and to continue as the owner and manager of housing in the traditional way. The big strategic decisions about the future direction of social housing have been made centrally, leaving tenants with the freedom to influence the timing of change at the local level and a choice as to which of the restricted list of (centrally defined) options to adopt. This is not, of course, to argue that tenant participation is always a waste of time and energy: far from it, because there is ample evidence that tenants can make a difference at the local level and within strictly defined limits. But the problems of social housing are too deep-rooted and intractable to be resolved in this way. As Goodlad (2001: 192) has pointed out, the contemporary context is not especially propitious for a successful tenant participation based strategy to redeem social housing. The residualization of social housing has resulted in a situation that makes involvement less, not more, likely: 'studies of political participation among British adults show that many of the socio-economic characteristics associated with least participation are found disproportionately among social housing tenants' (Goodlad, 2001: 192). Empowerment comes in different forms, and it can be argued that fifty years ago council tenants were empowered by the fact that most of them (the men anyway) had jobs – they had some political and economic power derived from their participation in the work force rather than direct interaction with the managers of their housing. The difference between the physical quality of the social housing stock then and now is striking, even allowing for the effects of ageing, suggesting that tenant participation has yet to make much impact in overall terms.

In addition to what might be seen as conventional tenant participation (through compacts) New Labour introduced the notion of Best Value (BV) as its replacement for compulsory competitive tendering; built into BV is the requirement that local authorities (and RSLs) consult and be accountable to local service users. But BV is much more than a means of developing public participation; it is a comprehensive system for setting targets and monitoring progress, with the underlying objective of continuous improvement. It is a centrally imposed framework, enabling central government to exert pressure on local performance, but with the rhetorical emphasis placed on local responsibility for setting standards, targets and means of achieving them. Introducing BV the government argued that CCT had failed, but also that:

> A culture in which authorities decide what services are to be provided on the basis of what suits them as providers is no longer an option ... [S]ustained improvements to services are more likely where those who use and pay for them are given a greater say in how they are run: in setting the appropriate standards, for example, and in deciding how those standards should be met and by whom. (DETR, 1998: 6)

Under the Local Government Act, 1999, a statutory duty was laid on local authorities to obtain best value by securing economic, efficient and effective services. This applied to all local government services, not just housing, but it did not apply directly to RSLs; however, English RSLs were quickly brought into the BV culture by the decision of the Housing Corporation to adopt a similar approach to regulation and monitoring performance. Best Value is based on several stages: first, service providers should carry out regular fundamental reviews of their work, challenging themselves to justify continuing to provide the service, comparing performance across a range of indicators, consulting local tax-payers and service users in setting new performance targets, and subjecting service to an array of tests of competitiveness. The government was careful to make it clear that there was no expectation that services should be privatized, or that competitive tendering would be employed (DETR, 1998: 20).

Second, the review process is intended to lead to the setting of demanding targets for efficiency and improvements in service quality. These are to be set out in local performance plans and progress is to be regularly monitored and reported to central government and the public at large. This inevitably means that service providers are drawn towards setting targets that they are confident about meeting, and that their subsequent behaviour is geared to demonstrating success.

Third, central government maintains a close watch on and exercises leverage over local performance through the work of a nationally constituted inspectorate. An inspectorate for local authority housing in England was established within the Audit Commission by the Local Government Act, 1999. A separate inspection system for RSLs was then set up by the Housing Corporation in 2002, and taken over in 2003 by the Audit Commission after a lively debate about where the unified service should be located:

> Whilst the Best Value regime draws upon many of the key elements of the previous reforms [of the Conservatives] and retains some important vestiges of the CCT regime, the way in which it has been introduced marks a very significant shift in central government's approach to the regulation of local authorities and the services for which they are responsible. In marked contrast to the previous administration's reliance on detailed legislation and prescription imposed from Whitehall and Westminster, the present government has sought to promote the 'modernisation' of local services through a process of persuasion and exhortation. (Martin, 2000: 213)

Best Value is a good example of the 'centralized decentralization' that is so characteristic of the new organizational settlement (Hoggett, 1996: 18); as governments have sought to decentralize operational responsibilities to local authorities and other service providers in the fragmented governance of public services they have simultaneously strengthened their control over resources and performance. This strengthening of the position of central government needs to be stressed, especially because of the rhetorical emphasis on devolution of decision making at every level. In the housing Green Paper of 2000, for example, the government referred to strengthening the strategic role of local authorities (although the subsequent decision to establish regional housing boards across England has thrown that commitment into question); the commitment to tenant participation has been noted above; housing was one of the services devolved to the Scottish Parliament and the Welsh Assembly.

Conclusion

For twenty-five years or more housing scholars have discussed and debated the residualization of social housing, but this chapter has sought to show that alongside that process there has been a gathering transformation of the organization of social housing. This is most apparent in the transfer of local authority housing to new landlords, but at the same time other important changes have been taking place in terms of the way social housing is financed and managed, and the mechanisms by which those responsible for it are held to account. The most obvious conclusion from the analysis presented here is that although local authorities continue to exist, and although government speaks piously of modernization and democratic renewal, in practice local government has a rapidly diminishing role in relation to social housing. The model of accountability through local democratic processes has been abandoned in favour of direct accountability to service users on the one hand and to central government (or its agents) on the other. Modernization of service provision has come to mean distancing services from the town hall and the adoption of a set of organizational practices based on managerialism as the successor to the old bureau-professionalism of the past. This is based on the 'tight–loose' approach (or centralized decentralization) which gives managers greater control over operations while leaving the centre in overall control. Implicit in the new managerialism is the elaborate apparatus of review, target setting and performance monitoring, regulation and inspection. The irony is that as social housing moves to organizations that are legally independent of the state those organizations are increasingly instruments of policy, delivering a national programme that is specified in much more detail than was ever the case in the past.

Whether this is better or worse than what is being replaced is not a question to be answered here. The point to be made is how different the organization of social housing is in the first decade of the twenty-first century compared with the arrangements that typified the postwar welfare state.

Chapter 11

Conclusion

Looking back to 1945 it is not surprising that living standards have improved dramatically, given that Britain was emerging from six debilitating, draining and damaging years of war. Among the most important indicators of change and improvement is the housing wellbeing of the people. Then there was a severe overall shortage of accommodation and great swathes of urban Britain consisted of ageing and neglected privately rented houses, built in an age when inside toilets and separate bathrooms were luxuries, and before electricity was widely available. Now there is a gross surplus of dwellings, the basic 'modern amenities' are taken for granted and over 90 per cent of dwellings have central or programmable heating (ODPM, 2001: 4). These are just some of many variables that could be invoked to indicate the transformation of the housing situation. How much of the improvement can be attributed to government policy and the welfare state is very difficult to determine, because of course it is impossible to know what would have happened in its absence. However, it is reasonable to suggest that without state intervention, especially in the early postwar period, there would have been many fewer new houses, particularly at affordable prices or rents, and much less replacement of obsolete stock. It follows that fewer new council houses after the war would have meant that there was less scope later to expand home ownership through the right to buy. The policy of full employment in the postwar welfare state also contributed to the privately financed repair, improvement and modernization of older housing.

In addition to the general marked improvement in the quality and quantity of accommodation available, the housing system itself has changed considerably and now works in quite different ways. Britain has ceased to be a place where most people rent their homes and instead has become a nation of home owners. In the process owner occupation has become a much more socially diverse tenure, while the role of social housing has changed to one of residual tenure of last resort, increasingly accommodating people with no earned income who therefore cannot afford market prices or rents. Both the rise of owner occupation and the residualization of social renting need to be understood in relation to the rise of consumer society. Owner occupation provides access to wealth accumulation and asset acquisition, underpinning high levels of debt fuelled consumption spending, in a way that renting does not. This means, on the one hand, that housing and the economy are bound together more intimately than in the past, and, on the other hand, that people excluded from owner occupation are also excluded from the same sorts of consumption spending. As Chapter 9 argued, these 'flawed consumers', many living in social renting, are the socially excluded.

Again it is important to stress that the housing system has its own dynamic, rooted in the market mechanism, and would have been subject to continual change even in the absence of policy action. Housing policy has to be understood as essentially supportive of the market throughout the period covered by this book. This distinguishes housing from some other areas of social policy. Housing policy has changed a lot over the period since 1945, partly in response to changes in the housing situation and partly in order to promote change in the tenure pattern. For more than twenty years after the war housing policy was dominated by high output objectives and by a desire to replace old, unfit houses through large scale redevelopment. These policy goals then gave way to concerns about the reform of housing finance and the privatization of council housing. After several decades in which successive governments saw local authority housing as part of the solution to problems located in the private market, after 1979 the position was reversed and council housing came to be seen as very much part of the problem, to which the private sector provided the answers. The prolonged support for council housing was based on persistent shortages and the perception that most people needed to rent, but once it became clear to politicians that further substantial expansion of working-class home ownership was feasible then their stance on council housing changed.

As mentioned in Chapter 2, some writers (for example, Kleinman, 1996) refer to the collapse of housing policy. Certainly, when compared with the importance attached to housing in early postwar general elections, it has become virtually a non-issue. The point was made in Chapter 7, however, that by the mid-1990s a new housing policy had coalesced around a new set of assumptions about what was needed and achievable; in practice this means less subsidy, a focus on the organizational restructuring of social renting, a diminished role for local authorities, and a return to urban regeneration and housing supply. In the present period, however, regeneration and supply are problems addressed in ways that are different from those employed in the earlier postwar decades.

Contemporary housing policy operates within a very different welfare state, in which 'big government' has become deeply unfashionable. In contrast to the late 1940s governments now try to do less, relying more on markets and placing responsibility for wellbeing on the shoulders of individuals and families. Across the world governments have decided that low taxation, less direct public service provision and more consumer choice are desirable. Globalization has caused governments to lose confidence in their ability to manage national economies and to deliver high quality services to all. The postwar settlements have been substantially renegotiated in ways that have been highlighted in previous chapters, and which can be summed up here as encouragement to individuals and families to take responsibility for housing themselves in the private sector, a residual social rented sector for groups lacking in purchasing power, and a shift to a managerialist, non-municipal social rented sector.

However, to focus solely on change would be a mistake, for there are also important areas of continuity. First, the idea that the market could and should provide for most people most of the time has underpinned British housing policy since at least the start of the twentieth century. For the first half of the century it was assumed that the majority of people needed to rent and that private enterprise would provide, once normal market conditions were restored, but in the last fifty years support for the market has been expressed primarily in terms of meeting the demand for owner occupation. Second, faith in the market has led to a second line of continuity, shaping how successive governments have approached social housing, seeing it as essentially complementary to private enterprise. In certain periods, after the two great wars when the market was most disrupted, this has meant meeting the bulk of new building (but in ways that have actually generated work for private builders, helping them to recover and sustaining them through difficult times), and in the longer run undertaking socially necessary tasks (that private enterprise could not or would not do in socially acceptable ways), such as replacing old unfit dwellings and accommodating the least well off.

Third, the poor have always tended to get the worst of the deal. In the market of course this is only to be expected, for it is in the nature of markets that the people with the most money have the widest choice and the best opportunities to secure the highest quality and most desirable products, while those with the least money have to make do with less choice and poorer quality. What is less expected is the way that housing policy measures have also tended to marginalize or even to ignore the poor. Given the previous point about the underlying assumption that the market would provide for the majority, it would have been logical to develop public housing as a residual service for the minority. However, this was not the course of policy development and the poor were only slowly and belatedly drawn into local authority housing. Historically there was a clash of rationalities: on the one hand was indeed the argument that if the local authorities were to provide housing at all then it should be for the least well off, those who were least well served by the market. On the other hand there was a case for saying that if the local authorities built for the rather better off then this would cost less in terms of subsidy provided by tax-payers, while at the same time freeing private accommodation into which the poor could afford to move. There was a moral undertone here, implying that the poor did not deserve decent subsidized houses, while the better off, securely employed working class did. In practice, for forty years or so after 1919 local authority housing tended to be mainly provided for (and occupied by) the better off working class. Municipal rent levels and lettings practices generally meant that the poor remained in the declining private rented sector. Slum clearance did have the effect of bringing more of the least well off into public housing, but at a time when the space standards were falling, or when the proportion of flats was increasing.

The key points here are, first that the least well off tended to miss out on council housing when it was at its best, and second, as social housing in general has become more accessible to this group it has been changing into a sector with relatively high levels of disrepair and low social standing. As was pointed out in Chapter 9, the poor were previously socially excluded from social housing and now they are excluded by it, a useful reminder of how social housing has changed over time.

Moving frontiers

The main purpose of this book has been to explore the relationship between housing and the welfare state in Britain over the last sixty years, and this section returns to the question of how to depict that dynamic relationship. The book is an attempt to reassess the housing–welfare relationship, questioning established accounts of both the postwar decades and the more recent past, and challenging the portrayal of housing as the wobbly pillar under the welfare state. If the welfare state is understood as a concept implying that governments have some sort of duty to guarantee all citizens a degree of wellbeing that is above mere subsistence (survival with dignity, as Bauman (1998: 45) has put it), then there remains scope for debate about precisely what level of wellbeing constitutes the socially acceptable minimum, and how it should be guaranteed. The balance of responsibility as between individuals and their families, voluntary charitable activity, private markets and the state is a set of moving frontiers (Finlayson, 1990). The frontiers were drawn up in different places for different services in the 1940s, and they have subsequently moved around a good deal, again in differing ways. So in thinking about housing and the welfare state it is necessary to specify particular temporal contexts: even if housing is judged to be the wobbly pillar now, it cannot be assumed that it was always the same.

As argued in Chapter 1, the way that housing is understood depends upon how the welfare state itself is conceptualized. First, a case can be made to say that housing was not only the wobbly pillar under the postwar welfare state, but that housing policy was barely touched by the welfare state project. If the focus is narrowly placed on the welfare state as a set of public services then housing does tend to stand out as being decidedly less decommodified than health and education. To the extent that decommodification is the key criterion then housing was, and remains, only weakly incorporated into the welfare state.

On the question of policy, the impact of the Second World War was to move the frontiers of public intervention and provision, and to move them different distances in different service areas. The key difference between housing and other areas was that whereas reforms in education and health, in particular, and to a lesser extent in relation to social security, rejected the market mechanism, in housing the basic assumption was that the market had been working pretty well before the war, and could be relied upon to do so again, once the difficult postwar transitional period had been negotiated. The evidence presented in Chapter 4 suggests that wartime planning within Whitehall for postwar housing was conducted more or less in isolation from any wider programme of social reform. The discussions were informed more by the lessons of the past, specifically the difficulties encountered in implementing the postwar housing programme in 1919, and the perceived successes of housing policy in the immediate prewar years of the late 1930s. It is significant that, in contrast to other areas, not only was housing policy formulated around support for the market but there was no sign of real, radical and long term reform. A commitment to building a lot of houses was not the same as, and should not be confused with, the notion of reform. In this context the welfare state appears as a post hoc ideological overlay on an area of policy that had a well established trajectory, to which it was planned to return as soon as circumstances permitted. The implementation of Macmillan's 'grand design' for housing after 1954 (Chapter 5) shows that this is indeed what happened: council house building was cut back and redirected towards slum clearance, and the market was set free.

The changes to housing policy that began to be implemented from 1954 mark it out as arguably the key turning point in postwar housing policy, the point when housing began to move away from heavy reliance on public sector building and reverted to a 1930s style of relationship between public and private sectors. At the stage when other spending ministers were resisting Treasury demands for public expenditure cuts, housing was taking the lead in reshaping policy. Over the next twenty years successive governments, both Conservative and Labour, expanded and extolled the market for owner occupation, experimented with deregulation and new ways of promoting private renting, and encouraged means testing as the way to target subsidies in the public sector. A Labour government went along with Tory plans to experiment with co-ownership and cost renting in the mid-1960s, and it was a later Labour government that introduced the 'option mortgage' arrangement designed to help low income home buyers who were not able to benefit from tax relief.

At one level, then, the welfare state had little impact on housing policy, and it seems reasonable to conclude that postwar housing policy was marching to its own tunes, composed in the 1920s and 1930s; but there is other evidence to consider. First, the sheer scale of the planned postwar housing programme, and the amount of replacement implied, as set out and agreed in 1943, indicates that housing policy was indeed affected by enthusiasm for building a better Britain. Second, the size of the building programme was partly a reflection of the acceptance of a full employment policy after the war (because building houses was seen as a good way of absorbing labour). Third, there is no doubt that once the term welfare state came into use, housing was understood to be part of it, probably because of its high political profile and level of expenditure. Fourth, in the event the scale of investment in the postwar housing programme far exceeded capital investment in other programme areas, such as hospitals and schools.

If we think of the welfare state in terms of a policy stance and ask whether governments pursued policies designed to enhance wellbeing, then the picture that emerges invites the conclusion that housing should not be seen as the wobbly pillar. The average level of housing wellbeing improved considerably during the thirty years after 1945, partly because of direct housing policies in terms of new building and slum clearance, partly because the housing market was quite closely regulated and partly because of the wider approach to economic management. All governments were proactive and interventionist in relation to the problems of shortage and poor quality; they were prepared to use the power of the state to boost supply and to over-ride the rights of property owners where public health was threatened. Apart from the experiment with creeping decontrol of private sector rents during the period 1957–65, the private rental market remained subject to control and tenants enjoyed security of tenure. The achievement of virtually full employment for most of the thirty years after 1945 (irrespective of whether that is attributed to policy or wider economic factors) undoubtedly had beneficial effects on housing: it helped to sustain tax revenues and minimize social security costs, which made high levels of public expenditure on housing possible; and it helped to raise average incomes, which in turn fed into sustained rising demand for owner occupation and private investment in repair and improvement work. But economic management went beyond achieving full employment; throughout the period there was relatively low inflation and a regulated mortgage market, both of which had beneficial effects for home owners. A further positive feature was the relative stability of the housing market; prices tended to rise over the years, and although there were some difficult periods, on the whole the housing market was not subject to the wild fluctuations of boom and slump that have become an apparently permanent feature of the market since the early 1970s.

It is interesting to note here that the classic welfare state coincided with what has been perceived by some writers to be a golden age for owner occupation (Murie, 1998: 96). Not only full employment but also a regulated capital market helped to make the costs of buying affordable for growing numbers of people. Full employment was a policy that dovetailed very neatly with a housing policy that encouraged people to become home owners.

Overall, then, it can be claimed that to focus on the narrow criterion of decommodification is misleading, and that the totality of government policy had broadly beneficial effects on housing wellbeing across all tenures. Public housing may not have been a universal service, but it was a site of social inclusion and the housing system as a whole was relatively egalitarian and low risk. Housing also reflected aspects of the social and organizational settlements, to the extent that the supply of new houses went mainly to families where the husband was employed in skilled and semi-skilled manual work, while elderly people, childless couples, single people and newly arrived people from the Commonwealth found it much more difficult. And in organizational terms the growth of municipal housing in the postwar period conformed very closely to the model of large scale bureaucratic services. This point is reinforced by remembering that not only were the housing associations virtually excluded from contributing to new building for fifteen years after 1945, but they were encouraged to devote themselves to precisely those groups that the local authorities were not helping.

Housing in the lead

Turning to the more recent period, it was suggested in Chapter 2 that it is conventional to see housing becoming more marginal to the welfare state. This conclusion is based on the impact of policies such as the right to buy, constraints on new building and an emphasis on providing for people in greatest need, especially the homeless, that have driven social housing towards an increasingly residualized position. The way that housing was singled out for privatization and investment cuts in the 1980s supported this sort of interpretation; if housing was not already the wobbly pillar the attacks by the Thatcherite Conservatives seriously undermined it. An alternative interpretation is to say that in fact the wider welfare state as a whole has begun to move in the same direction that housing has been travelling for many years.

The modernized welfare state that has been forged over the last twenty-five years or so is based on a freer, more open economy, a greater role for private markets, a reduced role for the state in key areas affecting wellbeing, heavier emphasis on individual choice, opportunity and responsibility and a fragmented pattern of service delivery organizations. In the modern welfare state, the government tries to do less for people, and leaves them to do more for themselves, a strategy that some have referred to a 'responsiblisation' (Garland, 1996). Housing fits very well in this context. Far from being marginalized and separated from the welfare state it can be argued that changes in housing are increasingly congruent with the wider trend and trajectory of the welfare state as a whole. Rather than divergence it is better to think in terms of convergence around a new set of assumptions and practices. Precisely because housing was never as decommodified as other services and because there was always a mixed economy of housing welfare, it had a head start in terms of the kind of modernization now emerging. Markets were well established and ideas such as responsibility and choice, that are at the heart of the modernizers' lexicon, were already embedded in housing policy discourse. Housing policy makers were developing ways of expanding the market for owner occupation and private renting from the 1950s; they were experimenting with alternatives to municipal provision from the 1960s and 1970s; they explored and exploited the potential for privatization in the 1980s and in the same decade used housing as a way of pioneering private finance; in the 1990s housing pushed ahead with moving municipal services *en bloc* into the independent not-for-profit sector. In the present period it seems that the end game for local housing authorities is being played out, as they continue to lose stock and find their strategic role leaking away to the regional level.

Housing in the early 2000s illustrates the implications of moving the frontiers of the welfare state. The retreat from big government meant drawing in the frontiers. By abandoning the policy of full employment in the mid-1970s the government made home ownership a riskier undertaking, but by cutting back the size and scope of the social rented sector, and by constantly denigrating it, successive governments have created a situation where most people in work find that they have no option but to take on the risk of buying. As Chapter 8 pointed out, housing policy has consistently encouraged the growth of owner occupation, by implication moving the frontier towards a smaller social rented sector. This was a policy that implied increasing numbers of working-class and low income purchasers, and it worked reasonably well when it was underpinned by full employment. But when unemployment rose to high levels and industrial restructuring led to a return of long term unemployment, the market quickly became a much riskier and less congenial way to satisfy individual housing needs. The subsequent emergence of an officially sanctioned flexible, insecure labour market has had serious implications for individual purchasers, who now have to bear potentially high levels of risk and uncertainty where before there was more comfort. This has been made worse by the series of boom and slump cycles in the British housing market over the last thirty years: the worst affected are people who lose their jobs in a housing market recession and then can neither maintain mortgage repayments nor sell their home.

The point was also made in Chapter 8 that the housing market reflects and amplifies inequalities generated in the labour market. The capacity of households to obtain suitable housing in the market relates directly to their employment status and level of remuneration. It follows that insecurely employed and single-earner households are disadvantaged compared with households where there are two earners, and low income households in general are also disadvantaged. The housing market amplifies inequalities to the extent that house prices reflect location and therefore those with the highest spending power will be able to secure access to houses in the most sought after neighbourhoods, closest to the most popular schools and other scarce resources. It is in precisely these same areas that house prices tend to increase most, thereby doubly rewarding their lucky owners. Increased risk, insecurity and inequality are exactly the sorts of contingencies that the postwar welfare state was proclaimed to tackle and reduce but which have made a comeback under modernization.

Despite the risks, and the high cost of buying in some parts of the country, owner occupation retains its popularity with a large majority of the population of Britain (memories of the housing market slump of the early 1990s seem to have faded), and as Hamnett (1999: 10) has pointed out the housing market is a gigantic lottery, in which the chances of winning are enough to keep drawing people in. Owner occupation is also highly popular with the advocates of choice, for the range of choices in the housing market can easily be made to contrast favourably with those in social renting. The growth of owner occupation can be seen as fundamentally important to the emergence of consumer society, not simply because it provides choice and is the best possible demonstration of one's standing as a successful consumer, but in terms of both its role as a source of wealth and a form of collateral for debt financed consumption, and the greater opportunities provided by ownership to spend money on decoration and improvement of the home. The freedom and autonomy of the owner occupier in this respect are much greater than that of tenants. Owner occupation may be expensive, but the more it costs the more status it confers and conveys, and the more spending power it generates. Choice and consumerism go together, but

Bauman (1998: 59) has argued that consumerism and the welfare state are at cross-purposes for, as he says, 'If the marketing of products cannot operate without promoting (through lip service at least) the cult of *difference* and choice, the idea of the welfare state makes little sense without appealing to the idea of the *sameness* of the human condition, human needs and human rights.' On this view the growth of owner occupation is directly inimical to the future of the welfare state.

This is also supported by another observation made by Bauman (1998: 90), namely that the poor are 'flawed consumers', and in a consumer society to be in that category is to be less than a full citizen; it is to be one of the socially excluded. This brings us to the question of the future of social renting, which is now widely understood to be increasingly residualized, occupied mainly by people who have no earned income. It is therefore a site of social exclusion, but in Chapter 9 it was argued that it is necessary to distinguish between residualization and social exclusion, on the grounds that tackling the latter was not the same as tackling the former. The focus of current policy is firmly on social exclusion, converting flawed consumers by getting them into paid work, rather than addressing residualization as such. It was argued in Chapter 9 that a strategy to turn the tide of residualization would imply broadening the social base of social housing, for example by consciously trying to draw in the young professionals in public sector jobs, the very people who are in fact targeted for the so-called 'key worker living' scheme, and which scrupulously avoids any reference to social renting. This may be taken as definitive evidence of the abandonment of social housing by the New Labour government of Tony Blair.

It is already explicit policy to abandon council housing as quickly as possible, by continuing to support the right to buy and stock transfer, although the people are rather less keen on the latter than is the government. Stock transfer is an evolving story, as discussed in Chapter 10, and it is likely that there will be more developments in the narrative before the last council house is sold (which could be around a hundred years after the first homes for heroes houses were completed). In the meantime, registered social landlords seem set to continue their expansion, becoming the second largest tenure category in a much shorter time. The transformation of the ownership and control of council housing shows what can happen to apparently entrenched public services in a relatively short run of years, and as the major responsibility of the lowest tier of local authorities it is possible that the demise of council housing might spell a similar fate for local government itself, at least across large areas of England.

If housing is indeed at the forefront of change in the welfare state then the intractability of the problems associated with a deeply residualized public sector and an unstable and highly unequal private market should give policy makers reasons to ponder. The prospects for the future appear to imply a self-reinforcing spiral in which the housing market amplifies the widening inequalities rooted in the labour market, and this is then further strengthened by the extent to which the better off secure access to the best schools, hospitals and other public services by their ability to pay premium prices in favoured housing markets. As a model for a reformed welfare state it leaves a lot to be desired.

References

Abel-Smith, B. and Titmuss, K. (1987) *The Philosophy of Welfare*, London: Allen & Unwin.

Abercrombie, N. and Warde, A. (2000) *Contemporary British Society*, Cambridge: Polity Press, 3rd edn.

Addison, P. (1977) *The Road to 1945*, London: Quartet.

Agus, M. R., Doling, J. and Lee, D.-S. (2003) *Housing Policy Systems in South and East Asia*, Basingstoke: Palgrave Macmillan.

Alcock, P. (1996) *Social Policy in Britain: Themes and Issues*, London: Macmillan.

Allen, J. and Hamnett, C. (eds) (1991) *Housing and Labour Markets: Building the Connections*, London: Unwin Hyman.

Anderson, I. and Sim, D. (eds) (2000) *Social Exclusion and Housing; Context and Challenges*, Coventry: Chartered Institute of Housing.

Atkinson, R. (2000) 'Combating Social Exclusion in Europe: the new urban policy challenge' *Urban Studies*, vol. 37, no. 5–6, pp. 1,037–55.

Audit Commission (1986) *Managing the Crisis in Council Housing*, London: HMSO.

Bacon, N. (2000) *Building for the Future: the homes we need and how to pay for them*, London: Shelter.

Balchin, P. and Rhoden, M. (2002) *Housing Policy: An Introduction*, London: Routledge, 4th edn.

Ball, M. (1986) 'Housing Analysis: time for a theoretical refocus?' *Housing Studies*, vol. 1, no. 3, pp. 147–65.

Banting, K. (1979) *Poverty, Politics and Policy*, London: Macmillan.

Barker, K. (2003) *Review of Housing Supply: Securing our Future Needs. An Interim Report*, London: Treasury and ODPM.

—— (2004) *Review of Housing Supply: Delivering Stability: Securing our Housing Needs, Final Report*, London: HMSO.

Barnett, C. (1986) *The Audit of War*, London: Macmillan.

Barnett, M. J. (1969) *The Politics of Legislation: The Rent Act, 1957*, London: Weidenfeld & Nicolson.

Barron, J., Crawley, G. and Wood, T. (1991) *Councillors in Crisis*, London: Macmillan.

Bartlett, W., Roberts, J. and Le Grand, J. (eds) (1998) *A Revolution in Social Policy: Quasi-market Reforms in the 1990s*, Bristol: Policy Press.

Bauman, Z. (1998) *Work, Consumerism and the New Poor*, Buckingham: Open University Press.

Beck, U., Giddens, A. and Lash, S. (1994) *Reflexive Modernisation: Politics, Tradition and Aesthetics in the Modern Social Order*, Cambridge: Polity Press.

Bennett, J. (2002) 'Low Cost Home Ownership Schemes in England and Wales' *Housing Finance*, Winter, pp. 35–42.

Bentham, G. (1986) 'Socio-tenurial Polarisation in the United Kingdom, 1953–1983: the income evidence' *Urban Studies*, vol. 23, no. 2.

Berghman, J. (1995) 'Social Exclusion in Europe: policy context and analytical framework' in Room.

Beveridge, W. (1942) *Report on Social Insurance and Allied Services*, London: HMSO.

—— (1948) *Voluntary Action*, London: Allen & Unwin.

Birchall, J. (1995) 'Co-partnership Housing and the Garden City Movement' *Planning Perspectives*, vol. 10, pp. 329–58.

Blair, T. (1998) *Leading the Way: A New Vision for Local Government*, London: Institute for Public Policy Research.

—— (2002) *The Courage of Our Convictions: Why Reform of Public Services is the Route to Social Justice*, London: Fabian Society.

Boddy, M. (1980) *The Building Societies*, London: Macmillan.

—— (1989) 'Financial Deregulation and UK Housing Finance: government–building society relations and the Building Societies Act, 1986' *Housing Studies*, vol. 4, no. 2, pp. 92–104.

Boelhouwer, P. and van der Heijden, H. (1992) *Housing Systems in Europe, Part 1*, Delft: Delft University Press.

Bogdanor, V. and Skidelsky, R. (eds) (1970) *The Age of Affluence 1951–64*, London: Macmillan.

Boleat, M. (1982) *The Building Society Industry*, London: Allen & Unwin.

—— (1997) 'The Politics of Home Ownership' in Williams, P. (ed.) *Directions in Housing Policy*, London: Paul Chapman Publishing, pp. 54–67.

Booth, P. and Crook, A. (eds) (1986) *Low Cost Home Ownership*, Aldershot: Gower.

Bowley, M. (1945) *Housing and the State 1919–1944*, London: Allen & Unwin.

Bramley, G. (1990) *Bridging the Affordability Gap*, London: Association of District Councils/House Builders Federation.

—— (1993) 'The Enabling Role for Local Housing Authorities' in Malpass and Means.

—— (1997) 'Housing Policy: a case of terminal decline?' *Policy and Politics*, vol. 25, no. 4, pp. 387–407.

—— Munro, M. and Pawson, H. (2004) *Key Issues in Housing Policy: Policies and Markets in 21st Century Britain*, Basingstoke: Palgrave Macmillan.

Brehony, K. and Deem, R. (2003) 'Education Policy' in Ellison, N. and Pierson, C. (eds) *Developments in British Social Policy*, London: Palgrave.

Brooke, S. (1992) *Labour's War: The Labour Party during the Second World War*, Oxford: Clarendon Press.

Brown, M. and Payne, S. (1994) *Introduction to Social Administration in Britain*, London: Hutchinson, 7th edn.

Browne, D. (2004) Speech by the Minister for Work to the Work Foundation, 1 April, www.dwp.gov.uk/mediacentre/pressrelease/2004/april/emp0104-wlness.asp

Buck, N., Gordon, I., Hall, P., Harloe, M. and Kleinman, M. (2002) *Working Capital: Life and Labour in Contemporary London*, London: Routledge.

Building Societies Association (1979) *BSA Bulletin*, no. 20, London: Building Societies Association.

Burden, T., Cooper, C. and Petrie, S. (2000) *'Modernising' Social Policy: unravelling New Labour's welfare reforms*, Aldershot: Ashgate.

Burnett, J. (1985) *A Social History of Housing 1815–1985*, Newton Abbot: David & Charles, 2nd edn.

Burns, W. (1963) *New Towns for Old*, London: Leonard Hill.

Burrows, R. (1997) *Contemporary Patterns of Residential Mobility in Relation to Social Housing in England*, York: Centre for Housing Policy, University of York.

—— (1999) 'Residential Mobility and Residualisation in Social Housing in England' *Journal of Social Policy*, vol. 28, no. 1, pp. 27–51.

Burrows, R. (2003) *Poverty and Home Ownership in Contemporary Britain*, Bristol: Policy Press.

—— and Loader, B. (eds) (1994) *Towards a Post-Fordist Welfare State?* London: Routledge.

Butler, T. and Robson, G. (2003) 'Plotting the Middle Classes: gentrification and circuits of education in London' *Housing Studies*, vol. 18, no. 1, pp. 5–28.

Byrne, D. (1999) *Social Exclusion*, Buckingham: Open University Press.

—— and Damer, S. (1980) 'The State, the Balance of Class Forces and Early Working Class Housing Legislation', *Housing, Construction and the State*, London: Political Economy of Housing Workshop.

Cairncross, A. (1985) *Years of Recovery*, London: Methuen.

—— (1992) *The British Economy since 1945*, Oxford: Basil Blackwell.

Calder, A. (1969) *The People's War: Britain 1939–45*, London: Jonathan Cape.

Cantle, T. (1986) 'The Deterioration of Public Sector Housing' in Malpass (1986).

Carr, H., Sefton-Green, D. and Tissier, D. (2001) 'Two steps forward for tenants?' in Cowan and Marsh.

Churchill, W. S. (1952) *Winston S Churchill Wartime Speeches, vol. 3 1943–45* (complied by C. Eade) London: Cassell.

Clapham, D. and Maclennan, D. (1983) 'Residualisation of Public Housing: a non-issue' *Housing Review*, January–February.

Clapham, D., Kemp, P. and Smith, S. (1990) *Housing and Social Policy*, London: Macmillan.

Clarke, J. and Newman, J. (1997) *The Managerial State*, London: Sage.

Clarke, J., Gewirtz, S. and McLaughlin, E. (2000) *New Managerialism, New Welfare?* London: Sage.

Clarke, P. (1996) *Hope and Glory: Britain 1900–1990*, Harmondsworth: Penguin.

Cohen Committee (1971) *Housing Associations*, London: HMSO.

Cole, I. and Furbey, R. (1994) *The Eclipse of Council Housing*, London: Routledge.

—— and Goodchild, B. (1995) 'Local Housing Strategies in England' *Policy and Politics*, vol. 23, no. 1, pp. 49–60.

Coleman, A. (1985) *Utopia on Trial*, London: Hilary Shipman.

Coleman, D. (2000) 'Population and Family' in Halsey and Webb.

Committee on Local Expenditure (1932) *Report of the Committee on Local Expenditure (England and Wales)* London: HMSO, Cmd 4200.

Cooper, C. and Hawtin, M. (eds) (1997) *Housing, Community and Conflict*, Aldershot: Arena.

Council of Mortgage Lenders (2004) *The CML Mortgage Market Manifesto: Taking the Past into the Future*, London: Council of Mortgage Lenders.

Cowan, D. and Marsh, A. (eds) (2001) *Two Steps Forward: Housing Policy into the New Millennium*, Bristol: Policy Press.

Cox, A. (1984) *Adversary Politics and Land: The Conflict over Land and Property in Postwar Britain*, Cambridge: Cambridge University Press.

Cox, P., Whitely, J. and Brierley, P. (2002) 'Financial Pressures in the UK Household Sector: evidence from the British household panel survey' *Bank of England Quarterly Bulletin*, Winter, pp. 410–19.

Craig, F. W. S. (1970) *British General Election Manifestos 1918–1966*, Chichester: Political Conference Publications.

—— (1975) *British Election Manifestos 1900–1974*, London: Macmillan.

Cullingworth, J. B. (1975) *Environmental Planning, vol. 1, Reconstruction and Land Use Planning 1939–1947*, London: HMSO.

—— (1979) *Essays on Housing Policy*, London: Allen & Unwin.

—— (1980) *Environmental Planning 1939–1969, vol. iv, Land Values, Compensation and Betterment*, London: HMSO.

Cutler, J. (1995) 'The Housing Market and the Economy' *Bank of England Quarterly Bulletin*, August, pp. 260–9.

—— (2002) 'UK House Prices – an accident waiting to happen?' *Housing Finance*, Autumn, pp. 11–25.

Damer, S. (1980) 'State, Class and Housing: Glasgow 1885–1919' in Melling, (1980).

Darley, G. (1990) *Octavia Hill: A Life*, London: Constable.

Daunton, M. (1983) *House and Home in the Victorian City*, London: Edward Arnold.

—— (1987) *A Property Owning Democracy?* London: Faber & Faber.

Davies, T., Nulty, S. and Smith, P. (2000) *What Works?*, Bristol: Policy Press.

Dean, H. (ed.) (2004) *The Ethics of Welfare*, Bristol: Policy Press.

Dean, H. and Woods, R. (1999) *Social Policy Review 11*, Luton: Social Policy Association.

Dennis, N. (1972) *Public Participation and Planners' Blight*, London: Faber & Faber.

Dennis, R. (1989) 'The Geography of Victorian Values: philanthropic housing in London, 1840–1900' *Journal of Historical Geography*, vol. 15, no. 1, pp. 40–54.

Department of Health (2000) *The NHS Plan: a plan for investment, a plan for reform*, London: The Stationery Office.

Department of Health and Social Security (1984) *For Richer for Poorer? DHSS Cohort Study of Unemployed Men*, Research report no. 11, London: HMSO.

DETR (1998) *Modernising Local Government: Improving Local Services through Best Value*, London: DETR.

—— (1999) *Towards an Urban Renaissance*, Final report of the Urban Task Force, London: The Stationery Office.

DETR (2000) *Quality and Choice: The Housing Green Paper*, London: The Stationery Office.

Digby, A. (1989) *British Welfare Policy: Workhouse to Workfare*, London: Faber & Faber.

DoE (1971) *Fair Deal for Housing*, London: HMSO, Cmnd 4728.

—— (1977a) *Housing Policy: A Consultative Document*, London: HMSO, Cmnd 6851.

—— (1977b) *Housing Policy Technical Volume I*, London: HMSO.

—— (1985) *Home Improvement: A New Approach*, London: HMSO, Cmnd 9513.

—— (1987) *Housing: The Government's Proposals*, London: HMSO, Cm 214.

—— (1992) *Local Authority Housing in England, Voluntary Transfers: Consultation Paper*, London: DoE.

Doling, J. and Stafford, B. (1989) *Home Ownership: The Diversity of Experience*, Aldershot: Gower.

Donnison, D. (1967) *The Government of Housing*, Harmondsworth: Penguin.

—— (1982) *The Politics of Poverty*, Oxford: Martin Robertson.

—— (1989) 'Foreword' in M. Smith, *Guide to Housing*, London: Housing Centre Trust.

—— and Ungerson, C. (1982) *Housing Policy*, Harmondsworth: Penguin.

—— Cockburn, C. and Corlett, T. (1961) *Housing Since the Rent Act*, Welwyn Garden City: Codicote Press.

Doogan, K. (2001) 'Insecurity and Long Term Employment' *Work, Employment and Society*, vol. 15, no. 3, pp. 419–41.

Dorling, D. and Cornford, J. (1995) 'Who has Negative Equity: house price falls in Britain have hit different groups of home buyers' *Housing Studies*, vol. 10, no. 2, pp. 151–78.

Dudley Report (1944) *Design of Dwellings*, Report of a sub-committee of the Central Housing Advisory Committee, London: HMSO.

Duncan, S. (1990) 'Do House Prices Rise that Much? A dissenting view' *Housing Studies*, vol. 5, no. 3, pp. 195–208.

Dunleavy, P. (1981) *The Politics of Mass Housing in Britain*, Oxford: Clarendon Press.

—— and Hood, C. (1994) 'From Old Public Administration to New Public Management' *Public Money and Management*, July–September, pp. 9–16.

Durbin, E. (1985), *New Jerusalems: The Labour Party and the Economics of Democratic Socialism*, London: Routledge & Kegan Paul.

Early, F. and Mulholland, M. (1995) 'Women and Mortgages' *Housing Finance*, no. 25, (February), pp. 21–7.

Elliott, L. and Atkinson, D. (1998) *The Age of Insecurity*, London: Verso.

Ellison, N. and Pierson, C. (eds) (1998) *Developments in British Social Policy*, London: Macmillan.

—— (2003) *Developments in British Social Policy 2*, Basingstoke: Palgrave Macmillan.

Engels, F. (1844) *The Condition of the Working Class in England in 1844*, London: Panther Books.

Englander, D. (1983) *Landlord and Tenant in Urban Britain, 1838–1918*, Oxford: Clarendon Press.

English, J. (1982) 'Must Council Housing Become Welfare Housing?' *Housing Review*, September–October.

—— Madigan, R. and Norman, P. (1976) *Slum Clearance*, London: Croom Helm Environment Committee, (1995) *Department of the Environment Memorandum on Provision for Social Housing*, First Special Report, Session 1994–95, London: HMSO, HC 442.

Esping-Andersen, G. (1990) *The Three Worlds of Welfare Capitalism*, Cambridge: Polity Press.

—— (ed.) (1996) *Welfare States in Transition*, Cambridge: Polity Press.

Fainstein, S., Gordon, I. and Harloe, M. (1992) (eds) *Divided Cities: New York and London in the Contemporary World*, Oxford: Basil Blackwell.

Fawcett, H. and Lowe, R. (1999) *Welfare Policy in Britain: The Road from 1945*, London: Macmillan.

Ferlie, E., Ashburner, L., Fitzgerald, L. and Pettigrew, A. (1996) *The New Public Management in Action*, Oxford: Oxford University Press.

Fielding, S., Thompson, P. and Tiratsoo, N. (1995) *'England Arise!' The Labour Party and Popular Politics in 1940s Britain*, Manchester: Manchester University Press.

Finlayson, G. (1990) 'A Moving Frontier: voluntarism and the state in British social welfare 1911–1949' *Twentieth Century British History*, vol. 1, no. 2, pp. 183–206.

Foot, M. (1973) *Aneurin Bevan: A Biography. Vol. 2, 1945–1960*, London: Davis-Poynter.

Ford, J. (1984) *Mortgage Arrears*, Loughborough: University of Loughborough.

—— (1988) 'Managing or Mismanaging Mortgage Arrears? The case of the building societies' *Housing Studies*, vol. 3, no. 1, pp. 40–50.

—— (2003) 'Housing Policy' in Ellison and Pierson, (2003), pp. 153–9.

—— Burrows, R. and Nettleton, S. (2001) *Home Ownership in a Risk Society*, Bristol: Policy Press.

Forrest, R. and Murie, A. (1983) 'Residualisation and Council Housing: aspects of the changing social relations of housing tenure' *Journal of Social Policy*, vol. 12, no. 1, pp. 453–68.

—— (1988) *Selling the Welfare State: The Privatisation of Public Housing*, London: Routledge.

—— (1994) 'Home Ownership in Recession' *Housing Studies*, vol. 9, no. 1, pp. 55–74.

Forrest, R., Lansley, S. and Murie, A. (1984) *A Foot on the Ladder?* Working Paper 41, School for Advanced Urban Studies, University of Bristol.

Forrest, R., Murie, A. and Williams, P. (1990) *Home Ownership: Differentiation and Fragmentation*, London: Unwin Hyman.

Foucault, M. (1977) *Discipline and Punish*, Harmondsworth: Penguin.

Francis, M. (1995) 'Economics and Ethics: the nature of Labour's socialism, 1945–1951' *20th Century British History*, vol. 6, no. 2, pp. 220–43.

Franklin, J. (ed) (1998) *The Politics of Risk Society*, Cambridge: Polity Press.

Fraser, D. (1973) *The Evolution of the British Welfare State*, London: Macmillan, 2nd edn 1984.

Furbey, R., Reid, B. and Cole, I. (2001) 'Housing Professionalism in the United Kingdom: the final curtain or a new age?' *Housing, Theory and Society*, vol. 18, nos 1–2, pp. 36–49.

Gallie, D. (2000) 'The Labour Force' in Halsey and Webb.

Garland, D. (1996) 'The Limits of the Sovereign State: strategies of crime control in contemporary society' *British Journal of Criminology*, vol. 36, no. 4, pp. 445–71.

Garside, P. (1995) 'Central Government, Local Authorities and the Voluntary Housing Sector, 1919–1939' in A. O'Day (ed.), *Government and Institutions in the Post-1832 UK*, Lampeter: Mellon Press.

Gaskell, S. M. (1986) *Model Dwellings: From the Great Exhibition to the Festival of Britain*, London: Mansell.

Gauldie, E. (1974) *Cruel Habitations*, London: Allen & Unwin.

Gay, O. (1987) 'Prefabs: a study of policy making' *Public Administration*, vol. 65 (Winter), pp. 407–22.

Gibb, K. (2003) 'Transferring Glasgow's Council Housing: financial, urban and housing policy implications' *European Journal of Housing Policy*, vol. 3, no. 1 (April), pp. 89–114.

Gibson, M. and Langstaff, M. (1982) *An Introduction to Urban Renewal*, London: Hutchinson.

Giddens, A. (1998) 'Risk Society: the context of British politics' in J. Franklin, (ed.), *The Politics of Risk Society*, Cambridge: Polity Press.

—— (1998b) *The Third Way*, Cambridge: Polity Press.

Ginsburg, N. (1979) *Class, Capital and the Welfare State*, London: Macmillan.

—— (1992) *Division of Welfare*, London: Sage.

—— (1999) 'Housing' in Page and Silburn.

Gittus, E. (1976) *Flats, Families and the Under Fives*, London: Routledge & Kegan Paul.

Gladstone, D. (1999) *The Twentieth Century Welfare State*, London: Macmillan.

Glennerster, H. (1995) *British Social Policy since 1945*, Oxford: Basil Blackwell.

—— (1999) 'A Third Way?' in Dean and Woods.

—— and Hills, J. (1998) (eds) *The State of Welfare: The Economics of Social Spending*, Oxford: Oxford University Press, 2nd edn.

Glynn, S. (1999) 'Employment, Unemployment and the Labour Market' in Page and Silburn.

Goodlad, R. (1993) *The Housing Authority as Enabler*, Harlow: Longman/ Coventry: Chartered Institute of Housing.

—— (2001) 'Developments in Tenant Participation: accounting for growth' in Cowan and Marsh.

Gordon, D. and Pantazis, C. (eds) (1995) *Breadline Britain in the 1990s*, Aldershot: Ashgate.

Gough, I. (1979) *The Political Economy of the Welfare State*, London: Macmillan.

—— (1983) 'Thatcherism and the Welfare State' in S. Hall and M. Jacques (eds) *The Politics of Thatcherism*, London: Lawrence & Wishart.

Gray, F. (1979) 'Consumption: council house management' in Merrett.

Green, H. and Hansbro, J. (1995) *English Housing in 1993/94: A Report of the 1993/94 Survey of English Housing*, London: HMSO.

Griffiths, R. and Stewart, M. (eds) (1998) *Social Exclusion in Cities: The Urban Policy Challenge*, Bristol: University of the West of England, Faculty of the Built Environment, Occasional Paper 3.

Gyford, J., Leach, S. and Game, C. (1989) *The Changing Politics of Local Government*, London: Unwin Hyman.

Hall, P. (1952) *The Social Services of Modern England*, London: Routledge & Kegan Paul.

Halsey, A. H. (1987) 'Social Trends Since World War II' in *Social Trends 1987*, London: HMSO.

—— and Webb, J. (2000) *Twentieth Century British Social Trends*, London: Macmillan, 3rd edn.

Hamilton, R. (2003) 'Trends in Households' Aggregate Secured Debt' *Bank of England Quarterly Bulletin*, Autumn, pp. 271–9.

Hamnett, C. (1984) 'Housing the Two Nations: socio-tenurial polarisation in England and Wales, 1961–81' *Urban Studies*, vol. 21, no. 4, pp. 389–405.

Hamnett, C. (1991) 'A Nation of Inheritors? Housing inheritance, wealth and inequality in Britain' *Journal of Social Policy*, vol. 20, no. 4, pp. 509–36.

—— (1999) *Winners and Losers: Home Ownership in Modern Britain*, London: UCL Press.

—— (2003) *Unequal City*, London: Routledge.

—— and Seavers, J. (1996) 'Home Ownership, Housing Wealth and Wealth Distribution in Britain' in Hills.

Harloe, M. (1978) 'The Green Paper on Housing Policy' in M. Brown and S. Daldwin (eds), *The Year Book of Social Policy in Britain 1977*, London: Routledge & Kegan Paul.

—— (1981) 'The Recommodification of Housing' in M. Harloe and E. Lebas (eds), *City, Class and Capital*, London: Edward Arnold.

—— (1985) *Private Rented Housing in the United States and Europe*, Beckenham: Croom Helm.

—— (1995) *The People's Home? Social Rented Housing in Europe and America*, Oxford: Basil Blackwell.

Harris, B. (2004) *The Origins of the British Welfare State: Social Welfare in England and Wales, 1800–1945*, Basingstoke: Palgrave Macmillan.

Harris, J. (1977) *William Beveridge: A Biography*, Oxford: Clarendon Press.

Hawksworth, J. and Wilcox, S. (1995) *Challenging the Conventions*, Coventry: Chartered Institute of Housing.

Hay, C. (1999) *The Political Economy of New Labour*, Manchester: Manchester University Press.

Heery, E. and Salmon, J. (eds) (2000) *The Insecure Workforce*, London: Routledge.

Henderson, J. and Karn, V. (1987) *Race, Class and State Housing: Inequality and the Allocation of Public Housing in Britain*, Aldershot: Gower.

Hennessy, P. (1993) *Never Again: Britain 1945–1951*, London: Vintage.

Hill, M. (2000) *Understanding Social Policy*, Oxford: Basil Blackwell, 6th edn.

Hills, J. (1991) *Unravelling Housing Finance*, Oxford: Clarendon Press.

—— (1996) *New Inequalities: The Changing Distribution of Income and Wealth in the United Kingdom*, Cambridge: Cambridge University Press.

—— (1998) 'Housing: a decent home within the reach of every family?' in Glennerster and Hills.

Hoggett, P. (1996) 'New Modes of Control in the Public Service' *Public Administration*, vol. 74 (Spring), pp. 9–32.

Holmans, A. (1987) *Housing Policy in Britain: A History*, London: Croom Helm.

—— (1995a) *Housing Demand and Need in England, 1991 to 2011*, York: York Publishing Services.

—— (1995b) 'The Changing Relationship between Tenure and Employment' in Green and Hansbro, pp. 105–17.

—— (1997) 'UK Housing Finance: past changes, the present predicament and future sustainability' in P. Williams.

—— (2000) 'Housing' in Halsey and Webb.

—— Morrison, N. and Whitehead, C. (1998) *How Many Homes Will We Need?* London: Shelter.

House of Commons (1980) *Enquiry into Implications of the Government's Expenditure Plans 1980–81 to 1983–84 for the Housing Policies of the Department of the Environment*, First Report of the House of Commons Select Committee on the Environment, Session 1979–80, HC 714, London: HMSO.

Housing Corporation (2003a) *A Home of My Own: Report of the Government's Home Ownership Task Force*, London: Housing Corporation.

—— (2003b) *Re-inventing Investment*, London: Housing Corporation.

—— (2004) *Investment Bulletin 2004*, London: Housing Corporation.

Huber, E. and Stephens, J. (2001) *Development and Crisis of the Welfare State*, Chicago: University of Chicago Press.

IPPR (Institute for Public Policy Research) (2000) *Housing United: final report of the IPPR Forum on the future of social housing*, London: IPPR.

Jackson, A. A. (1973) *Semi-Detached London*, London: Allen & Unwin.

Jarmain, J. R. (1948) *Housing Subsidies and Rents*, London: Stevens.

Jevons, R. and Madge, J. (1946) *Housing Estates: A Study of Bristol Corporation Policy and Practice Between the Wars*, Bristol: University of Bristol.

Jones, H. (1991) 'New Tricks for an Old Dog? The Conservatives and social policy, 1951–55' in A. Gorst, L. Johnson and W. Scott Lucas (eds), *Contemporary British History 1931–61*, London: Pinter.

Jordan, B. (1996) *A Theory of Poverty and Social Exclusion*, Cambridge: Polity Press.

Joseph Rowntree Foundation, (1995) *Inquiry into Income and Wealth*, York: Joseph Rowntree Foundation.

Karn, V. (1993) 'Remodelling a HAT: the implementation of the housing trust legislation 1987–92' in Malpass and Means.

—— Kemeny, J. and Williams, P. (1985) *Home Ownership in the Inner City: Salvation or Despair*, Aldershot: Gower.

Kemeny, J. and Lowe, S. (1998) 'Schools of Comparative Research: from convergence to divergence' *Housing Studies*, vol. 13, no. 2, pp. 161–76.

Kemp, P. (1993) 'Rebuilding the Private Rented Sector?' in Malpass and Means.
—— (1999) 'Housing Policy under New Labour' in T. Brown (ed.), *Stakeholder Housing*, London: Pluto Press.
—— (2000) 'Housing Benefit and Welfare Retrenchment' *Journal of Social Policy*, vol. 29, no. 2.
—— and Williams, P. (1991) 'Housing Management: an historical perspective' in S. Lowe and Hughes.
Kerr, H. (1981) 'Labour's Social Policy 1974–79' *Critical Social Policy*, vol. 1, no. 1, pp. 5–17.
Kleinman, M. (1996) *Housing, the State and Welfare in Europe*, Cheltenham: Edward Elgar.
—— (2002) *A European Welfare State?* Basingstoke: Palgrave.
Labour Party (1934) *Up with the Houses! Down with the Slums!*, London: Labour Party.
—— (1942) *The Old World and the New Society: A Report on the Problems of War and Peace Reconstruction*, London: Labour Party.
Lambert, C. and Malpass, P. (1998) 'Rules of the Game: Competition for Housing Investment' in Oatley, N. (ed), *Cities, Economic Competition and Urban Policy*, London: Paul Chapman Publishing.
Langan, M. and Clarke, J. (1993). 'The British Welfare State: foundation and modernisation' in Cochrane, A. and Clarke, J. (eds), *Comparing Welfare States: Britain in international context*, London: Sage.
Laski, H., Jennings, I. and Robson, W. (1935) *A Century of Municipal Progress*, London: Allen & Unwin.
Le Grand, J. (1991) 'Quasi-markets and Social Policy' *Economic Journal*, vol. 101, pp. 1,256–67.
Lee, P. (1998) 'Housing Policy, Citizenship and Social Exclusion' in A. Marsh and D. Mullins (eds), *Housing and Public Policy*, Buckingham: Open University Press.
—— and Murie, A. (1997) *Poverty, Housing Tenure and Social Exclusion*, Bristol: The Policy Press.
Levitas, R. (1998) *The Inclusive Society? Social Exclusion and New Labour*, London: Macmillan.
Lindsay, C. (2003) 'A Century of Labour Market Change: 1900 to 2000' *Labour Market Trends*, March, pp. 133–44.
Local Government Board (1919) *Manual on the Preparation of State-aided Housing Schemes*, London: HMSO.
Loughlin, M., Gelfand, M. and Young, K. (1985) *Half a Century of Municipal Decline 1935–1985*, London: Allen & Unwin.
Lowe, R. (1989) 'Resignation at the Treasury: the Social Services Committee and the failure to reform the welfare state, 1955–57' *Journal of Social Policy*, vol. 18, no. 4, pp. 505–27.
—— (1993) *The Welfare State in Britain since 1945*, London: Macmillan.
—— (1994) 'Lessons from the Past: the rise and fall of the classis welfare state in Britain, 1945–76' in A. Oakley and A.S. Williams (eds), *The Politics of the Welfare State*, London: UCL Press.
Lowe, S. (2004) *Housing Policy Analysis: British Housing Policy in Cultural and Comparative Context*, Basingstoke: Palgrave Macmillan.

Lowe, S. and Hughes, D. (1991) *A New Century of Social Housing*, Leicester: Leicester University Press.

MacDonagh, O. (1958) 'The Nineteenth Century Revolution in Government: a reappraisal' *Historical Journal*, vol. 1, pp. 52–67, quoted in Fraser (1973).

MacGregor, S. (1985) 'Making Sense of Social Security? Initiatives and implementation 1979–83' in P. Jackson (ed.), *Implementing Government Policy Initiatives: The Thatcher Administration 1979–83*, London: Royal Institute of Public Administration.

Mack, J. and Lansley, S. (1985) *Poor Britain*, London: Allen & Unwin.

Maclennan, D. (1994) *A Competitive UK Economy: The Challenge for Housing Policy*, York: Joseph Rowntree Foundation.

—— Meen, G., Gibb, K. and Stephens, M. (1997) *Fixed Commitments, Uncertain Incomes: Sustainable Owner Occupation and the Economy*, York: Joseph Rowntree Foundation.

Macmillan, H. (1969) *Tides of Fortune 1945–1955*, London: Macmillan.

Madanipour, A., Cars, G. and Allen, J. (eds) (1998) *Social Exclusion in European Cities*, London: Jessica Kingsley.

Malpass, P. (ed.) (1986) *The Housing Crisis*, Beckenham: Croom Helm.

—— (1987) 'Utopia in Context: state, class and the restructuring of the housing market in the twentieth century', in N. Teymur, T. Markus and T. Woolley (eds), *Rehumanising Housing*, London: Butterworths.

—— (1990) *Reshaping Housing Policy: Subsidies, Rents and Residualisation*, London: Routledge.

—— (1993) 'Housing Policy and the Housing System Since 1979' in Malpass and Means (1993).

—— (1997) 'Rents within Reach' in J. Goodwin and C. Grant (eds), *Built to Last? Reflections on British Housing Policy*, London: Shelter.

—— (1998) *Housing, Philanthropy and the State: A History of the Guinness Trust*, Bristol: UWE, Faculty of the Built Environment, Occasional Paper 2.

—— (2000a) 'The Discontinuous History of Housing Associations in England' *Housing Studies*, vol. 15, no. 2 (March), pp. 195–212.

—— (2000b) *Housing Associations and Housing Policy: A Historical Perspective*, London: Macmillan.

—— (2000c) 'Public Utility Societies and Housing and Town Planning Act, 1919: a reassessment of the introduction of Exchequer subsidies' *Planning Perspectives*, vol. 15, no. 4, pp. 1–16.

—— (2001) 'The Uneven Development of "Social Rented Housing": Explaining the Historically Marginal Position of Housing Associations in Britain' *Housing Studies*, vol. 16, no. 2, pp. 225–42.

—— (2003) 'Private Enterprise in Eclipse? A reassessment of British housing policy in the 1940s' *Housing Studies*, vol. 18, no. 5, pp. 645–59.

—— and Jones, C. (1996) 'The Fourth Experiment? the Commissioner for Special Areas, the Ministry of Health and the North Eastern Housing Association' *Planning Perspectives*, vol. 11, pp. 303–21.

—— and Means, R. (eds) (1993) *Implementing Housing Policy*, Buckingham: Open University Press.

—— and Mullins, D. (2002) 'Local Authority Housing Stock Transfer in the UK: from local initiative to national policy' *Housing Studies*, vol. 17, no. 4, pp. 673–86.

—— and Murie, M. (1982) *Housing Policy and Practice*, London: Macmillan.

—— (1990) *Housing Policy and Practice*, London: Macmillan, 3rd edn.

—— and Murie, M. (1999) *Housing Policy and Practice*, London: Macmillan, 5th edn.

——, Warburton, M., Bramley, C. and Smart, G. (1993) *Housing Policy in Action*, Bristol: School for Advanced Urban Studies, University of Bristol.

Marsh, A. and Mullins, D. (1998) 'The Social Exclusion Perspective' *Housings Studies*, vol. 13, no. 6, pp. 749–59.

Marsh, D. and Rhodes, R. (eds) (1992) *Implementing Thatcherite Policies*, Buckingham: Open University Press.

Marshall, T. H. (1950) *Citizenship and Social Class*, Cambridge: Cambridge University Press.

Martin, S. (2000) 'Implementing 'Best-Value': local public services in transition' *Public Administration*, vol. 78, no. 1, pp. 209–27.

Marwick, A. (1968) *Britain in the Century of Total War*, London: Bodley Head.

—— (1982) *British Society since 1945*, Harmondsworth: Penguin.

McCutcheon, R. (1975) 'High Flats in Britain 1945 to 1971' in *Political Economy and the Housing Question*, London: Political Economy of Housing Workshop.

McGuire, C. (1981) *International Housing Policies: An International Analysis*, Toronto: Lexington Books.

McNicol, J. (1987) 'In Pursuit of the Underclass' *Journal of Social Policy*, vol. 16, pp. 293–318.

Means, R. and Smith, R. (1994) *Community Care Policy and Practice*, London: Macmillan.

Melling, J. (ed.) (1980) *Housing, Social Policy and the State*, Beckenham: Croom Helm.

Merrett, S. (1979) *State Housing in Britian*, London: Routledge & Kegan Paul.

—— (1982) *Owner Occupation in Britain*, London: Routledge.

Middlemas, K. (1986) *Power, Competition and the State, vol. 1, Britain in Search of Balance 1940–61*, London: Macmillan.

Ministry of Health (1925) *5th Report of the Ministry of Health*, London: HMSO, Cmd 2450.

—— (1931) *12th Annual Report of the Ministry of Health, 1930–31*, London: HMSO, Cmd 3937.

—— (1933a) *14th Annual Report of the Ministry of Health, 1932–33*, London: HMSO, Cmd 4372.

—— (1933b) *Report of the Departmental Committee on Housing*, London: HMSO, Cmd 4397 (Moyne Report).

—— (1934) *15th Annual Report of the Ministry of Health, 1933–34*, London: HMSO, Cmd 4663.

Ministry of Reconstruction (1918a) *Housing in England and Wales: Memorandum by the Housing Panel on the Emergency Problem*, London: HMSO, Cd 9087.

Ministry of Reconstruction (1918b) *Housing (Financial Assistance) Committee: Interim Report on Public Utility Societies*, London: HMSO, Cd 9223.
—— (1944) *Employment Policy* (White Paper) London: HMSO, May, Cmd 6527.
—— (1945) *Housing* (White Paper), Cmd 6609.
Minogue, M., Polidano, C. and Hulme, D. (eds) (1998) *Beyond the New Public Management*, Cheltenham: Edward Elgar.
Mishra, R. (1984) *The Welfare State in Crisis*, London: Macmillan.
MoHLG (Ministry of Housing and Local Government) (1953) *Houses – the Next Step*, London: HMSO, Cmd 8996.
—— (1955) *Report of the Ministry of Housing and Local Government 1950–51 to 1954*, London: HMSO, Cmd 9559.
—— (1961) *Housing in England and Wales*, London: HMSO, Cmnd 1290.
—— (1963) *Housing*, London: HMSO, Cmnd 2050.
MoHLG (Ministry of Housing and Local Government) (1965) *The Housing Programme 1965–70*, London: HMSO, Cmnd 2838.
—— (1968) *Old Houses into New Homes*, London: HMSO, Cmnd 3602.
Morgan, K. (1984) *Labour in Power 1945–51*, Oxford: Clarendon Press.
—— (1999) *The People's Peace: British History since 1945*, Oxford: Oxford University Press, 2nd edn.
Morris, P. (1969) *Put Away: A Sociological Study of Institutions for the Mentally Retarded*, London: Routledge & Kegan Paul.
Morris, S. (2001) 'Market Solutions for Social Problems: working class housing in nineteenth century London', *Economic History Review*, vol. 54, no. 3, pp. 525–45.
Morton, J. (1991) *'Cheaper Than Peabody': Local Authority Housing from 1890 to 1919*, York: Joseph Rowntree Foundation.
Mullen, T. (2001) 'Stock Transfer' in Cowan and Marsh.
Munro, M. (2000) 'Riding the Roller Coaster: household responses to changing housing market risk' in Taylor-Gooby.
Murie, A. (1977) 'Council House Sales Mean Poor Law Housing' *Roof*, vol. 2, no. 2 (March), pp. 46–9.
—— (1994) 'Housing: on the edge of the welfare state' in D. Gladstone (ed.), *British Social Welfare: Past, Present and Future*, London: UCL Press.
—— (1997) 'The Social Rented Sector, Housing and the Welfare State in the UK' *Housing Studies*, vol. 12, no. 4, pp. 437–61.
—— (1998) 'Secure and contented citizens? Home ownership in Britain' in Marsh, A. and Mullins, D. (eds), *Housing and Public Policy*, Buckingham: Open University Press.
—— and Ferrari, E. (2003) *Reforming the Right to Buy in England*, Birmingham: Centre for Urban and Regional Studies, University of Birmingham.
—— and Nevin, B. (2001) 'New Labour Transfers' in Cowan and Marsh.
Murray, C. (1990) *The Emerging British Underclass*, London: Institute of Economic Affairs.
National Housing Committee (1934) *A National Housing Policy*, London: King & Son.
Newman, J. (2000) 'Beyond the New Public Management?' in Clarke, Gewirtz and McLaughlin.

NFHA (1985) *Inquiry into British Housing*, London: National Federation of Housing Associations.

ODPM (2001) *English House Condition Survey 2001*, London: ODPM.

—— (2002) *Recent Trends in the UK Property Market*, Housing Statistics Summary no. 14, London: ODPM.

—— (2003) *Sustainable Communities: Building for the Future*, London: ODPM.

—— (2004a) *Annual Report*, www.odpm.gov.uk

—— (2004b) *Key Worker Living: Settle for More*, London: ODPM.

—— (2004c) *£3.5 billion Boost for New Affordable Housing*, News Release, 24 March.

OECD (1997) 'Is Job Security on the Increase in OECD Countries?' *Employment Outlook*, Paris: OECD.

Offe, C. (1982) 'Some Contradictions of the Modern Welfare State' *Critical Social Policy*, vol. 2, no. 2, pp. 7–16.

—— (1984) *Contradictions of the Welfare State*, London: Hutchinson.

Office of Public Service Reform (2002) *Reforming Our Public Services*, www.pm.gov.uk/opsr

ONS (2004) *Fewer Workless Households*, www.statistics.gov.uk/cci/nugget_print.asp?ID=409

Orbach, L. (1977) *Homes Fit for Heroes: A Study of the Evolution of British Public Housing 1915–21*, London: Seeley, Service.

Osborne, D. and Gaebler, T. (1992) *Reinventing Government*, London: Plume.

Owen, D. (1965) *English Philanthropy 1660–1960*, London: Oxford University Press.

Pacione, M. (ed.) (1997) *Britain's Cities: Geographies of Division in Urban Britain*, London: Routledge.

Page, D. (1993) *Building For Communities*, York: Joseph Rountree Foundation.

Page, R. and Silburn, R. (eds) (1999) *British Social Welfare in the Twentieth Century*, London: Macmillan.

Pawson, H. (2004) 'Reviewing Stock Transfer' in Wilcox.

—— and Fancy, C. (2003) *Maturing Assets: The Evolution of Stock Transfer Housing Associations*, Bristol: Policy Press.

Peach, C., Rogers, A., Chance, J. and Daley, P. (2000) 'Immigration and Ethnicity' in Halsey and Webb.

Pierson, C. (1991) *Beyond the Welfare State?*, Cambridge: Polity Press.

Pinto, R. (1993) *The Estate Action Initiative: Council Housing Management and Effectiveness*, Aldershot: Avebury.

Pole Report (1944) *Private Enterprise Housing*, report of the private enterprise sub-committee of the Central Housing Advisory Committee, London: HMSO.

Powell, M. (ed.) (1999) *New Labour, New Welfare State?: The 'Third Way' in British Social Policy*, Bristol: The Policy Press.

—— (ed.) (2002) *Evaluating New Labour's Welfare Reforms*, Bristol: The Policy Press.

—— and Hewitt, M. (2002) *Welfare State and Welfare Change*, Buckingham: Open University Press.

Power, A. (1987) *Property Before People*, London: Allen & Unwin.

Priemus, H. and Dieleman, F. (1999) 'Social Housing Finance in the European Union: Developments and Prospects' *Urban Studies*, vol. 36, no. 4, pp. 623–31.

Rhodes, R. (1996) 'The New Governance: governing without government' *Political Studies*, vol. xliv, pp. 652–67.

—— (1997) *Understanding Governance: Policy Networks, Governance Reflexivity and Accountability*, Buckingham: Open University Press.

—— (1999) Foreword, in Stoker.

—— (2000) Foreword, in Stoker.

Robb, B. (1967) *Sans Everything*. London: Nelson.

Robbins Report (1963) *Higher Education: Report*, London: HMSO, Cmnd 2154.

Robinson, R. (1986) 'Restructuring the Welfare State: an analysis of public expenditure, 1979/80–1984/85' *Journal of Social Policy*, vol. 15, no. 1, pp. 1–21.

—— and O'Sullivan, A. (1983) 'Housing Tenure Polarisation: some empirical evidence' *Housing Review*, July–August.

Robson, W. (1976) *Welfare State and Welfare Society*, London: Allen & Unwin.

Room, G. (1990) *'New Poverty' in the European Community*, London: Macmillan.

—— (1991) *National Policies to Combat Social Exclusion*, First Annual Report of the EC Observatory, Bath: University of Bath.

Room, G. (1995) *Beyond the Threshold: The Measurement and Analysis of Social Exclusion*, Bristol: Policy Press.

Royal Commission on the Housing of the Working Classes (1885a) *Report*, London: HMSO, C.4402.

—— (1885b) *Minutes of Evidence*, London: HMSO.

Rubinstein, D. (ed.) (1974) *Victorian Homes*, Newton Abbot: David & Charles.

Saunders, P. (1990) *A Nation of Home Owners*, London: Unwin Hyman.

—— and Harris, C. (1988) *Home Ownership and Capital Gains*, Working Paper 64, Urban and Regional Studies, University of Sussex.

Savage, S. and Atkinson, R. (eds) (2001) *Public Policy Under Blow*, London: Palgrave.

Skidelsky, R. (2000) *John Maynard Keynes: Fighting for Britain 1937–1946*, London: Macmillan.

Skifter Andersen, H. (2002) 'Excluded Places: the interaction between segregation, urban decay and deprived neighbourhoods' *Housing, Theory and Society*, vol. 19.

—— (2003) *Urban Sores: On The Interaction between Segregation, Urban Decay and Deprived Neighbourhoods*, Aldershot: Ashgate.

Skilleter, K. (1993) 'The Role of Public Utility Societies in Early British Town Planning and Housing Reform' *Planning Perspectives*, vol. 8, pp. 125–65.

Smith, J. (2001) 'Key Trends in Mortgage Lending 1985–2000: results from the survey of mortgage lenders' *Housing Finance*, no. 50 (May), pp. 16–23.

—— (2002) 'CML market research results 2001' *Housing Finance*, no. 53 (Spring), pp. 13–27.

—— (2003) 'Mortgage Equity Withdrawal: evidence from CML market research' *Housing Finance*, Spring, pp. 50–63.

Smith, S. (1989) *The Politics of 'Race' and Residence: Citizenship, Segregation and White Supremacy in Britain*, Cambridge: Polity.

Social Exclusion Unit (1998) *Bringing Britain Together: A National Strategy for Neighbourhood Renewal*, London: Social Exclusion Unit.

—— (2004) *Tackling Social Exclusion: Taking Stock and Looking to the Future*, London: ODPM.

Somerville, P. (1998) 'Explanations of Social Exclusion: where does housing fit in?' *Housing Studies*, vol. 13, no. 6, pp. 761–80.

Speight, G. (2000) *Who Bought the Inter-war Semi? The Socio-economic Characteristics of New-house Buyers in the 1930s*, Oxford: University of Oxford, Discussion Papers in Economic and Social History, no. 38.

Stedman Jones, G. (1971) *Outcast London*, Oxford: Clarendon Press.

Stephens, M. (1993) 'Finance for Owner Occupation in the UK: the sick man of Europe?' *Policy and Politics*, vol. 21, no. 4, pp. 307–17.

Stoker, G. (1991) *The Politics of Local Government*, London: Macmillan, 2nd edn.

—— (ed.) (1999) *The New Management of British Local Governance*, London: Macmillan.

—— (2000) *The New Politics of British Local Governance*, London: Macmillan.

Supple, B. E. (1981) 'Income and Demand 1860–1914' in R. Floud and D. McKlosky (eds), *The Economic History of Britain since 1700, vol. 2 1860 to the 1970s*, Cambridge: Cambridge University Press, pp. 121–43.

Swenarton, M. (1981) *Homes For Heroes*, London: Heinemann.

—— and Taylor, S. (1985) 'The Scale and Nature of the Growth of Owner Occupation in Britain between the Wars' *Economic History Review*, vol. 38, part 3, pp. 373–92.

Sykes, R., Palier, B. and Prior, P. (eds) (2001) *Globalisation and European Welfare States*, London: Palgrave.

Tarn, J. (1974) *Five Per Cent Philanthropy: An Account of Housing in Urban Areas between 1840 and 1914*, Cambridge: Cambridge University Press.

Taylor, A. J. P (1965) *English History 1914–1945*, London: Oxford University Press.

Taylor-Gooby, P. (ed.) (2000) *Risk, Trust and Welfare*, Basingstoke: Palgrave.

Thomas, A. (1986) *Housing and Urban Renewal*, London: Allen & Unwin.

Thompson, G., Frances, J., Levacic, R. and Mitchell, J. (eds) (1991) *Markets, Hierarchies and Networks: The Co-ordination of Social Life*, London: Sage.

Timmins, N. (1996) *The Five Giants: A Biography of the Welfare State*, London: Fontana.

Titmuss, R. (1958) *Essays on 'the Welfare State'*, London: Allen & Unwin.

—— (1968) *Commitment to Welfare*, London: Allen & Unwin.

—— (1976) *Social Policy: An Introduction*, London: Allen & Unwin.

Tomlinson, J. (1995) 'Welfare and the Economy: the economic impact of the welfare state, 1945–1951' *20th Century British History*, vol. 6, no. 2, pp. 195–219.

Torgersen, U. (1987) 'Housing: the Wobbly Pillar under the Welfare State' in B. Turner, J. Kemeny and L. Lundqvist (eds), *Between State and Market: Housing in the Post-Industrial Era*, Stockholm: Almqvist & Wiksell.

Townsend, P. (1976) *Sociology and Social Policy*, Harmondsworth: Penguin.

—— (1979) *Poverty in the United Kingdom*, Harmondsworth: Penguin.

Townsend, P. and Bosanquet, N. (eds) (1972) *Labour and Inequality*, London: Fabian Society.

Treasury Select Committee (2004) *Restoring Confidence in Long Term Savings: Endowment Mortgages*, London: The Stationery Office, HC 394.

Tucker, J. (1966) *Honourable Estates*, London: Gollancz.

United Nations (1958) *Financing of Housing in Europe*, Geneva: Economic Commission for Europe.

Usher, D. (1987) *Housing Privatisation: The Sale of Council Estates*, Bristol: School for Advanced Urban Studies, University of Bristol, SAUS working paper 67.

Vale, B. (1995) *Prefabs: A History of the UK Temporary Housing Programme*, London: Spon.

Vass, J. (2003) 'Affordability: have we reached breaking point?' *Housing Finance*, Autumn, pp. 24–34.

Viet-Wilson, J. (2000) 'States of Welfare: a conceptual challenge' *Social Policy and Administration*, vol. 34, no. 1, pp. 1–25.

Waldegrave, W. (1987) *Speech in Bristol, 28 August*, London: Conservative Central Office.

Walker, A. and Walker, C. (eds) (1997) *Britain Divided: The Growth of Social Exclusion in the 1980s and 1990s*, London: Child Poverty Action Group.

Walker, R. (1998) 'New Public Management and Housing Associations: from comfort to competition' *Policy and Politics*, vol. 26, no. 1, pp. 71–87.

Waller, P. (1984) 'Charles Booth' in P. Barker (ed.), *Founders of the Welfare State*, London: Heinemann.

War Office (1944) *Statistics Relating to the War Effort in the United Kingdom*, London: HMSO, Cmd 6564.

Ward, S. (1994) *Planning and Urban Change*, London: UCL Press.

White, J. (1980) *Rothschild Buildings: Life in an East End Tenement Block 1887–1920*, London: Routledge & Kegan Paul.

White, M. (1983) *Long-term Unemployment and Labour Markets*, London: Policy Studies Institute.

Whitehead, C. (1979) 'Why Owner Occupation?' *CES Review*, May.

—— and Kleinman, M. (1992) *A Review of Housing Needs Assessments*, London: Housing Corporation.

Whiteside, N. (1996) 'Creating the Welfare State in Britain, 1945–1960' *Journal of Social Policy*, vol. 25, no. 1, pp. 83–103.

Wilcox, S. (1993) *Housing Finance Review 1993*, York: Joseph Rowntree Foundation.

—— (1999) *Housing Finance Review 1999/2000*, London: CIH/CML.

—— (2003a) *Can Work – Can't Buy*, York: Joseph Rowntree Foundation.

—— (2003b) *UK Housing Review 2003/2004*, London: CIH/CML.

—— (2004) *UK Housing Review 2004/2005*, London: CIH/CML.

Wilding, P. (1972) 'Towards Exchequer Subsidies for Housing, 1906–1914' *Social and Economic Administration*, vol. 6, no. 1, pp. 3–18.

—— (1973) 'The Housing and Town Planning Act 1919 – a study in the making of social policy' *Journal of Social Policy*, vol. 1, no. 4, pp. 317–34.

Williams, F. (1989) *Social Policy: A Critical Introduction*, Cambridge: Polity Press.

Williams, P. (ed.) (1997) *Directions in Housing Policy: Towards Sustainable Housing Policies for the UK*, London: Paul Chapman.

—— (2003) 'Owning up – Where is Home Ownership Going?' in Wilcox.

Williamson, O. (1975) *Markets and Hierarchies: Analysis and Anti-trust Implications*, New York: Free Press.

Wohl, A. (1977) *The Eternal Slum*, London: Edward Arnold.

Woods, R. (2000) 'Social Housing: managing multiple pressures' in Clarke, Gewirtz and McLaughlin.

Yates, D. (1982) 'The English Housing Experience: an overview' *Urban Law and Policy*, vol. 5, pp. 203–33.

Young, G. (1991) 'Our Shared Commitment' *Roof*, November–December, 8.

Yuen, B. (2003) 'Singapore' in Agus, Doling and Lee.

Index

Note: the terms 'prewar' and 'postwar' refer to the Second World War unless otherwise stated.